PRENTICE-HALL SERIES IN WORLD RELIGIONS

ROBERT S. ELLWOOD, JR., EDITOR

BEYOND "THE PRIMITIVE":
THE RELIGIONS OF NONLITERATE PEOPLES

_____ *SAM D. GILL*

HINDUISM: A CULTURAL PERSPECTIVE

_____ *DAVID R. KINSLEY*

ISLAM: A CULTURAL PERSPECTIVE

_____ *RICHARD C. MARTIN*

AMERICAN RELIGION:
A CULTURAL PERSPECTIVE

_____ *MARY FARRELL BEDNAROWSKI*

Mary Farrell Bednarowski

United Theological Seminary of the Twin Cities

*AMERICAN
RELIGION
a cultural
perspective*

Prentice-Hall, Inc., Englewood Cliffs, New Jersey 07632

Library of Congress Cataloging in Publication Data

Bednarowski, Mary Farrell.
   American religion.

   (Prentice-Hall series in world religions)
   Bibliography: p.
   Includes index.
   1. United States—Religion.   I. Title.   II. Series.
BL2525.B43 1984   291'.0973   83-22895
ISBN 0-13-029059-9

For my father and in memory of my mother,
whose happy life together taught me early that
there are many paths to heaven's gate.

Printed in the United States of America

1 2 3 4 5 6 7 8 9 10

ISBN 0-13-029059-9

Prentice-Hall International, Inc., *London*
Prentice-Hall of Australia Pty. Limited, *Sydney*
Prentice-Hall Canada Inc., *Toronto*
Prentice-Hall of India Private Limited, *New Delhi*
Prentice-Hall of Japan, Inc., *Tokyo*
Prentice-Hall of Southeast Asia Pte. Ltd., *Singapore*
Whitehall Books Limited, *Wellington, New Zealand*
Editora Prentice-Hall do Brasil Ltda., *Rio de Janeiro*

Contents

1 celebrating diversity:
religion in a plural society 1

2 coming to terms with diversity:
the other side of celebration 15

3 washed in the blood of the lamb:
revivalism in america 29

4 "the peering eyes": science and religion
in nineteenth-century america 38

5 visible saints: biography in american religious history 47

6 "the law knows no heresy": dissent in american religion 65

7 sacred and secular images of the eternal:
religion and the arts 78

8 making sense of the universe:
belief and doctrine in american religion 94

9 ritual response to the eternal:
worship in american religions 116

10 gathering together: some aspects of organization
in american religions 138

11 "many paths to heaven's gate": concluding remarks 160

bibliography 166

glossary 170

index 177

Foreword

The Prentice-Hall Series in World Religions is a new set of introductions to the major religious traditions of the world, which intends to be distinctive in two ways: (1) Each book follows the same outline, allowing a high level of consistency in content and approach. (2) Each book is oriented toward viewing religious traditions as "religious cultures" in which history, ideologies, practices, and sociologies all contribute toward constructing "deep structures" that govern peoples' world view and life-style. In order to achieve this level of communication about religion, these books are not chiefly devoted to dry recitations of chronological history or systematic exposition of ideology, though they present overviews of these topics. Instead the books give considerable space to "cameo" insights into particular personalities, movements, and historical moments that encourage an understanding of the world view, life-style, and deep dynamics of religious cultures in practice as they affect real people.

Religion is an important element within nearly all cultures and itself has all the hallmarks of a full cultural system. "Religious culture" as an integrated complex includes features ranging from ideas and organization to dress and diet. Each of these details offers some insight into the meaning of the whole as a total experience and construction of a total "reality." To look at the religious life of a particular country or tradition in this way, then, is to give proportionate attention to all aspects of its manifestation: to thought, worship, and social organization; to philosophy and folk beliefs; to liturgy and pilgrimage; to family life, dress, diet, and the role of religious specialists like monks and shamans. This series hopes to instill in the minds of readers the ability to view religion in this way.

I hope you enjoy the journeys offered by these books to the great heartlands of the human spirit.

ROBERT S. ELLWOOD, JR., editor
University of Southern California

Preface

American Religion: A Cultural Perspective is an introduction to the subject of religion in America.* As such, one of its chief purposes is to provide speculations about religion in general in American life. What place does religion have in a culture in which church and state are separate, in which religious affiliation is optional, a private matter, nobody's business but one's own? And how do we make sense of the fact that, in spite of separation of church and state, even the briefest analysis of American culture will reveal that religious issues and values are intertwined with many other aspects of American culture—among them political trends, swings in the economy, education, scientific discoveries, developments in psychology and sociology, wars, the arts? A second, most basic purpose of this book is to make available specific details about religion in particular in America, about the many, many religious groups that are at home in America—what their members believe, how they worship, and how they try to live their lives in accordance with their beliefs.

However, the format of this book, part of a series published by Prentice-Hall, has allowed me the latitude to branch out in both method and content from some of the more traditional ways of looking at religion in America, to explore areas that do not always receive much attention and are likely to be treated in separate volumes, such as dissent, the arts, and ritual. I have particularly enjoyed the opportunity to include biographical materials in this book, in order to demonstrate how particular people in American religious history have struggled to articulate and act upon their religious beliefs. As essential as it is to have "factual" material about religious systems, it is difficult to feel the urgency of the theological and political issues under discussion if we have no idea of how they have affected people's lives. Because of the variety of topics covered, then, the methodological approach varies from chapter to chapter. I have tried to avoid jargon that is peculiar to any one discipline and at the same time have attempted to include and define terms that the student of American religion is likely to encounter over and over again.

As far as the content of the book is concerned, one issue is uppermost, and that is choice of the extended examples that are so important in the format of the book. This is a brief book on a vast subject, and anyone who engages in such an enterprise is well aware of the apprehensions involved in selecting examples that are both representative and inclusive. Two instances may suffice to illustrate what I mean. The chapter "Visible Saints" is biographical in nature and gives details of the lives of one eighteenth-century leader and three twentieth-century personalities. In making these selections, I decided to sacrifice historical balance to considerations of inclusiveness, particularly of race and gender. For the chap-

---

* I have followed convention in referring to the United States as "America" but acknowledge the growing recognition that such usage is provincial in its exclusion of other Americans in the Western Hemisphere.

ter on ritual, "Ritual Response to the Eternal," I made a different kind of decision. After decrying throughout the book that too many studies of American religion have not gone much beyond a discussion of the three "great faiths," I chose to describe a Lutheran Sunday service, a Roman Catholic baptism, a Jewish Bat Mitzvah, and an Ojibwa wake service. Only the wake service could be considered a departure from the routine. Yet, it is my conviction that we seldom go to church or synagogue or temple with each other; we are not familiar with some of the most common ritual expressions of one another's beliefs. And so, in an introduction to American religion, it seemed wiser to omit descriptions of a nineteenth-century Shaker dance ritual or the Zen Buddhist practice of *zazen* and to concentrate a little more on what should be familiar to us but isn't.

Finally, in the matter of general tone or writing style, I have not tried to conceal the fact that this study of American religion has been filtered through my own experiences. This is more evident in some chapters than in others, for example in the introductory chapter and the chapter on ritual. Although I have used scholarly sources and have worked to be as accurate as possible in my descriptions and assessments of various aspects of religion in America, it is not beside the point that I am a woman, a Roman Catholic, the child of a "mixed" marriage between a Lutheran and a Catholic, a faculty member in a Protestant seminary, and an inhabitant of the Upper Midwest. I myself have found it helpful that in recent years scholars are becoming more willing to acknowledge that personal experiences have influenced their scholarly work, and it is my hope that those of you who read this book will consciously bring to it your own experiences as complementary filters to mine.

Acknowledgments and expressions of gratitude have become somewhat formulaic in a preface, but they are very much heartfelt. No one writes a book alone. I very much appreciate the fact that Robert Ellwood asked me to write this book in the first place, and I am grateful to him for advice during the whole project. Further, I owe many thanks to United Theological Seminary for sabbatical time and to Barbara J. Nelson and Marian Hoeft for their typing skills. The help I received from my colleagues at United and the willingness of my friends and neighbors to invite me to share in their worship have convinced me even more firmly that it is simply not possible to learn about religion and religions from books alone. My husband, Keith, and my children, Betsy and Paul, gave me the gift of normalcy during a time when it is a great temptation to take oneself too seriously.

1

celebrating diversity: religion in a plural society

The first time I taught a course on religion in America a student asked me none too gently why the syllabus contained no references to black or Native American religions. At the time it must have seemed too woefully obvious to say, simply, "Because I never thought of it," and I recall sputtering defensively about the need to cover all the major religious groups in America before going on to some of the marginal groups. In truth, the course I had taught could more accurately have been called "Mainstream Protestantism in America," for it covered almost exclusively the history and development of the major Protestant religions in America—the Congregationalists, the Baptists, the Methodists, the Episcopalians, and the Presbyterians. The course began with the Puritan settlements in New England in the seventeenth century, ranged through the waxing and waning of religious revivalism in the eighteenth and nineteenth centuries, chronicled Protestantism's encounter with science and religious skepticism beginning at the end of the eighteenth century and continuing through the present, and concluded with the controversy between Fundamentalism and Modernism in the twentieth century. In spite of my own upbringing as an American Catholic, Catholicism, like Judaism, received only two or three days' worth of attention, with a few minimal references to utopian groups in the nineteenth century. And, it did not occur at the time either to me or to my critic that the course made no mention of the fact that women, for the most part, have experienced American religions very differently from men.

The next time I taught the course I thought I was a little wiser, and I included not only the Protestant, Catholic, and Jewish mainstreams, but more diverse groups as well: eastern and occult religions, Native American and black traditions, and "new" religions. This time a student cried out in frustration, "But they're all the same!" At first I had no idea what she meant, but it gradually became clear that this student was overwhelmed by the very diversity of religions that I had been so eager to convey. She was disillusioned by the seemingly endless number of religious groups in America and thought she sensed a kind of crassness in the origins and histories of all these religions. Each one began to seem just like another—human-made cure-alls tailored to the needs of a credulous public. Apparently, in my zeal to be as inclusive as possible in referring to the multiplicity of forms that religious expression has taken in American culture, I had failed to convey the wonderful creativity of the human spirit that had produced so many responses to the questions which both plague and inspire us in our efforts to be whole persons, whether American or not: What is the nature of the divine? What is the essence of human nature? Is it good? evil? a mixture of both? What is the basis of reality? How should we live our lives? To study religion in America without reference to these broader questions, no matter how complete the list of groups might be, is to present a compendium of lifeless facts without the power to convince anyone that it is worthwhile to study them.

Both these incidents occurred more than ten years ago, but they remain vivid memories and reminders to me that a study of religion in America, particularly an introduction, requires a healthy balance between telling too much about a few religions that have been dominant in American culture, thereby failing to convey the immense religious diversity that characterizes America; or, on the other hand, spilling out a little information about a great number of religious groups, in which case we end up with an overwhelming amount of factual information—names of religions, the dates of their arrival in the United States, and a little something about their beliefs and rituals—without much sense of the place these movements have found in American culture or of the spirit that has moved their followers. Studying religion in America in this fashion—that is, by emphasizing diversity above all else—is a little like trying to acquire a foreign language by learning only the vocabulary without delving into grammatical constructions. We end up not knowing what to do with the information we actually do have, because we don't know how to put things together.

This book is an attempt to find that balance between too much and too little for the beginning student of American religion. To that end, the chief theme of this book is that of diversity of religious expression, and we will take some advice from the American philosopher and psychologist William James, who suggested in *The Varieties of Religious Experience* that "a large acquaintance with particulars often makes us wiser than the possession of abstract formulas."[1] What kind of "particulars" are we talking about? First, it is necessary to be aware that a discussion of religion in America must refer not only to what have been called the

---

[1] William James, *The Varieties of Religious Experience* (New York: Mentor, 1958), p. ix. Originally published in 1902.

mainstream traditions, such as Protestantism as it finds expression among the Baptists, the Methodists, the Episcopalians, the Presbyterians, the Congregationalists, the Disciples of Christ, and the Lutherans, as well as the other two "great faiths," Catholicism and Judaism; we must also consider groups that have been called "marginal" or "non-normative" or "cults" in their history, such as Mormons and Christian Scientists, Spiritualists and Theosophists, followers of Meher Baba or the Reverend Sun Myung Moon, practitioners of Hare Krishna, feminist witchcraft, or Zen. Nor can we forget that race and gender have figured significantly in the formation of various religious groups. Second, our acknowledgement of pluralism and diversity in American religion must extend to disciplines as well as to religious movements. We have much to learn about religion in America from the traditional experts such as the religious historian and the theologian, but the sociologist, the artist, the poet, and the psychologist have a great deal to teach us as well. Third, we must indicate that there are many different definitions of "religion" itself that are illuminating.

There are three definitions that are particularly helpful in this study. William James speaks of religion as "the feelings, acts, and experiences of individual men in their solitude, so far as they apprehend themselves to stand in relation to whatever they may consider the divine."[2] It is a definition that stresses the private, personal, and experiential aspects of religion and can provide insights into the conversion experience—for example, that of a man like Jonathan Edwards, who will be discussed in a later chapter.

The second definition is quite broad. It is that of the Protestant theologian Paul Tillich, who refers to religious systems as based on "ultimate concerns," those matters that affect us most deeply as human beings, such as the meaning of life and death and our destinies as individuals in a universe that sometimes seems meaningless. Because it is a definition that extends beyond the obviously religious—that is, doctrines, rituals, and moral codes—it is especially useful in looking at art or literature in American culture as they may express meanings without delineating actual religious content.

Two sociologists, Charles Glock and Rodney Stark, provide us with a third definition. They acknowledge the validity of James's and Tillich's definitions but want to include in their own definition a reference to "institutionalized systems of beliefs, symbols, values, and practices," or in other words, to emphasize what people do, what they value, and what kinds of groups they gather into as a result of their religious beliefs.[3] Glock and Stark's definition motivates us to remember that a study of religion must extend beyond the abstract and be concerned with the ways in which people put their beliefs together with the other parts of their lives—their politics, their jobs, their families.

Before we go too much further and run the risk of putting forth too much too

---

[2] *Ibid.*, p. 42.

[3] Charles Glock and Rodney Stark, *Religion and Society in Tension* (Chicago: Rand McNally and Company, 1965), p. 17.

soon in the way of definitions and the names of specific religious groups, it is time to look at the setting in which this study of religion takes place—American culture. As essential as it is to emphasize the diversity of religious expression in America, it is just as necessary to speak in more general terms about the place of religion as an institution in America. We are looking at religion in a nation that insists upon the separation of church and state and a nation whose Constitution guarantees both free exercise and nonestablishment—that is, the freedom to practice our various religions as we see fit (or not to) and the assurance that one religion will not be given rights and privileges denied any others.

Historically, there are different opinions as to why this separation of church and state was necessary. It is interesting to recall that, by contrast, the governments of the early settlements in America of the English, French, and Spanish were very much dominated by religious concerns and practices. One theory, attributed to Roger Williams, is that the church must be protected from the "corruptions" of the state. A second view, that of Thomas Jefferson, is the reverse—that the state must be saved from the interference of the church. Put forth by James Madison, a third view holds that both church and state are better off if power is decentralized and diffused, and there is competition among various religions rather than domination by one.

Whatever the variety of theories underlying the principle, most Americans are committed to the separation of church and state as essential to freedom of religion, and that separation has been zealously guarded over the last two centuries. One need only look at some of the decisions rendered by the United States Supreme Court in cases concerning religion to see how very careful the justices have been to make sure that no individual is prevented from practicing his or her religion, unless it can be demonstrated that the practice is in some way dangerous to the public welfare or even to the individual—and whether there really is danger is often a matter of great debate. The court must further see to it that a decision in no way grants special consideration to any one religion. "The law knows no heresy," proclaimed one court decision in the nineteenth century (*Watson* v. *Jones,* 1872), by which the justices were trying to indicate that the government and the courts had no power to decide which religious beliefs are right and which are wrong or whether one religion is more "true" than another. That decision, they said, is up to the individual conscience.

One might speculate that in a nation which guarantees no special favors to any one religion and in which there is no state religion, religion itself might become a matter of some indifference to the citizens. In many ways, just the reverse has been the case. In the eyes of much of the rest of the world, America is perceived as a hotbed of religious fervor and activity in which hundreds of religious groups flourish—more than 1,200, in fact. There have been numerous attempts by scholars to understand why this has been the case in America and not in countries with somewhat similar beginning histories, like Australia and Canada. Some have considered that it might be that very competition between religions that James Madison anticipated as a result of separation of church and state which accounts for the flourishing of religious activity in America. As early as 1832, Alexis de Tocqueville, a young Frenchman visiting the United States, remarked that "religion in America takes no direct part in the government of society, but it must be regarded as the first of their political institutions." Tocqueville claimed that this opinion was not peculiar to one class, "but it belongs to the whole nation and to every rank of society."[4] More than one hundred years later, the sociologist Will Herberg in *Protestant, Catholic, Jew* depicted American society as highly religious (he was writing during a period of renewed interest in religion after World War II). As partial evidence Herberg cited a study indicating that four-fifths of American adults believe that the Bible is "the revealed word of God."[5] In a more recent study Leo Rosten, author of *Religions in America,* claims that as many as 98 percent of Americans over twenty-one believe in God, although they would not all define "God" in the same way.[6]

But there is more to the story than these indications of widespread behavior would lead us to think. At the same time that he was making his observations about the proliferation of religious belief in America, Tocqueville registered a reservation, saying that he did not know whether all Americans had a sincere faith in their religion, "for who can search the human heart?" he asked. Herberg, too, was aware that at the same time that America was an intensely religious society, it was also highly secular, that is, greatly concerned with worldly and material things. For example, according to another study Herberg cites, even though such a high percentage of Americans believe in the Bible as divinely revealed, 53 percent of those questioned could not name one of the first four books of the New Testament, the four Gospels. Finally, Rosten informs us that less than half of the American population attends religious services with any regularity. However, this piece of information needs further explanation. We might assume that in a culture in which almost the total adult population expresses some sort of belief in God, certainly more than half would attend weekly religious services. Nonetheless, the number that actually do attend is much greater in America than in any of the other industrialized nations. In England, for example, weekly church attendance is estimated variously at only between 6 and 11 percent of the population.

Making matters even more complicated in the study of American religion is the fact that, although every religion is equal under the law, it is not true that each religion has equal status in American culture. It is more socially acceptable in most parts of the country to be an Episcopalian than it is to be a member of a Pentecostal denomination that emphasizes gifts of the Holy Spirit such as healing and speaking in tongues. Hostile reaction to "new" religions gives us ample evidence that legal validity does not automatically bring with it public acceptance.

---

[4] Alexis de Tocqueville, *Democracy in America,* ed. Phillips Bradley, Vol. I (New York: Knopf, 1963), p. 305. Originally published in 1835.

[5] Will Herberg, *Protestant, Catholic, Jew: An Essay in American Religious Sociology* (New York: Anchor Books, 1960), p. 2.

[6] Leo Rosten, ed., *Religions of America: Ferment and Faith in an Age of Crisis* (Simon and Schuster, 1975), pp. 18–20. An even newer study suggests 94 percent.

The very fact that historians and sociologists, psychologists, and theologians speak of "marginal" religions indicates that some religions are more dominant and influential in American life than others. Furthermore, we know that relationships among religious groups in America have not always been amicable, as we shall see in the next chapter. Americans have burned convents and painted swastikas on synagogues and shouted at and hit Jehovah's Witnesses who refused to salute the flag.

There has been and continues to be dissension of various sorts not only among members of different religions, but within individual groups as well. As much as we are inclined to celebrate religious diversity as a highly desirable aspect of American culture, we have to admit that religious pluralism can have implications for Americans' personal lives that are not at all positive. We are all familiar with incidents in which one person marries someone of another faith with resulting bitterness in both families. And we hear only too often lately about families torn apart when a member joins what is referred to as a "cult."

As accepting as we are of religious pluralism on many levels, there is a curious kind of etiquette that adheres to the subject of religion in America. Precisely because there is separation of church and state, and religious affiliation is a voluntary matter, a matter of choice, there is a strong sense that religion is a private matter, and no one's business but one's own. We learn even as children that it is not polite to ask another person to what religion he or she belongs and it is a kind of social truism that to discuss religion or politics at a party is to ask for a more volatile conversation than we may have anticipated. This privatization of religion in America helps partly to account for the fact that we almost never go into one another's churches and synagogues except for special occasions. We pass each other's houses of worship day after day and know almost nothing about their interiors or the beliefs that are acted out in the rituals that take place there.

This certainly isn't the whole story, however, of the place of religion in American culture. Even though it is considered impolite to ask personal questions about Americans' religious beliefs, at the same time there is intense public conversation about religious issues that have a bearing on the separation of church and state. There are extremely strong feelings on either side of the debate about whether or not abortion should be legal and whether or not there should be public funds available for abortion. School boards and legislatures alike do battle over the appropriateness of prayer in public schools, whether or not creationism should be taught along with evolutionary theory in high school biology classes, how best to celebrate holidays such as Christmas in the public schools, and whether it is unconstitutional to say a prayer at a public high school commencement service.

All of this is to say that there are "rules" in American culture governing religious behavior, many of them unwritten, that have emerged from trying to find the most appropriate ways to deal with religion in a culture that is pluralistic. Sometimes the forum for discussion of these rules is someone's living room; other times it is the United States Supreme Court. We will observe in more detail in later chapters how some of these "rules" of the culture operate in the area of religious beliefs and behavior as Americans struggle to live out their conviction that religious pluralism is more conducive to the common good than a state religion.

The following chapters of this book will take into account, then, both the diversity of religious expression in American culture as well as references to the overall culture itself in relation to religion. The assumption is, of course, that there is a dialogue between religion in America, in all its many forms, and the culture, that religions are both influenced by and influence the culture, and indeed, that religions are a part of the culture even though some religious groups might see themselves standing apart from "the world." Endlessly varied voices enter this dialogue. Part I of the book assesses the relationship between religions and American culture primarily from a historical perspective. Chapter 2 reviews the gradual development of religious pluralism in America and the struggle of Americans to deal with the social and political realities of the separation of church and state. Chapter 3 looks at a particular aspect of religion in America, the revival, and provides some theories as to how revivalism has influenced patterns in the secular culture. Chapter 4 describes the effects of the rise in importance of science and the scientific method on various religions at the end of the nineteenth century. Chapters 3 and 4 are meant to function in contrast with each other, with Chapter 3 detailing the ways in which a form of religious expression has had implications for American self-identity and political behavior and Chapter 4 a turnabout of that process and an example of how science, an institution of the secular culture, forced religions to respond to its new discoveries and assumptions about the nature of reality. Chapter 5 makes use of the biographies of four American religious leaders and their attempts to live their lives with integrity according to the beliefs they espoused and to bring their interpretations of these beliefs to bear upon the historical times in which they found themselves. Chapter 6 relates some characteristics of religious dissent in general in America along with extended examples of three dissenting groups in the culture. Chapter 7 departs somewhat from the historical perspective to look at several ways in which the arts, specifically architecture, literature, and painting, have contributed to our understanding of religion in America.

Part II of this book takes up three aspects of the study of religion: theology or belief systems, ritual, and sociology, in this case referring to some of the bases on which Americans have organized themselves into religious groups. The movement in these chapters is from a general discussion of each topic to specific examples of theological thinkers, rituals, and organizations as they reveal both unique contributions to American religion and a reflection of the values of American culture. To illustrate: Isaac Meyer Wise, whose life is analyzed in Chapter 7, provides us with information about issues that were peculiar to Reform Judaism in nineteenth-century America and at the same time gives us insights into some of the ways in which values concerning religion in American culture shaped ritual and belief among Reform Jews.

Before moving on to the next chapters, we can make use of two final reminders of the diversity we will encounter. The first is the time line that concludes this chapter. It offers a lengthy list of events in the course of American religious history covering everything from theological developments to the founding of universities to the arrival of various immigrant groups in America. Such a list can be overwhelming, first because as long as it is, we know that it represents only the smallest fraction of religious activity over the centuries, and second because we also know that each item points to the long and complicated story that lies behind it. Nonetheless, it can be a helpful list and one that attests to the great variety of religious groups and religious events in America. But, at this point, the beginning of a study, there is not much life to it. In fact, I recommend reading it over again after the conclusion of the book. In the meantime, to infuse the beginning of our study of religion in America with more vitality it helps to have some motivation that stems from personal experience. In truth, we don't need a book or a list of facts to convince us that there is religious diversity in America. The evidence is all around us; we just need to open our eyes.

Within ten minutes I can drive from my home in a large city in the Upper Midwest to more than sixty churches and synagogues that attest to the immense variety of religious expression in America. There are five Roman Catholic churches, thirteen Lutheran congregations, three Episcopalian, two Presbyterian, four United Methodist, and seven Baptist churches. There are three congregations of the United Church of Christ (whose ancestry lies in New England Congregationalism and the evangelical reformed tradition), two Christian Science churches, a Church of Divine Science, a Unitarian Universalist church, and a Friends' (Quaker) meeting house. There is one congregation each of the Evangelical Free Church, the Jehovah's Witnesses, Evangelical Covenant, Seventh Day Adventist, Christian Reformed (of Dutch ancestry), Disciples of Christ, also known as the Christian Church, Assemblies of God, the Church of the Nazarene, and a Metaphysical church called The Universal Temple of Love. In an old mansion on one of the city's lakes there is a Zen meditation center. Another old home houses a branch of The Church Universal and Triumphant. Close by is a Greek Orthodox church. There are four synagogues in the neighborhood—two Conservative congregations, one Reform, and one Orthodox. Not far away there is a United Church of Christ that serves an American Indian congregation, and a few blocks farther there is a black Pentecostal church led by a locally known woman evangelist.

Any one of us could travel around our neighborhoods and find this same evidence of religious diversity. Our lists of religious groups might differ in length according to whether we live in a large city, a small town, or a rural area. And the religious bodies that are most numerous would differ according to what part of the country we live in. For example, we would encounter many more Baptist groups in a Southern area, numerous Lutheran congregations in the Midwest, and much more evidence of Eastern religions in California and Hawaii. Each of these religious groups has a story to tell about its history in America. Some of them, such as the Congregationalists, Baptists, Episcopalians, Presbyterians, and Methodists, are among the earliest religions to achieve large membership and prominence in America. Others, among them Catholics, Lutherans, Jews, and Greek Orthodox, began to grow during the nineteenth and early twentieth centuries as great waves of immigrants began arriving from northern and western and then southern and eastern Europe. There are dissenting groups represented in our neighborhoods, such as the Quakers, who came to America in the seventeenth century, and the Unitarians, whose denomination began to emerge in the eighteenth century. There are "new" religions as well, Christian Science, for example, founded in the nineteenth century, the Church Universal and Triumphant, which is less than thirty years old, and Zen Buddhism, with a long tradition in other cultures and relatively new only to American culture. And there are black and Native American congregations with long, painful histories of dominance by and accommodation to white Christianity.

How do we make come alive all of those manifestations of religious pluralism in our neighborhoods that we have taken for granted for so long? Let us say that, for once, instead of passing by with unseeing eyes that church on the corner near the bus stop or the synagogue down the street from our old elementary school, we walk in just before a service begins. We enter with a spirit of what one of my colleagues, Robert Bryant of United Theological Seminary, calls "critical empathy," that is, a desire to learn and a regard for what we shall see that is not judgmental but instead seeks to understand the surroundings and the rituals in a way that fosters a feeling of compassion for the many ways in which we as human beings in American culture have tried to make sense of the places and times in which we have found ourselves.

As we wait for the service to begin, we have time to speculate about the history of this group in America. How long has it been a part of American culture? Has it been a denomination that was easily accommodated into the culture, or has it had to struggle for acceptance? Do its members belong to a particular ethnic group or economic class or race or age group? Or is its membership obviously mixed in various ways? As we think about these things we look at our surroundings. What are the symbols of this particular religion as they are incorporated into the architecture and the interior of the building? Are there paintings or statues or candlesticks or banners that proclaim the symbols of the tradition? Or does the interior give evidence of a denomination that feels strongly about simplifying its places of worship? As the service begins, we notice the priest or minister or rabbi and what he or she is wearing. Is it street clothes or elaborate vestments or a simpler kind of clerical garb such as a stole (a narrow strip of cloth, often embroidered in some way, that is worn over the shoulders and hangs down in front) or a special kind of collar? Is there a member of the clergy present at all? We may have chosen to visit a religious group that has no ordained clergy and thus no one obviously "in charge" of the service. As the service proceeds, does it appear to be highly ritualized—that is does it appear to follow an obviously prescribed order in which there are many prayers and elaborate actions that have been performed in just this way thousands of times before? Or is the service simpler, with perhaps just the singing of hymns, reading from Scripture, and a sermon? Does the service appear to be more spontaneous than ritualized, with congregation and clergy speaking and singing as they are moved to do so? Is it possible to ascertain from the service what the theological beliefs of the group might be? Can we come close to understanding how it is that they perceive the nature of God? Or whether or not they consider human nature as essentially good or essentially evil or a mixture of both? Are there ethical expectations for the group expressed during the service? That is, can we figure out how this denomination expects its members to live their lives?

As the service ends and we mingle with members of the congregation, we may set aside the American notion that it is not polite to ask people about their religious beliefs and inquire, if someone is willing to answer, how their religious views affect other parts of their lives. Does their religious belief help them to come to terms with struggles in their lives—personal, perhaps, or financial? Does it influence how they vote or what they eat or what they wear or how many children they have or whether or not they go to doctors or accept blood transfusions? Are there aspects of their religion with which they disagree, over which they might feel it necessary to leave the formal practice of religion or to join another denomination?

All of these observations and questions have relevance for the following chapters of this book, as we make an attempt to understand the different aspects of religious diversity in America, and the ways in which the culture accommodates such diversity. In keeping with this emphasis on pluralism, the next chapter will trace very briefly both the growth of diversity in American religion and the gradual development of the concept of religious tolerance. Both the major religious traditions and groups that have gone a different path from what we call the mainstream have had their share in this two-part story. A history of religious development can, of course, encompass many different foci, from the growth of organizations to biographies of leaders to doctrinal developments or disputes. This particular historical account will pay attention to the encounters of various religions in America with one another and the realities of a culture that guarantees separation of church and state and freedom of religious practice but that cannot go so far as to ensure that the maintaining of a religiously diverse society is free from struggle.

This time line is meant to indicate the entry point of many religions into American culture, as well as to mark some of the significant events in the relationship of various religions to American culture as a whole.

1200–1400	The Southeastern Ceremonial Complex, a pre-Columbian ritual movement (Natchez, Choctaw, Creek Cherokee, Yuchi) reaches its peak.
1492	Columbus visits "America" and claims it for the Catholic monarch of Spain.
1500	Pueblo culture flourishes in the Southwest.

1513	Ponce de Leon reaches Florida.
1565	St. Augustine, Florida, is founded by Spanish Catholics.
1607	Jamestown, Virginia, is settled by Anglicans.
1608	French Jesuits begin missionary work among the Indians in the St. Lawrence Valley.
1620	Separatist Puritans arrive in Plymouth, Massachusetts.
1628	A Dutch Reformed church is established in New Amsterdam (New York).
1630	Non-Separatist Puritans begin to settle in Massachusetts Bay (Boston).
1634	Maryland is chartered by Lord Calvert as a Catholic colony.
1636	Harvard College is chartered to train ministers.
1639	Roger Williams, exiled from Massachusetts, begins what is considered to be the first Baptist church in America in Rhode Island.
1640	The Bay Psalm Book, the first book published in North America, appears in Massachusetts. A short-lived Swedish Lutheran congregation is set up in Delaware.
1649	The Act of Toleration in Maryland grants freedom of religious practice to Christians.
1656	Two Quaker women are jailed upon their attempt to enter Boston.
1658	A small number of Jews arrives in Rhode Island.
1681	William Penn charters Pennsylvania as a Quaker colony but extends religious freedom to all.
1683	Presbyterians begin to settle in the Philadelphia area.
1697	Jesuit mission for Indians established at San Xavier del Bac in Arizona.
1701	Yale College is chartered.
1707	First Presbytery in America founded by a group of Presbyterian ministers.
1734	First Great Awakening begins in earnest in Massachusetts.
1740	George Whitefield, English revivalist preacher, spreads religious enthusiasm throughout the Eastern seaboard colonies.
1735	John Wesley, founder of Methodism, arrives in America.
1741	Jonathan Edwards preaches "Sinners in the Hands of an Angry God" at Enfield, Connecticut. Moravians arrive in Pennsylvania.
1746	Jonathan Edwards publishes *A Treatise Concerning Religious Affections.* The College of New Jersey (Princeton) is chartered.
1763	Touro Synagogue built in Newport, Rhode Island.
1769	First of the California missions established in San Diego, California.

1774	Mother Ann Lee, founder of the Shakers, arrives in New York with eight followers.
1776	Thomas Jefferson writes *The Declaration of Independence,* invoking the colonists' God-given right to revolt against royal tyranny.
1791	The Bill of Rights, with the First Amendment's guarantee of religious freedom and disestablishment, is added to the Constitution.
1799	The Second Great Awakening begins in Cane Ridge, Kentucky.
1800	A Boston woman organizes the Boston Female Society for Missionary Purposes.
1814	African Methodist Episcopal Church formed in Philadelphia.
1820s	Charles Grandison Finney speads his revivalist techniques through the Midwest. Unitarianism has become a strongly felt religious influence in New England.
1827	Joseph Smith has a religious experience that leads to the founding of Mormonism.
1834	Catholic convent burned in Charlestown, Massachusetts.
1838	Ralph Waldo Emerson, a Transcendentalist, delivers the Harvard "Divinity School Address," questioning the divinity of Jesus. John Humphrey Noyes assembles his community of what will become the Oneida Perfectionists in Vermont.
1841	Brook Farm, a Transcendentalist community, is established in Massachusetts.
1843	William Miller, an adventist preacher, announces that the world will end in 1844.
1846	Isaac Meyer Wise arrives in America and begins his attempts to reform Judaism.
1847	The potato famine in Ireland brings nearly one million Irish Catholics to America by 1850.
1852	Harriet Beecher Stowe publishes *Uncle Tom's Cabin,* the most famous anti-slavery book of all time.
1853	Antoinette Brown becomes the first ordained woman in the Congregational Church.
1857	President James Buchanan assembles troops to send against the Mormons.
1860–1865	The Baptist, Methodist, and Presbyterian churches all separate into regional denominations over the issues of slavery and states' rights.
1866	Mary Baker Eddy has a religious experience that leads to the discovery of Christian Science.
1870s	The revivalist Dwight Moody and the gospel singer Ira Sankey begin to promote urban revivalism.
1875	Mary Baker Eddy publishes *Science and Health with Key to the Scriptures.* Madame Helena Blavatsky and Colonel Henry Olcott found The Theosophical Society.

1881–1882	Czarist pogroms in Russia motivate large-scale Jewish immigration to America.
1884	Third Plenary Council in Baltimore urges that every Catholic parish have its own school.
1885	The Pittsburgh Platform puts forth principles for Reform Judaism.
1889	Robert Ingersoll publishes "Why Am I an Agnostic."
1891	First Greek Orthodox parish organized in New York.
1899	Pope Leo XIII publishes *Testem benevolentiae,* condemning "Americanism" among Catholics.
1880s	Holiness Revival sweeps Methodism.
1900–1910	The Social Gospel movement is at the peak of its influence.
1902	William James publishes *The Varieties of Religious Experience.*
1908	The Church of the Nazarene is formed from Pentecostal and Holiness groups. The Federal Council of Churches of Christ in America (Protestant) is organized.
1918	The Eighteenth Amendment ushers in the age of Prohibition.
1919	Father Divine's Peace Mission Movement is set up on Long Island.
1920s	Neo-orthodoxy is diminishing American theological optimism.
1922	Harry Emerson Fosdick preaches "Shall the Fundamentalists Win?"
1925	The Scopes "monkey trial" over the teaching of evolution takes place in Tennessee.
1928	The National Conference of Christians and Jews is formed. Alfred E. Smith, the first Catholic to run for president, is defeated.
1932	Dorothy Day and Peter Maurin found the Catholic Worker Movement.
1933	Jews begin to leave Germany because of Hitler's persecution.
1943	The Supreme Court exempts Jehovah's Witnesses from saluting the American flag.
1950	The National Council of Churches of Christ in America is formed.
1952	Scientology is incorporated as a church in California.
1957	The United Church of Christ is formed by a merger of Congregational and Evangelical Reformed churches.
1960	Black Muslim membership is estimated at 100,000. John F. Kennedy is elected the first Catholic president.
1962	Vatican II begins in Rome. San Francisco Zen Center is established, largest of the American Zen centers.

1963	Martin Luther King preaches the "I Have a Dream" sermon at the Lincoln Memorial.
1964	A California Supreme Court decision permits Native Americans to use peyote in their religious ceremonies.
1966	The Hare Krishna movement comes to America.
1967	Robert Bellah publishes his essay on civil religion in America. The Catholic Charismatic movement begins in Pittsburgh.
1973	Sun Myung Moon shifts the primary base for the Unification Church to America.
1975	The Native American Theological Association is founded in Minneapolis.
1979	The Episcopal Church votes to ordain women.
1982	Hispanic Catholics are estimated to constitute one-third of the American Catholic population. Several major Lutheran denominations begin plans for unity.
1983	The Presbyterian Church of the United States (South) and the United Presbyterian Church (North) are reunited after being apart since the Civil War.

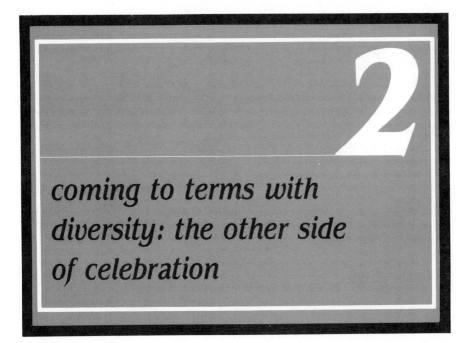

coming to terms with diversity: the other side of celebration

In *A Religious History of the American People,* Sydney Ahlstrom recounts a disagreement over Quakers that took place in 1657 between the commissioners of the Puritan colonies and the governor of Rhode Island. Fearful of what they considered the Quakers' dangerous belief in the possibility of human perfection and their conviction that the inspiration of the Inner Light was available to all, Christian or not, the Puritans engaged in both the punishment and the exile of Quakers. By 1657, Rhode Island had already become a refuge for dissenters, including Quakers, and the Puritans considered their presence too close for comfort. Thus, they asked the governor of Rhode Island to prevent Quakers from settling, or even landing, in Rhode Island. The governor (interestingly, one of Benedict Arnold's ancestors) refused to entertain such a request. He answered the Puritans by saying that Rhode Island did not interfere in matters of conscience, and, further, that he considered it a much less dangerous practice to permit Quakers to settle in Rhode Island than ''the course taken by you to send them out of the country.''[1]

This is a small incident, one that occurred more than 300 years ago, before the United States was even a nation. But it introduces the two themes that form the basis of this chapter, a historical overview of religion in America. The first is the continuing entry of various religious groups into American culture, whether the indigenous religions of the Native Americans; the imported religions of Europeans, Africans, and Asians; religions founded in America, or religious move-

---

[1] Sydney Ahlstrom, *A Religious History of the American People* (New Haven, Connecticut: Yale University Press, 1972), p. 178.

15

ments formed by splits from already existing groups. Second, there is the theme of the gradual unfolding over time of the idea of religious diversity as more conducive to the common good than a state, or established, religion. It was to be more than 100 years after the incident mentioned above before the Constitution confirmed that no one could be either persecuted or sent "out of the country" for his or her religious beliefs, but even earlier than 1657 religious diversity was very much a reality in the American colonies—an accepted reality in colonies such as Pennsylvania and Rhode Island and a situation that caused much consternation and turmoil in Puritan colonies such as Massachusetts. In spite of the tremendous influence of Puritanism over American culture, in this particular matter of religious freedom their practice of exiling dissenters did not prevail. Instead there came to be a gradual acceptance that a religiously plural society would be the norm in America and such a society could function best by granting freedom to all who came.

It is very important, however, to emphasize the *gradual* nature of the idea of religious pluralism, for to indicate that Americans have lived out the Constitutional guarantee of religious freedom with great ease would be misleading indeed. The success stories of Americans' abilities to live in a heterogenous society—the Constitutional guarantee of religious freedom, Supreme Court decisions upholding that guarantee, the absence of religious warfare, parochial school systems, interfaith dialogues and liturgies, interdenominational seminaries—must be balanced by a look at the less pleasing aspects of that same history; for example, the persecution of Catholics, the virtual ghettoizing of Jews by means of restrictive real estate covenants, the burning of black churches, the physical attacks on Jehovah's Witnesses, and the near obliteration of Native American religions.

In general, the swiftness with which a religion came to be acceptable in American culture hinged upon whether it was perceived to be sufficiently "American" in its doctrines, its liturgy, and its value system. Obviously, under these criteria religions such as Catholicism and Judaism were bound to suffer because they were perceived as foreign religions. But it was not only "foreign" religions that were found lacking. The religions of Native Americans were not looked upon by most Americans of European descent as religions at all, but rather pagan practices. Mormonism, a religion founded in America and one whose teachings form a kind of theological compendium of American values, was deprived of its religious charter by the Supreme Court in 1890 on the basis of its belief in the practice of polygamy. A belief in polygamy, the Court declared, went against "the common sense of mankind" and could not be upheld as a religious belief under the Constitution.

We will discover, then, as we briefly investigate more than four centuries' worth of religious belief and practice, that it is not enough merely to list all the religions that have found their home in America. We also need to place them against the backdrop of American culture as a whole as well as within the context of their relationships with one another. Citizens of the United States in the late twentieth century take religious freedom and separation of church and state for granted, and we find it almost impossible to comprehend how astonishingly radical these two concepts appeared to our sixteenth-, seventeenth-, and even eighteenth-century ancestors, no matter in what part of the world they lived. Thus, to repeat, any history of religion in America must proceed from at least two perspectives: one involves changes over time in the number of religions in America, because of the constant addition of religious groups to the culture by the various means mentioned at the beginning of the chapter; the other has to do with changes in the definitions of "religion," "religious freedom," and "separation of church and state" as Americans have acted out their conviction that freedom of religion is a necessary part of American culture.

THE SIXTEENTH CENTURY

The history of religious pluralism in America predates the history of European settlement by hundreds, even thousands, of years. The Spanish settlers who arrived in America in the sixteenth century and encountered Indian tribes in Florida and in the Southwest could not have known that the peoples they met made up only a fraction of the tribes living on the continent and that their cultures, including means of livelihood, world view, and tribal organization, differed drastically from one another. Further, the Spanish, as well as the French and the English who came after them during the next two centuries, did not realize that what they observed of Native American cultures had religious significance. Because the European understanding of religion was restricted to that which had to do with churches and sets of doctrines, the newcomers did not recognize the pervasively religious orientation of Native American cultures. In *Native American Religions,* Sam Gill points out that in order to understand the role that religion has played in American Indian cultures, it is necessary to define religion broadly as "actions, processes, and symbols" that order life and give it meaning and purpose, and to look for such manifestations in many different places: "[I]n the stories of creation, of heroes, of tricksters, of fools. . . . [I]n architecture, art, and orientations in the landscape. . . . [I]n ritual drama, costumes, masks, and ceremonial parapher-nalia . . . related to hunting, farming, and fishing."[2] Religious activities among Native Americans were not restricted to only one aspect of life that could be easily observed and marked off, and, thus, the Europeans, unable to interpret what they saw in terms of their own understanding of religion, came to the conclusion that Indians were "pagans," having no religion at all.

There were other aspects of religion among Native Americans that differed very greatly from that of Europeans. Although it is important to emphasize that Indian religions and cultures were highly different from one another, it is also possible to make some generalizations about similarities in contrast with Euro-

---

[2] Sam Gill, *Native American Religions: An Introduction* (Belmont, California: Wadsworth Publishing Co., 1982), pp. 11–12.

pean religions that help us to comprehend why the lack of understanding between Europeans and Native Americans has been so overwhelming, so destructive, and so long-lasting. Indians did not share the European interpretation of the ''truth'' of one religion over all others. They took it for granted that there would be many different deities, stories of creation, and rituals among tribes depending upon their region and their means of livelihood. In addition, Indians had no concept of the story of the Fall and of a creation corrupted by human sin and in need of divine redemption. Their world views were more holistic than the Europeans' and did not break apart so drastically into warring components of spirit and matter, sacred and profane. Finally, Indians did not look upon land ownership as an individual matter; land belonged to the community or to no one.

All of these differences help to explain the virtual disintegration of many Indian cultures over the period of time that stretched from the first encounters with European cultures in the sixteenth century through to the present time. The religious diversity among Native American religious systems certainly did not disappear after the sixteenth century; it persists to this day. But it is during this century that we can begin to observe the domination of one way of being religious—Western European—over another—Native American—that has so greatly defined the course of religious history in America.

THE SEVENTEENTH CENTURY

The Spanish who came to the South and Southwest and the French who arrived in the Northeast during the sixteenth century brought their Roman Catholicism with them. They claimed land for their respective crowns and were, in essence, seeking to establish European religion, culture, and economic influence in North America. The seventeenth century, however, saw the arrival of settlers, particularly from England, with another purpose in addition to that of extending European settlements and seeking fortunes. The English Puritans, in whose country the Reformation had caused the most turmoil, came to America to found a new society, free from what they considered the corruptions of church and state left over in Europe from medieval times. The Puritans, who came to Plymouth in 1620 and to Massachusetts Bay (Boston) in 1630, were not the only English settlers in America. By 1650 there were Baptists and Quakers in Rhode Island, as well as Quakers in Pennsylvania and New Jersey and Anglicans in Virginia. All of these groups have their own histories of adaptation to and growth in American culture. From one perspective, however, the Puritans' story is the one that has had the most influence on America's self-understanding and that has shaped the stories of all of us who have come after them, no matter what our religious beliefs might be. This seventeenth-century group of dissidents came to America with the intention of forming not just another settlement, but a new kind of society formed on the basis of a covenant with God. For the Puritans there was something sacred—something innocent, we might even say—about the very land that they settled. They spoke of America as a new Israel and of themselves as chosen people.

Because they saw the successes and failures of their society so closely tied to God's will, the Puritans interpreted not just religious affairs, but economic and political goings-on as well, as signs of God's favor or disfavor. When times were bad, the Puritans feared that they had displeased God and were deserving of punishment for a breach of the very covenant upon which their society was founded. The year 1692, for example, was a particularly unfortunate one. Crops failed, there was much sickness, and there was uneasiness over relationships with the English crown. This was also the year of the Salem Witchcraft trials, and it appeared to many Puritans that the difficulties visited upon them were a result of diminished religious fervor.

This sense of America as a nation set apart by God and the connection between America's fortunes to divine pleasure or displeasure has persisted through the twentieth century. The doctrines of Puritanism upon which this interpretation of America was based have long since dissipated. What remains is the same sense of chosen-ness, although it has lost its religious underpinnings—most Americans could not trace their understanding of America as a nation especially chosen by God to the history of Puritanism. Nonetheless, it is a heritage carried down to us from a relatively small group of believers in the seventeenth century.

One thing the Puritans did not bequeath to their offspring from many nations was their conviction that religious dissidents must be kept out of the community. By the end of the seventeenth century, it was simply not feasible to keep dissenters out of even those colonies in which there were established religions. Religious diversity had long since become a reality in North America, and the anecdote with which this chapter begins is testimony to the fact that even by the mid–seventeenth century there were voices raised against the practice of exiling those who disagreed with the establishment's religious beliefs. There were some Catholics, many of them in Maryland, which had been settled by the Catholic Lord Calvert, and there were Jews in both Rhode Island and New York, although not many. Still, it is not possible to say, really, that religious tolerance—that is, the granting of civil rights and social privileges to all comers—was widespread. If religious diversity was a reality, religious tolerance had a long way to go.

THE EIGHTEENTH CENTURY

At the beginning of the eighteenth century, there was religious diversity, as we have seen, but there were few clues to the huge variety of religious beliefs and practices that would come to characterize American culture in the nineteenth and twentieth centuries. Nor was there much evidence of the large numbers of Americans who would be associated with institutional religion in later centuries or of the religious fervor among the population that would so amaze and puzzle Europeans. By 1700, it is safe to say, with a few exceptions a pall had fallen upon religious piety in the American colonies. The fact of established religions in some of the colonies—Massachusetts, Connecticut, and Virginia among them—did not necessarily mean liveliness in the practice of the particular religion. In fact, there was a widespread sense that the religious intensity that had marked at least the first three to four generations of settlers, particularly in the Puritan colonies, had waned noticeably even before the turn of the century and that the idea of a covenant between God and God's chosen people on the American continent was not nearly as compelling as it had once been. In addition to the many who could be considered lukewarm in their devotion to religion, there were thousands more who practiced no religion and had never set foot in a church.

Two events of the eighteenth century, the Great Awakening during the first half, and the American Revolution during the second, drastically changed the complexion of religious diversity in America. The Awakening, which we shall look at in more detail in the next chapter, provided an impetus both for renewed religious fervor in America and for the spread of a particular way of being religious. The Revolution resulted in a new nation, one of the foundations of which was the separation of church and state and the conviction that no one religion could be established or given special privileges over any other. Thus, if the Awakening prompted the revival of religious piety, the Revolution made it possible for America to become the home of many different religions, all equal under the law.

Because the Great Awakening came at a time when there was great fear in New England and beyond that God had lost interest in America and was displeased by the lack of fervor among the chosen, the churches of the colonies were more than ready to hear the cries of those preachers who shouted of the depravity and sinfulness of the population and at the same time promised that God's mercy would be given to those who repented. Sermons that put forth the wretchedness of sinners and elicited from listeners shrieks and moans of repentance were the marks of the revival experience. The revival technique and the response to it began to spread widely in the 1730s. The religious historian Winthrop Hudson claims that the Awakening "was 'Great' because it was general. People everywhere were caught up in the movement, and its influence was spread by innumerable local pastors, passing itinerants, and lay exhorters. No one could escape the excitement or avoid the necessity to declare himself friend or foe."[3]

Because the Awakening, which continued on through the 1750s, was so widespread geographically and because it cut across denominational lines, it had a unifying effect on both religious and national concerns. The theological tenor of the Awakening was thoroughly Protestant in nature with its overwhelming emphasis on human depravity along with the accessibility of God's freely given mercy to those who would repent. Congregationalists, Baptists of various kinds, Presbyterians, even Anglicans and later Methodists, could all acknowledge the validity of the revival experience for their own denominations. On the practical side, the revivals increased church membership, bringing back many who had become indifferent and drawing in for the first time thousands who had never

---

[3] Winthrop S. Hudson, *Religion in America,* third edition (New York: Charles Scribner's Sons, 1981), p. 76.

been church members. Politically speaking, the Awakening provided a bond that cut across colonial borders and renewed and reconfirmed the concept so important in the early years of settlement, particularly in New England—that God had a special destiny in store for America that would leave Europe behind.

By 1760 the Great Awakening had died down, but, as it turned out, it was to be the first of numerous widespread revivals in American religious history, the next one less than fifty years later on the frontiers of Kentucky, Ohio, and Tennessee. Each time these awakenings have served the dual function of increasing religious enthusiasm and church membership and of deepening national consciousness, often in times of crisis.

The other event of nearly cataclysmic proportions with which we are concerned in the eighteenth century is the American Revolution and its connections with religion. Given the early patterns of religious history in America and the force with which the Great Awakening erupted and was maintained over a period of many years, it seems astonishing that when independence from England was won fewer than twenty years after the Awakening died out, the Constitution for the new nation did not establish some form of Protestantism as the national religion. Let us start with the more negative reasons why this was not the case: apathy and fear. In spite of the recent history of the Awakening, the last quarter of the eighteenth century was marked by a time of spreading religious indifference during which time only one person in about twenty was a church member. These were the years of the Enlightenment, a period of rationalism that saw the growing departure from belief in a depraved and helpless humanity upon a sovereign God and a much greater reliance upon and optimism about the rights and capabilities of the individual person. Sydney Ahlstrom speculates that the guarantee of religious freedom in America may have proceeded as much from indifference to organized religion as from a conviction of its importance.[4] Fear of the dominance of one religion over another was also a factor. By the time of the Revolution, religious pluralism, at least of the Protestant sort, had reached a point where it was not so clear which religion was the top contender for establishment, and there was a fear that Anglicanism might win. Tied as it was to a British rule that seemed more and more hateful and to an Episcopal form of governance (rule by bishops) that many colonists had sought to escape, Anglicanism generated much more apprehension as a candidate for the established religion than it did approval.

There are also more positive wasy to interpret the fact that the Revolution resulted in freedom of religion. By 1776 the thought was common that plurality of religious belief could foster the kind of dynamism of religious activity among many different groups that a state religion was more likely to stifle. In other words, competition had more benefits than dangers for religion. Furthermore, the Great Awakening had revealed many of the common elements among what would become the mainstream Protestant groups of the nineteenth and twentieth cen-

---

[4] Ahlstrom, p. 379.

turies, diminishing the concern that by granting religious freedom to others, one was endangering one's own system of beliefs and the freedom to practice them.

By 1799, the year during which the Second Great Awakening began, an observer could see the legacy of both the first Great Awakening and the years of the Enlightenment as they found outlets among different religions in America. The numbers of Baptists and Methodists with their evangelical form of Christianity had increased greatly to the extent that they would remain among the four largest Protestant denominations up to the present time. On the other hand, the Enlightenment philosophy of optimism concerning the power of human reason to make sense of the world and to keep it running smoothly once God had put it into motion had already produced Deism, a minimalist kind of religious outlook that did not achieve institutionalization but that was represented in disproportionately high numbers among those who founded the American nation—for example, George Washington, Thomas Jefferson, Thomas Paine, and Benjamin Franklin. The God of the Deists essentially minded its own business but was nonetheless a God to be worshiped and one who had an interest in the destiny of America. Another manifestation of Enlightenment views was Unitarianism, based on the "reasonable" doctrine that there was one God rather than three persons in one God. By the early nineteenth century many congregations that had had a Puritan heritage were Unitarian.

There were still no great numbers of Catholics and Jews in America at the end of the eighteenth century. Nor had the Lutherans more than a small representation. There were communal religions that had found a home in America before 1800, among them the Shakers, whose communities would flourish during the nineteenth century, and the members of the Ephrata Cloister in Pennsylvania. Protestantism, as it was practiced by Congregationalists, Anglicans, Presbyterians, Baptists, and Methodists, dominated American religion at this point in history. But the next century would be witness to forces that would shake that domination: the influx of millions of Catholic and Jewish immigrants, the founding of new religions, and the further splitting of Protestant religions into those that spoke to the head and those that appealed to the heart. Interwoven among all these developments, however, was the constant theme of America as a nation set apart by God for a special destiny, a theme that continued to be developed throughout the years of the nineteenth century and that affected not only mainstream Protestantism, but all those religions that came to be at home in America.

THE NINETEENTH CENTURY

There are so many story lines in the development of religious diversity in the nineteenth century that it is difficult to sort them all out. At the beginning of the century, the years of the Second Great Awakening, it appeared as if evangelical Protestantism, with its emphasis on enthusiastic religion and moral reform, would surely come to overwhelm all other forms of Protestantism and religion in general in America. In fact, the nineteenth century in America has been described as the ''triumph of evangelicalism,'' and the Baptists and Methodists who came out of this mold of religious piety have endured as major denominations to this day. There were too many other contenders, however, for one way of being religious to have dominated completely.

By the end of the century evangelical Protestantism had a strong rival in liberal Protestantism, a way of being religious that toned down enthusiastic expressions of piety, looked beyond the Bible for religious truth, and expressed its beliefs not so much in emphasis on rightness of doctrine but through doing good works in the world. The Social Gospel movement, which sought to eliminate poverty and economic injustice by reforming capitalism, is an example of this kind of religious expression. Along with more liberal forms of mainstream Protestantism, communal religions—the Shakers, Rappites, Amana Colonists, Harmonists, Oneida Perfectionists, Brook Farmers—flourished at different times during the nineteenth century, even if their settlements were small and usually not long-lived. In addition, religions of American origin sprang up, among them Mormonism (1827), Seventh Day Adventism (1840s), Spiritualism (1848), Christian Science (1866), and Theosophy (1875). In the meantime, the numbers of Catholics and Jews in America multiplied greatly through two different immigration periods: from northern and central Europe in the middle of the century and from southern and eastern Europe toward the end. Finally, by the time of the World Parliament of Religions held in Chicago in 1893, the interest in Eastern religions provided evidence that Americans were beginning to have some knowledge of non-Western religious beliefs.

As we might expect, all of these different expressions of religious belief and practice followed varying paths through the nineteenth century. In its many forms, mainstream Protestantism was so well established in American culture that its adherents could afford to turn away in part from a theological emphasis and put their energies into issues of moral reform. Beginning with the mission societies of the early part of the century, on through abolition, women's rights, temperance, and finally the Social Gospel Movement of the end of the century, Protestantism found expression in the attempt at purification of both the individual and society as a whole. This is not to say, however, that all Protestants agreed on these matters of reform. The issue of abolition, for example, split not only congregations, but entire denominations. Catholics and Jews were not, of course, indifferent to individual and social reform, but many of their struggles centered on the dual problem of trying to achieve acculturation within American society and at the same time retain their European heritage. The different ethnic groups represented within both Judaism and Catholicism made assimilation a highly complex task. For the communal and occult movements, as well as for religions such as Mormonism and Christian Science, survival was a matter of existing on the fringes of

American religious society for as long as it took to convince nonbelievers that they were respectable religions and not dangerous to society.

The point here is that in spite of the Constitution's guarantee of religious freedom for all as well as the reality of religious diversity in nineteenth-century America, it is simply not possible to say that each religion had achieved the same social acceptance as any other. Some were ''in'' and some were ''out.'' One way to get a good idea of which religions had achieved a high degree of acceptance in American culture and which had not is to consult a religious historian who wrote during the nineteenth century—a Protestant, in fact. Robert Baird (1798–1863) provides a good example of a religious historian who described the many religions that had found a home in America. Baird was a Presbyterian minister who promoted Protestantism in Europe and who wrote a history of religions in America in an effort to explain religious pluralism to Europeans. Because Baird was an historian, we would expect him to describe what he knew of religions in America. But he went further than that—he ''prescribed'' many of the characteristics of Protestantism as the norm for all religions, and he judged what he observed among other religions by Protestant criteria. Baird favored what he called the ''evangelical'' churches, which he named as the following: Episcopalian, Presbyterian, Methodist, Congregationalist, and Lutheran. In spite of the differences among them, he saw them all as being on the right track theologically: ''On no one point are all these churches more completely united, or more firmly established, than on the doctrine of the supremacy of Christ in His Church, and the unlawfulness of any interference with its doctrines, disciplines, and government.'' Baird looked upon many of the other religions in America not merely as examples of religious diversity but rather as ''non-evangelical'' and, in fact, in error. Baird was not only suspicious about their theologies, but concerned also as to whether they promoted the proper interpretation of separation of church and state. Baird numbered among the ''non-evangelicals'' Catholics, Jews, Unitarians, Mormons, and Shakers, an interesting combination of foreign, domestic, and liberal religions. What Baird thought they all had in common was the error of their ways: ''All those sects that either denounce or fail faithfully to exhibit the fundamental and saving truths of the Gospel.''[5] While Baird had to acknowledge that all religions in America were equal under the law, he did not see them by any means equal theologically.

By the end of the nineteenth century, Americans had already been astonishing Europeans for decades with the prolific nature of their religious behavior. And there is no denying the accuracy of Europe's perceptions. America was indeed a nation of many, many religions. However, if we look beyond mere numbers to see how specific religions were stratified socially and how they were regarded by historians, theologians, and the law, we find that mainstream Protestantism continued to be the arbiter of religious beliefs, values, and practices in

---

[5] Robert Baird, *Religion in America: A Critical Abridgement by Henry Warner Bowden,* originally published in 1842 (New York: Harper and Row, 1970), p. 208 and p. 257.

American culture, and its members to hold positions of social, economic, and political power. Further, the perception of America as a chosen nation continued to grow and to be articulated throughout the nineteenth century. And in spite of its Protestant beginnings in the Puritanism of seventeenth-century New England, this view of America as a nation set apart by God for a special destiny exercised authority over non-Protestants and nonbelievers alike and continued to have great currency well into the twentieth century.

THE TWENTIETH CENTURY

In the twentieth century we find a continuation of many of the stories that had their beginnings in the nineteenth century or even earlier. Among Protestants the theological debate went on between liberals and what came to be called "fundamentalists" regarding biblical interpretation and the role of the churches in American culture. Argument continued as well between those who espoused the Social Gospel movement with its optimistic view of human nature and neo-Orthodox theologians who feared that such optimism would render Americans incapable of seeing the reality of sin either in individuals or in the nation. The Protestant penchant for moral reform, so much a part of nineteenth-century piety, found an outlet in the Prohibition movement, a crusade that united many Protestant denominations, at least on that issue. American Catholics and Jews kept up their efforts at assimilation into American culture, at the same time trying to do so without loss of their unique identities. Both these groups experienced events that were nearly cataclysmic in nature during the twentieth century: for Jews it was the Holocaust of World War II, and for Catholics it was the second Vatican Council of the 1960s. New religions, too, sprang up during the twentieth century, among them Eastern imports like Zen Buddhism new only in their American environment; others like the I Am movement or black groups such as Father Divine's Peace Mission Movement and the Black Muslims were American products.

It is important to interject another perspective at this point into the analysis of religions in twentieth-century America. For the most part we have looked at the addition of religions to the culture by means of immigration, the splitting off from already-existing groups, and the founding of new religions. But we can also observe in the twentieth century a broadening of the very definition of *religion* to include organizations and concepts that would have been outside what was defined as religion or as religious in the nineteenth century, certainly far beyond anything Robert Baird would have described as "evangelical." There are Supreme Court decisions that can be quite helpful in making this point. However, a little background with which to begin is necessary.

The Constitution emerged from a historical context in which religious pluralism was very much a reality, but in which there was little doubt as to what constituted a religion—beliefs, organization, rituals—and what did not. The guarantees of free expression and disestablishment regarding religion are clear enough, but the framers of the Constitution could not have foreseen that within the next two centuries there would be great difficulty in actually determining the definition of religion. In colonial times religion was perceived as founded upon belief in a deity and characterized by some form of worship and a moral code. As Laurence Tribe, a professor of Constitutional law, points out, religion "was recognized as legitimate and protected only insofar as it was generally acceptable as 'civilized' by Western standards."[6] Thus, Catholicism and Judaism, for example, may have been regarded by many Protestants as foreign and unevangelical, but there was little dispute as to whether they were actually religions. There was not so much certainty about the new religions, Mormonism among them, and, as mentioned earlier in the chapter, in 1890 (*Davis* v. *Beeson*) the Supreme Court deprived the Church of Jesus Christ of Latter Day Saints, as it is officially referred to, of its charter, finding that its practice of polygamy, which went against "the common sense of mankind," rendered the church unacceptable as a religious or charitable organization. In other words, any organization, whatever its claims, could not both believe in polygamy and still be considered a legitimate religion. The church was recognized again when it officially discontinued polygamy in 1890.

By the twentieth century, the Supreme Court found that the legal understanding of what constituted religious belief in the nineteenth century was too narrow to serve in solving contemporary dilemmas. Another Supreme Court decision provides an illustration. *The United States* v. *Seeger* (1965) involved a dispute over the basis for conscientious objection, which in the past had been tied at the very least to belief in a Supreme Being. The Court did indeed rule that conscientious objector status must be tied to belief in a Supreme Being, but it broadened that phrase to encompass any sincere belief occupying "a place in the life of its possessor parallel to that filled by the orthodox belief in God of one who clearly qualifies for exemption."[7] Thus, in order to facilitate the adequate functioning of the First Amendment in twentieth-century America, the Supreme Court had to recognize the realities of various understandings of a belief in an ultimate power that moved outside the boundaries of traditional religion, and that, in fact, might be perceived as humanism by more orthodox believers.

Interwoven through all these separate stories of multiplying numbers of religions and the broadening of the definition of religion was a kind of waxing and waning of religious fervor during the twentieth century that seemed tied to a series of wars and to America's search for the best way to fulfill the role of a nation set apart by God for a special destiny. This is a pattern that we have already observed in the eighteenth and nineteenth centuries, but it emerges in different form in the twentieth. The concept of America as a chosen nation began to lose ground during the Korean War and to diminish even more while America was engaged in the

---

[6] Laurence H. Tribe, *American Constitutional Law* (Mineola, New York: Foundation Press, Inc., 1978), p. 257.

[7] Ibid., p. 830.

conflict in Vietnam. The eruption of protests during the 1960s and 1970s began as objections to the war in Vietnam, but they were finally directed also against organized religion and other institutions of society as well. Many young people and others not so young began to look upon the traditional religions as irrelevant and hypocritical and to turn to Eastern religions, to the occult, and to new religious movements such as Scientology, Hare Krishna, and Unificationism for answers to the questions they felt could no longer be found in the mainstream churches. The old-guard religions of Christianity and Judaism appeared for a while to be left behind in the search for new truths that appeared more fitting for a new age. However, the "new conservatives" of the 1970s and 1980s, such as the Moral Majority, remind us that the old ways and the old religions have not diminished greatly in numbers or in influence in contemporary America.

How has religious toleration fared in twentieth-century America? As in previous centuries, there have been both successes and failures. Protestantism in all its forms is still the chief religious influence in American culture, although the election of John F. Kennedy in 1960 as the first Catholic president and the appointment of Henry Kissinger in 1973 as the first Jewish secretary of state give some evidence of the loosening of unwritten, but very real, restrictions with regard to religion upon the holders of high public office in America. Anti-Semitism, unfortunately, is by no means dead in American culture, and there continues to be widespread hostility directed toward unusual religions, with new religions—"cults"—bearing the brunt of it, in a pattern similar to that of the nineteenth century when new religions such as Mormonism and Christian Science were the targets. On the other hand, the recent ecumenical movement, originating in the 1960s, has fostered dialogue among Protestants, Catholics, and Jews. Further, there has been a resurgence of interest in Native American and black religions, caused in part by the fact that historians have begun to recognize their neglect of these religious systems and to try to remedy that omission. And, after centuries of being restricted from ordination, women have begun to find a place among the clergy of many denominations and, in those groups that still do not ordain women, to exert more influence.

CONCLUSION

In each century since the seventeenth we have found evidence of religious pluralism as well as of the attempt to come to terms with it. The stories are by no means all happy, and if we are inclined to take religious toleration too much for granted from our vantage point of the late twentieth century, we need only probe into history very lightly to find how many struggles have been fought in its name—*within* denominations as well as among them. And yet, battles aside, the strong commitment to the principle of separation of church and state has remained constant since 1791. Americans to this day are for the most part in agreement with that seventeenth-century governor of Rhode Island who was convinced that it was much less frightening to try to assimilate diverse religious elements into society than it was to contemplate the perils of a state religion and of exiling religious dissenters. As we have seen over and over again, the effort involved in living out the reality of religious freedom is never-ending and takes a different form in each century.

An historical overview such as this one runs the risk of conveying a sense of tidiness about general patterns in American religious history that belies the complexity and downright messiness of the materials the historian encounters. To counteract the temptation to look at the historical patterns already mentioned in this chapter as neatly packaged concepts that smooth out too neatly the tensions inherent in them, the next two chapters will deal more specifically with eras and with people who have greatly influenced both American religion and culture, not only at the level of religious institutions but in more widespread ways as well. Chapter 3 concentrates on revivalism in America, a way of acting out religious beliefs that emerged in the eighteenth century and that is still very much a part of certain segments of American religious life. Chapter 4 deals with the growing prestige of science and the scientific method as it drastically affected the religious belief systems in the nineteenth century and continues to have strongly felt repercussions for religions in America up to the present.

washed in the blood
of the lamb: revivalism
in america

"Won't you come, won't you come, won't you come," exhorted the evangelist, "won't you come and be washed in the blood of the Lamb?" Weeping in response to the preacher's urgings and the singing of gospel hymns, men, women, and children filed to the front of the wooden tabernacle in southern Mississippi in the 1940s. They knelt in the sawdust before encouraging friends and relatives, confessed that they had been sinners, and then finally accepted Jesus as their savior. It was the yearly gathering of the Frost Bridge Camp Meeting, and people had come far out into the country to the camp grounds where they resided in the little wooden cabins—called "tents"—to participate in an experience of religious revival and renewal. My friend and colleague who is the source of this description has said that her childhood experiences of the camp meeting and the revival appear to be exact replications of those in the nineteenth century that she has read about. And the nineteenth-century meetings had their historical origins in the First Great Awakening of the eighteenth century.

Though the direct experience of the religious revival has not been a part of every American's experience, it is a rare person who has not been exposed in some way to the concept of revivalism, a particular pattern of stirring up religious feelings, whether through the electronics ministries of evangelists like Oral Roberts, early-morning broadcasts of the PTL (Praise the Lord) Club, the big-city crusades of Kathryn Kuhlman and Billy Graham, the talk-show appearances of Marjoe Gortner (former child healer turned actor), or even the reading of Sinclair Lewis's *Elmer Gantry*. Unfortunately, this kind of contact usually results in a superficial knowledge of the more sensational aspects of revivalism without much understanding of its theological underpinnings or the place of revivalism in American religious history. What has become in the twentieth century a way of acting out religious beliefs that is generally confined to more evangelical denominations and to rural and southern America was once a widespread phenomenon that cut across many denominations and regions in eighteenth- and nineteenth-century America. The word *revival* is used in American history in two different ways: first, to designate a specific event—for example, the yearly revival of a particular congregation; second, to point to a period in history, perhaps thirty or forty years, during which revivals occur with great frequency and intensity (these periods are also called "awakenings"). We need to look at both manifestations in order to understand revivalism in America.

Awakenings have occurred in American history during very different periods, but the specific revival events that they comprise have a sameness in content and structure that seems to transcend historical contexts. The revival in the singular sense is usually a series of days during which a preacher, sometimes from a neighboring church but often a traveling evangelist who specializes in revivals, preaches emotional appeals to an assembled crowd, exhorting them to abandon their sinful ways and accept Jesus. This description fits not only the early revival meetings held by various religious groups in America or the tent meetings that several denominations in a town might sponsor each summer, but also the massive meetings that evangelists such as Billy Graham hold in auditoriums all over the world. The services generally include the singing of hymns, prayers, testimonials by those present as to the good that Jesus has done in their lives, the evangelist's sermon, and the coming forward to acknowledge first repentance and then acceptance of salvation through Jesus. These statements of repentance and salvation are not quiet declarations made in private to the preacher; they are more likely to be shouted out and sometimes accompanied by screaming, fainting, or bodily gyrations. The emphasis is on religious feeling and spontaneity rather than on intellectual response, but at the same time these emotions are expressed within the framework just described—no matter how high the emotional pitch, what occurs is expected within the context of the revival.

The revival is a drama of contrasts: a sinking to the depths followed by a rising to the heights; wallowing in one's sense of oneself as a sinner and then a reveling in God's love and acceptance of the sinner. The theology of the revival comes out of the Reformation with its emphasis on both the separation between the human and the divine and the power of God's mercy to overcome that separation. The evangelist pounds home the sinfulness, the "creatureliness," of those assembled and the wrath of God that will be visited upon those who refuse to repent. In the most famous of all American revival sermons, "Sinners in the Hands of an Angry God," Jonathan Edwards terrified his listeners by describing them as spiders held over a fiery pit: "The God that holds you over the pit of hell, much as one holds a spider or loathsome insect over the fire, abhors you, and is dreadfully provoked; his wrath towards you burns like fire; he looks upon you as worthy of nothing else, but to be cast into the fire.''[1] After arousing both terror and, he hopes, repentance in the hearts of those gathered, the evangelist begs them to fling themselves upon the mercy of an all-powerful God who sent his only son to earn the grace of redemption for humankind through his death on the cross. Sometimes, in fact, there are two evangelists: one to preach on human sin and one to describe God's mercy to sinners. In the revival hymn ''Amazing Grace'' we have a vivid example of that contrast in emotions: ''Amazing Grace, how sweet the sound / That saved a wretch like me; / I once was lost, but now am found / Was blind, but now I see.'' These are not empty words sung to a pretty tune; rather, they speak of extremes of emotion, of radical chance in self-perception: the blind and wandering wretch—the sinner—finds safety, acceptance, and new vision in the sweetness of God's grace, freely given. In revival theology the individual is responsible for her or his own repentance, but the acting out of the drama in the presence of others undergoing the same experience has a tremendous effect of reinforcement.

As much as the preacher encourages the outpouring of emotion, there is always fear on the part of evangelists with integrity that feeling might so overcome reason in the revival process that the results could only be temporary and with no long-lasting effects for the person's life. A skilled preacher has tremendous power over the revival audience. Among the most overwhelming was George Whitefield, the eighteenth-century British evangelist who sparked the First Great Awakening in America. The story of Whitefield's effect on Benjamin Franklin is well known—Franklin went to hear Whitefield with great skepticism and ended up emptying his pockets for an offering—but apparently Whitefield was just as stirring to those who spoke no English. A German Lutheran minister in Pennsylvania, Henry Muhlenberg, told in his journal the story of a woman who also went to hear Whitefield. The woman walked forty miles into Philadelphia, where Whitefield was preaching, and ''on her return she asserted that never in all her life had she had such a quickening, awakening, and edifying experience as when she listened to this man. To be sure, she understood nothing of his English sermon. . . .''[2]

Theologians of revivalism in both the eighteenth and nineteenth centuries worried about this emotionalism. Jonathan Edwards (1703–1758) believed fervently in the necessity of religious feelings, or ''affections,'' but at the same time was dismayed by the extremes of physical contortions and loud noises that accompanied the expression of feeling. Edwards had seen the backsliding among many who had professed themselves saved during the heat of a revival, and he had

---

[1] Jonathan Edwards, "Sinners in the Hands of an Angry God," in *Basic Writings,* ed. Ola Elizabeth Winslow (New York: Signet, 1966), p. 159. Although this is an outstanding example of a revival sermon, it is actually not typical of Edwards's writings.

[2] *The Lutherans in North America,* revised edition, ed. E. Clifford Nelson (Philadelphia: Fortress Press, 1980), p. 70.

experienced the tragedy of a parishioner who committed suicide, apparently in despair that he had not experienced God's saving grace. Edwards did not deny that the outward manifestations of religious feeling came from God. In spite of that he felt compelled to look beyond those temporary signs to speculate not only on the state of the individual's soul, but at longer-lasting effects of saving grace—the living of a virtuous life after the fervor of the revival had died down. "The Author of our nature," Edwards said, "has not only given us affections, but has made them very much the spring of actions."[3] Three generations later Charles Grandison Finney (1792–1875), one of the great evangelists of the nineteenth century, expressed the same concerns. He warned against fanaticism and the tyranny of the emotions: "Whatever the feelings are, if the soul gives itself up to be controlled by feelings rather than by the law and gospel of God, as truth lies in the intelligence, it is not a religious state of mind." Finney also showed himself to be an excellent religious psychologist in his understanding of how revivals might affect children who had no real understanding of what was occurring. The child, Finney thought, was likely to be badly overwhelmed, and "the result of all such efforts and such excitements among children is to make them skeptics."[4]

Up to this point the discussion has centered on the revival experience itself with some of its implications for the individual, and the description has had a kind of ahistorical quality to it. It is, of course, dangerous to lump together phenomena of many different eras, but I think it is safe to say that the emotional experience of the revival—the conviction of one's sinfulness followed by the overwhelming relief that one is saved in spite of it—has a sameness to it whether it has occurred in Jonathan Edwards's congregation in Northampton, Massachusetts, in 1742; at Cane Ridge, Kentucky, in 1800; at one of Billy Sunday's revival sermons in Spokane, Washington, in 1909; or in any one of many Jesus People's churches in the 1980s. This is not to say, however, that the phenomenon of the revival in American religious history is a simple one. The implications for the study of revivalism are endless. We could trace the history of evolving forms for the revival, such as Charles Grandison Finney's use of the "anxious seat" or "mourner's bench" during the Second Great Awakening; we could look at church records to see what effect revivals had on increasing church membership for a variety of denominations, or investigate how revivals have affected moral reform on such issues as temperance. We could easily discover many, many incidents of divisiveness and bitterness engendered by revivals, resulting not only in personal acrimony between individuals, but in the splitting of congregations or even denominations as they struggled to define the most appropriate means of religious expression. The role of women during revivals is another fruitful subject for study, since women were sometimes afforded greater freedom of public expression during revivals but were also subjected to innumerable sermons that defined

[3] Edwards, "A Treatise Concerning Religious Affections," in *Basic Writings*, p. 192.

[4] Charles Grandison Finney, *Reflections on Revival*, compiled by Donald Dayton (Minneapolis: Bethany Fellowship, Inc., 1979), p. 38.

the home as their appropriate sphere. The relationship between black and white revivalism is a further subject to ponder, not only in regard to theological concepts but also concerning different modes of emotional expression, hymns, and structural format. Finally, we might analyze the appeal that the revival model has had for the Catholic and Lutheran charismatic movements that have emerged since the 1960s. The list of possibilities goes on, but, now that we have looked at the revival in the singular sense, it is time to place this way of being religious in America in a broader context.

One of the most interesting aspects of revivalism in American religious history is its periodic occurrence over the course of three centuries. Historians generally agree upon two distinct periods of extended revivalism without much quarrel: the First Great Awakening, 1725–1769, and the Second Great Awakening, 1800–1830. There is occasional mention of a minor awakening in the 1850s. William McLoughlin, an eminent historian of revivalism in America, speaks of a third Great Awakening from 1890 to 1920 and claims also that we are now in the midst of another that began in 1960 and may end in 1990.[5] How do we account for these occasional eruptions of extended revivalism in American history? One obvious answer is to suggest a kind of cultural head/heart swing of the pendulum. After a time of religious fervor that expresses itself in tightly argued, closely adhered-to theological formulations with emphasis on that which is structured and reasonable, there may follow a breaking forth into a much more emotional expression of that same theology. To put this another way, when the head runs out of answers to the questions of life's meaning, the believer may turn to the heart. Another common pattern in the frequency of awakenings is that they have followed periods of (1) widespread doubt about the adequacy of religious piety and (2) fears over the corruption of morality whether in a particular group or in the culture as a whole. The First Great Awakening occurred just at the point in American religious history when the Puritan world view was beginning to crumble, and the awakening restored what turned out to be a temporary sense that the old ways still prevailed.

William McLoughlin has another theory about awakenings. He ties their appearance to periods of identity crisis in America and broadens their significance from religion, and specifically Protestant religion, to all the institutions of society: family, education, politics, and economics. McLoughlin sees the awakening as following a period of overall distress and fear that the old ways have become empty and useless and must either be abandoned or given a new life.[6] These periods of disorientation force an examination, and usually a revival, of a core of commonly held American values: the belief in the chosen-ness of America as a nation; the worth of the individual and the common person; the right to economic stability, at least, if not wealth, that hard work supposedly guarantees; the confidence that a

[5] William G. McLoughlin, *Revivals, Awakenings, and Reform: An Essay on Religion and Social Change in America* (Chicago: University of Chicago Press, 1978).

[6] Ibid., Chapter 1, "Awakenings as Revitalizations of Culture," pp. 1–23.

democratic form of government is the best there is; and the faith that an education can ensure success and must be available to all.

The First Great Awakening occurred before America was a nation, and although there was great emphasis on America as a special land set apart by God, there was not the adulation of democracy that became apparent after the Revolution. This series of revivals involved a looking to the past, not the future, and its general theme centered on decrying the religious complacency of the present in contrast with the fervor of earlier Puritanism. The awakening followed a time of great concern on the part of Puritan clergy that God's convenant with New England was in grave danger, and that the people of the colonies had earned God's displeasure and wrath. As evidence, they looked to declining church membership, crop failures, and sickness, increasing quarrels between ministers and congregations, and growing tension over bad relationships with England. When George Whitefield appeared in the 1730s after remarkable success in England, all was in readiness for a receptive population to be awakened to its own sense of abject sinfulness and helplessness but also to a conviction that, if they would only repent, God in his mercy would save both individuals and communities. Revivals were set off, McLoughlin says, "like a string of firecrackers," from New England to Georgia.

By the time of the Second Great Awakening, almost fifty years later, America was no longer a collection of colonies, but a new nation that had experienced a revolution. The questions that arose during these years show greater concern for national identity than for God's displeasure. As the new nation prospered, faith in individual ability and autonomy increased, and the influence of the Enlightenment, just previous, with its optimistic view of human nature and emphasis on the power of human reason, gave rise to a feeling that once God had set America on its special way, its citizens were perfectly capable of carrying on without much interference from the Divine Architect. This is not to say that exhortation about human sinfulness and the need to repent were missing from the Second Awakening, but rather to indicate a different tone produced by a different historical context. This awakening looked ahead to new possibilities rather than back at times considered to be more pious. The sense of America as a land set apart by God to fulfill a special destiny had persisted from early Puritan times, and now that concept had matured from the idea of a "land" to that of a nation. In the years from 1800 to 1830, revivals stressed the concept of "self-help" in contrast with the themes of human helplessness and dependence on God that had pervaded the revivals of the First Awakening.

This idea of America as a nation with a special destiny took on somewhat xenophobic proportions during the Third Great Awakening. By 1890 the Civil War, that tremendous threat to national identity and the sense of chosen-ness, was a generation past. America had experienced the huge influx of immigrants from northern and western Europe and was beginning to realize that great numbers were still to come from southern and eastern Europe and the Orient. In addition, the churches were having to come to terms with the discoveries of science (the topic of the next chapter), and much of the rhetoric of the Third Awakening deals with the search for national identity and national values. Here again we have an awakening that looks to the past, to those earlier years of the nineteenth century when it seemed there was greater clarity about what it meant to be "American," white, Anglo-Saxon, Protestant, with commonly held values about the relationship between virtue, hard work, and ethnic makeup. One picks up the same tone that was present in the First Awakening: that the future is dependent upon the revitalization, in fact the restoration, of the past. Billy Sunday, among the most famous of the preachers of this awakening, gave sermons that are good indications of this outlook, which feared racial, ethnic, and religious diversity as a threat to the stability of America and also the world. Sunday proclaimed in one sermon, "It so happens that America is placed in a position where the fate of the world depends largely upon her conduct. If we lose our heads down goes Civilization." At another point Sunday said, "Sixty-nine percent of our criminals are either foreign-born or of foreign parents."[7] Sunday and evangelists like him considered white Protestant evangelicalism synonymous with Americanism, and they, along with thousands of followers, saw themselves awakened to an obligation to see to it that newcomers conformed to the theology of the revival as well as to the moral piety—no drinking, no dancing, no smoking, no cards—that emerged from it. The immenseness and, finally, the impossibility of the task helps to account for the stridency, anger, and righteousness that characterize many of the revival sermons at the turn of the century.

The Fourth Great Awakening, in which we are all participants, has had a very different quality to it from those previous, and yet one can detect in the years from 1960 onward many of the same patterns, chief among them a concern for American identity that has produced two sets of answers as to the nature of American-ness. One answer has involved an opening of our eyes to the narrowness of previous definitions of "American" as well as to the fact that Protestant Christianity, American destiny, and world stability are not tied together in such tight knots as had once been supposed. The future seems less full of promise and the past more filled with error than at previous times in American history. That may sound like a gloomy assessment of American culture as a whole, but it has promoted nonetheless greater skills of self-criticism as a nation, as well as a better-developed capacity to view ethnic, racial, and religious diversity as positive contributions to the culture rather than as threatening obstacles to national unity that must be assimilated into a narrowly defined whole. Another faction in American culture, however, advocates conservative politics with conservative religion and has had an appeal for members of many different religious groups. One can interpret this voice as speaking for a part of the culture that longs for the certainties that are perceived as having existed in the past. As we have already seen, a looking longingly toward the past for the piety of earlier times is not a new

---

[7] William G. McLoughlin, *Billy Sunday Was His Real Name* (Chicago: University of Chicago Press, 1955), p. 278.

manifestation in American culture. A new understanding, a revitalization, occurs as those strains of the culture that would look backward meet elements that look toward different and new interpretations of American culture and reality. To see these forces as merely hostile to one another, however, is to overlook the possibility of a creative rather than a destructive tension between apparent polarities, a tension that is redolent with the kind of energy needed to redefine American values as the historical context changes.

We have looked at two different, but related, phenomena in American religious and cultural history: one, the revival in the singular sense, as a way of acting out religious beliefs about individual sin and salvation that are peculiar to a particular kind of Protestantism;[8] and the other, the awakening, both an extended series of revivals and a secularization of the revival process, which, according to at least one interpreter, has the power to push the revival concern with sin and salvation outside the boundaries of the obviously religious and into a questioning of national identity. During the times of awakening that have occurred at intervals in American history, the fears about national security and destiny, the loss of faith in common values and once-revered institutions, generally accompanied by a highly shaky economy, give way to a renewed confidence in American culture as full of promise and possibility, but with a reordered understanding of what "American" really means. Up through the Third Awakening, these new understandings that came out of past awakenings tended to be highly nationalistic in nature with much emphasis on America's chosen-ness by God as a leader and an exemplar for other nations of the world. If McLoughlin is on the right track, those of us who are living through the present awakening will begin to see the outlines of a definition of American-ness that enlarges on those of the past. McLoughlin's speculations as to what forms these changes in national identity might take are worth quoting at length for several reasons: not only because of his use of religious imagery, but because the images are more inclusive than exclusive; they enlarge the circle of those who would be counted among the "saved," and they give promise of an understanding of American identity that draws not only from its Judaeo-Christian heritage, but also from the contributions of groups that were once considered "other"—Native Americans, Orientals, blacks, and women:

> Such a reorientation will most likely include a new sense of the mystical unity between man and nature. The godhead will be defined in less dualistic terms, and its power will be understood less in terms of an absolutist, sin-hating, death-dealing "Almighty Father in Heaven" and more in terms of a life-supporting, nurturing, empathetic, easygoing parental (Motherly as well as Fatherly) image. The nourishing spirit of mother earth, not the wrath of an angry father above, will dominate religious thought (though different faiths and denominations will communicate this ideal in different ways). Sacrifice of self will replace self-aggrandizement as a definition of virtue; helping others will replace competitiveness as a value; institu-

---

[8] Jay Dolan, an historian of American Catholicism, also applies the patterns of revivalism to nineteenth-century American Catholicism in *Catholic Revivalism: The American Experience, 1830–1900* (Notre Dame, Indiana: University of Notre Dame Press, 1978).

tions will be organized for the fulfillment of individual needs by means of cooperative communal efforts rather than through the isolated nuclear family.[9]

If McLoughlin's description of a new understanding of American culture sounds intensely optimistic, it nonetheless has a basis in the psychology of revivalism—the belief that radical transformation of an individual person or of a whole culture is possible—through what the revivalist preacher would call the power of God's saving grace and what the cultural historian is more likely to see as the creative potential inherent in the act of redefining American identity as it comes up against historical events that call into question commonly held national values.

---

[9] McLoughlin, *Revivals, Awakenings, and Reforms*, pp. 214–15.

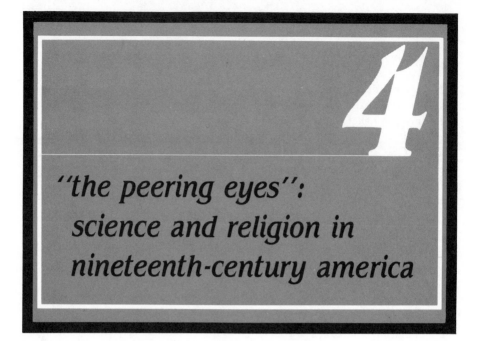

"the peering eyes": science and religion in nineteenth-century america

The previous chapter on revivalism emphasized one particular way of being religious in America along with the theories of an historian who sees that kind of religious behavior as incorporated into the way in which the culture as a whole comes to self-understanding. In this chapter we will look at the relationship between religion and culture from another angle: the way in which a nonreligious phenomenon—the growing cultural dominance of the scientific method in America—has affected religious beliefs and the practice of religion. In 1829 Edgar Allan Poe published a poem, "Sonnet—To Science," in which he decried the influence of science, or "cold philosophy," upon the poetic imagination:

> *Science! true daughter of Old Time thou art!*
>> *Who alterest all things with thy peering eyes.*
> *Why preyest thou thus upon the poet's heart.*
>> *Vulture, whose wings are dull realities?*
> *How should he love thee? or how deem thee wise,*
>> *Who wouldst not leave him in his wandering*
> *To seek for treasure in the jewelled skies,*
>> *Albeit he soared with an undaunted wing?*
>
> *Hast thou not dragged Diana from her car?*
>> *And driven the Hamadryad from the wood*
> *To seek a shelter in some happier star?*
>> *Hast thou not torn the Naiad from her flood,*

> *The Elfin from the green grass, and from me*
> *The summer dream beneath the tamarind tree?!*[1]

To say that Poe had in mind in this poem the effects that science would eventually have upon religious belief would be pushing interpretation beyond the actual text, but there is no doubt that as early as 1829 he sensed that science had the potential to de-mystify the universe, to separate the material and the spiritual, the "natural" and the "supernatural," into two separate realms governed by two distinct sets of laws. "Daughter of Old Time," Poe called science, and he might have said as well, "daughter of fact, of experiment, of physical proof," for the rise of faith in the method of science imposed upon American culture as well as that of other nations offered a different means by which to understand the nature of reality. Although the so-called "warfare" between science and religion is said to have commenced at the time of Charles Darwin's publication of *The Origin of Species* in 1859, its roots go back to the Renaissance. And thirty years earlier than *The Origin* Poe could sense the pain, the bewilderment, the anger, and the fear that would arise from a head-on confrontation of one view of reality that looked to the eternal and transcendence of the material with another whose view of reality had its basis in the time-bound entities of the physical universe.

There have been periods of greater and lesser intensity in the confrontation between science and religion—the world wars marked a period of hiatus—but the patterns of opposition and suspicion have remained a constant factor in American culture from the nineteenth century up to the present with arguments between creationists and evolutionists reminiscent of the Scopes trial in Tennessee in 1925 when a young teacher was accused of teaching evolutionary theory in violation of state law. To be fair, there have also been creative dialogues between science and religion, as in the contemporary cooperation between scientists and theologians to come up with guiding principles that will help sort out the ethical dilemmas inherent in advances in medical technology, among them organ transplants and *in vitro* fertilization. Actually, any generation in American religious history could provide us with the raw material to study the many varieties of interchange between science and religion. But one of the most fruitful time spans to look at are the years between 1875 and 1900, a time that Arthur M. Schlesinger identified in 1932 as "a critical period in American religion," and that is particularly illustrative of the many ways in which organized religion came to terms with the pressures of the particular age. According to Schlesinger, the price of survival for most religions during this period was change: "However disturbing to defenders of the old-time religion, the ceaseless bending of creeds and practices to the changing needs of society has been the price of survival."[2] During this time period we have

---

[1] Edgar Allan Poe, "Sonnet—To Science," *The Complete Poetical Works of Edgar Allan Poe*, ed. James A. Harrison (New York: Thomas Y. Crowell & Company, 1902), p. 22.

[2] Arthur M. Schlesinger, "A Critical Period in American Religion, 1875–1900," Proceedings of the Massachusetts Historical Society, 64 (June, 1932), 523.

the opportunity to observe what form change took among Protestants, Catholics, and Jews as they responded to the demand that religion, as well as science, be accessible to demonstrable proof. And we note, also, that the expanding role of science in giving meaning to reality resulted in the formation of new religious groups that attempted to break the tension between religion and science.

In 1890 Robert C. Ingersoll, an avowed and well-known American agnostic, stated as starkly as anyone what he considered the impossibility of maintaining religious beliefs in the face of scientific discoveries:

> The same rules of probability must govern in religious questions as in others. There is no subject—and can be none—concerning which any human being is under any obligation to believe without evidence. Neither is there any intelligent being who can, by any possibility, be flattered by the exercise of ignorant credulity. The man who, without prejudice, reads and understands the Old and New Testaments will cease to be an orthodox Christian. The intelligent man who investigates the religion of any country without fear and without prejudice will not and cannot be a believer.[3]

No one, said Ingersoll, to put it even more bluntly, who has any intelligence or awareness could possibly sustain a belief in the traditional truths of religion. Ingersoll was a controversial person, of course, but he had his followers. And even those who dismissed what he had to say either with disgust or with anger could not help but pause a bit at his argument. What developments had made Ingersoll so sure of his case? By 1890 advances in scholarship that pertained to religion had contributed to a growth of religious skepticism in American culture, an inability on the part of many to believe in either the divine origins of the universe or in the reasonableness of adhering to any particular set of religious beliefs. Scholarship in archaeology, geology, philology, anthropology, and comparative religions led to doubts about truths that many religious believers had always taken for granted: the divine origins of the Bible, the age of the earth and of the human race as 4004 years old, the creation of different languages at the Tower of Babel, the stories of the Creation and of the Great Flood. For some, undermining of religious beliefs by the discoveries of science came as a relief. Andrew Carnegie, for example, claimed in *The Gospel of Wealth* that he was relieved to abandon the superstitions of Christianity and to embrace evolution (which at the time seemed to many to be antithetical to religion) as his new faith. There were others, though, millions of them, for whom the conflict between science and religion was the cause of great anguish. Unable and unwilling to abandon a belief in God and in religion, yet drawn intellectually by the revelations and promises of science, they felt acutely a sense of abandonment in an indifferent universe. The old beliefs were crumbling and there was nothing with which to replace them except a horrible suspicion that humanity was alone, that death was the end of everything, that the universe was

---

[3] Robert C. Ingersoll, "Why Am I an Agnostic?" *American Issues*, 4th Edition Revised, eds. Merle Curti, Willard Thorpe, Carlos Baker, Joseph A. Dowling (Philadelphia: J. B. Lippincott Company, 1971), pp. 230–31.

only an empty and lifeless space from which the creator, if there had ever been one, had long since disappeared.

There came a point in the nineteenth century when organized religion could no longer ignore the implications of science for their beliefs and practices, but because America is a religiously plural society, the responses to the threats of science were by no means universal. For many, the most basic question raised was this one: what does science have to say to religion and to humanity about questions of ultimate meaning? The most conservative answer was "Nothing." There were those who felt strongly that scientists and scholars did not have the right to delve into the mysteries of religion, either to prove or disprove its doctrines; it was blasphemous to do so and only invited doubts. And to invite doubts was sinful in itself.

Some responses, on the other hand, were more compromising in nature, one of which was the "two revelations" theory, which claimed that religion and science were parallel disciplines and there was no need for conflict between them. Science was concerned with the natural world, and religion and theology were meant to concentrate on the supernatural. If the discoveries of science had a function for religion according to this theory, it was to add further to the glorification of the divine creator, who was capable not only of creating the universe in six days but of making it appear that it had taken millions of years to evolve. Thus the workings of the supernatural would be revealed in the natural and there need be no conflict between them. Another variation on the theme of compromise was the attempt to move religion away from the kind of theological speculation about final causes that might bring it into conflict with science and concentrate instead on doing good works in the present. According to this understanding of the role of religion, its purpose was not to make pronouncements about the age of the earth or the origins of the human species, but rather to bring people into a closer relationship with God and with their fellow humans. The Social Gospel movement of the late nineteenth and early twentieth centuries emerged from this interpretation of religion's place in the scheme of things. In full flower by 1910, its followers understood the Christian task to be the improvement of society by stamping out poverty and injustice. Those who espoused the Social Gospel based their efforts on a confidence that human nature could indeed gain control of social forces, and one of the prominent theologians of the movement, Walter Rauschenbusch (1861–1918) spoke of the latent perfectability in human nature. The Social Gospel movement was influenced not only by the conflict between science and religion, but perhaps even more by the poverty and disorientation generated by massive immigration, ever-increasing industrialization, and the movement of millions from rural areas into the cities. But whatever the complexity of its origins, it provided a means by which many could set aside their religious doubts and take refuge in action.

It does not take the student of religion long to realize that these different answers to the crisis occasioned by the dispute between religion and science were also in conflict with each other. In the conservative stance, a refusal to negotiate with science, we see the beginnings of American fundamentalism of the twentieth century, which emerged in combination with the evangelical piety and enthusiastic religion we have already encountered in a brief look at revivalism. The more liberal approach, which involved some form of dialogue or compromise with science, would take shape through the efforts of theologians who saw as their task the retaining of basic religious beliefs, along with an accommodation of those beliefs to the discoveries of science.

While many millions of church-going Americans looked to the religions in which they had been raised for answers to the questions posed by the discoveries of science, there were others who found more consolation in the formation of new religious movements. Mormonism, officially organized by Joseph Smith in 1830, and Spiritualism, whose followers trace its American beginnings to 1848, were active before 1875; Christian Science was discovered by Mary Baker Eddy in 1866, and Theosophy was founded by Helena Blavatsky in 1875. All four of them spoke to the difficulties encountered in the struggle to believe in the teachings of traditional religions in the face of so much evidence that seemed to promise their demise. And all of them made pronouncements on the nature of reality, whether material or spiritual or both, that went beyond the orthodoxies of mainstream religions in nineteenth-century America. In unique ways, each of them snapped the tension between matter and spirit, saying to their followers, "You need no longer be confused; we have the answer."

Mormonism did not ask of its followers that they believe in two kinds of reality, the spiritual and the material, so divorced from each other as to make reconciliation seem impossible. Instead, Mormon theology spoke of spirit as "invisible matter," differing not in essence from matter but in degree. The divine itself was not totally "other" from the human, but a being of the same flesh and bones as humans who had earned its present divine status. This was not a God, then, so inaccessible by nature and so removed from earthly concerns that the laws of science could appear to take its place as the agent of creation. Spiritualism had a different answer to offer to the question of whether the spiritual did indeed exist. This was a religious movement founded on the belief that the spirits of the dead could return to communicate with those still on earth. In addition to the obvious consolation it offered that life existed beyond the grave, Spiritualism also assured its believers that the communication of the spirits through mediums provided physical, irrefutable, scientific evidence of the reality of the spiritual and, in turn, of religious beliefs. In Christian Science, Mary Baker Eddy turned in a third direction by declaring that matter, including the material world and the human body, was illusory—that pain, sickness, poverty, and evil resulted from our participation in that illusion; if we ceased to believe in their reality, they would disappear. According to Eddy, the healings of Christian Science offered proof that a true understanding of the perfection of God's creation could do away with all suffering, physical and mental. Finally, Theosophy held an eclectic combination of religious beliefs with particular emphasis on Hinduism. Madame Blavatsky called

Theosophy a "religion, a science, and a philosophy," and this new movement had in common with Spiritualism and Christian Science its insistence that one did not have to "believe" the truths of religion; it was possible to "know." Among the operative words in all of these new religious movements are *proof* and *knowledge,* giving us a strong sense of the desire on the part of the nineteenth-century Americans to have certainty in the face of the grave doubts about the nature of reality endemic in nineteenth-century American society.

The stories of Catholics and Jews and their encounters with the advances of science differ, but not totally, from those of Protestants. Although their arrival in the New World predated that of Protestants, their coming in great numbers did not take place until the nineteenth century, during which their all-consuming concern was assimilation into American culture. As immigrant religions Judaism and Catholicism were involved in trying to come to terms with what it meant to be Jewish or Catholic in America, in contrast with what it had meant in the countries from which they had come. In the process, they tried also to maintain both their religious and ethnic identities. For Catholics, the encounter with science was only a part of a larger picture that involved the fears of Pope Leo XIII that the Catholic Church in America was assimilating itself to American culture to the extent that it was dangerous to doctrine. Thus, during the last quarter of the nineteenth century, American Catholics experienced the peculiar irony of being thought too "foreign" by many Protestants and too "American" by the pope. Anti-Catholic feeling, which had eased off somewhat during the Civil War, erupted again in the 1880s, and many Catholics felt the need to defend themselves from Protestant fears that their true loyalty was to a "foreign potentate," the pope.

Leo XIII, in the meantime, had written an encyclical in 1899, *Testem benevolentiae* (the title of an encyclical comes from its first two words, not necessarily from its contents), that condemned such excesses of American culture as "a rejection of external spiritual direction as no longer necessary; the extolling of natural over supernatural values; the preference of active over passive virtues; the rejection of religious vows as not compatible with Christian liberty; and the adoption of a new method of apologetics and approach to non-Catholics."[4] It is a fascinating and instructive exercise in historical interpretation to read Andrew Greeley's contemporary phrasing of these very same points. Far from viewing them negatively, Greeley, a priest and sociologist, claims that these were the very attitudes that should have been encouraged rather than condemned, and indeed he sees them as prevailing in post–Vatican II American Catholicism: "openness to non-Catholics, strong social concern, consultation with clergy and the laity in decision making, optimism about the modern world, willingness to conduct a dialogue with anyone, endorsement of scientific and technical progress."[5]

---

4 "Americanism," *New Catholic Encyclopedia,* Vol. 1, 1967, pp. 443–44.

5 Andrew Greeley, *The American Catholic: A Social Portrait* (New York: Basic Books, Inc., 1977), p. 35.

What was called the "Americanist" controversy in Catholicism came to a kind of dead end with liberal bishops such as John Ireland of St. Paul and John Spalding of Peoria denying that they had held any erroneous opinions and conservative bishops thanking the pope for saving American Catholicism. Thus, beset by hostility from without and controversy within, American Catholicism saw the challenge of science as only one of many pressures with which it needed to contend. Undergirded by neo-Thomism, the natural-law philosophy of Thomas Aquinas (d. 1274) revitalized in the early twentieth century, American Catholicism, in contrast with much of Protestantism, was actually able to maintain an optimistic and coherent world view that held together both the natural and the supernatural. It was not until after Vatican II that Catholicism in America experienced the crisis of meaninglessness and felt the same anguished fear that doctrines had failed to keep up with the reality of contemporary society. At that time Catholics, too, were set adrift to face the dilemmas of modern existence without the comfort of a church that up to then had appeared to be changeless in an ever-changing world.

In many ways the experiences of American Jews during the last quarter of the nineteenth century parallels that of Catholics. Viewed by Protestants as "foreign," Judaism was also an immigrant religion with the same need to understand itself in the context of American religious pluralism, as well as to come to terms with the questions engendered by the pressure for assimilation into American culture. Also, like Catholicism, Judaism had within itself the potential for disputes among different ethnic groups—for example, between German Jews and later-arriving Russian and Eastern European Jews. Further, there were controversies between liberal and conservative factions divided over issues of liturgical reform. Although anti-Semitism had a later start in American culture than did anti-Catholicism, by the 1880s it was becoming more and more obvious: private schools began to be closed to Jewish students, as were many private clubs in the business community; advertisements for summer hotels refused admittance to Jewish guests; law and medical schools of private universities had acknowledged, if unwritten, quotas for Jewish students. All of these experiences among American Jews were familiar to Catholics.

On the other hand, American Judaism seems to have felt the effects of science on religious beliefs and practices more acutely than did Catholics in the nineteenth century and in that respect had more in common with much of Protestantism. The faith in progress and the optimism about human nature and potential that scientific advances promoted instilled in many American Jews a desire for a religion that could withstand the rigors of scientific analysis. For example, the response of one rabbi to scientific ways of understanding religion sounds remarkably like those of Protestants cited earlier in the chapter. Having returned from Biblical study in Europe, Felix Adler (1851-1933) concluded that "the Mosaic religion is, so to speak, a religious mosaic and . . . there is hardly a single stone in it which can with certainty be traced to the authorship of Moses." Adler thought that if he were to stand before his congregation and preach the law of Moses, the words "would stick in my throat."[6] Adler ceased rabbinical practice and founded the Ethical Culture Society in 1876, a humanistic group for the "unchurched" dedicated to the moral reform of society.

To a lesser extent than groups like the Ethical Culture Society, Reform Judaism in nineteenth-century America tried also to divest Judaism of its supernatural elements, while at the same time hanging on to the "essence" of Judaism. Reform Judaism was greatly concerned with matters of liturgy and practice, but it also delved into theological beliefs, and its exponents maintained a stance that reflected Reform's development in an era whose hopes were more rooted in scientific progress than in religious tradition. In fact, the famous Pittsburgh Platform put together in 1885 was considered a break with traditions thought to be irrelevant for nineteenth-century American Jews. The principles of the Platform are full of evidence that Reform Judaism had no quarrel with science, and like their liberal Protestant counterparts its leaders felt that Judaism could accommodate scientific discoveries by purging itself of supernaturalism: for example, "We hold that the modern discoveries of scientific research in the domain of nature and history are not antagonistic to the doctrines of Judaism, or the Bible reflecting the primitive ideas of its own age, and at times clothing its conception of divine Providence and Justice dealing with man in miraculous narratives." Or on the same note, "We recognize in Judaism a progressive religion, ever striving to be in accord with the postulates of reason."[7] The Platform nevertheless affirmed very strongly Reform's connections with the rest of Judaism in its attempt to do two very difficult things: reflect the scientific wisdom of the age in all its secular manifestations and at the same time offer to Reform Jews an identity that was fitting for America and for the inheritors of thousands of years of Jewish tradition.

Arthur M. Schlesinger was speaking chiefly of American Protestantism when he cited adaptation as the price for religion's survival in America—the "ceaseless bending of creeds and practices," as he called it. We can see, however, that the influence of science upon religion during those last years of the nineteenth century was so pervasive that there was no way for Judaism or Catholicism to escape what Poe had called the "peering eyes" of science that seemed to call into question every doctrine, every long- and lovingly held belief about a spiritual reality that could not withstand the call for demonstrable, physical proof of its existence. Thus, religions in America in the nineteenth century had to answer the challenge of science and at the same time hold on to those doctrines and practices that are essential to the identity and integrity of the particular religious movement—without which its insights into the meaning of human existence did not seem worth pursuing.

We who live at the end of the twentieth century are no strangers, either, to

---

[6] Nathan Glazer, *American Judaism,* second edition revised (Chicago: University of Chicago Press, 1976), p. 45.

[7] Jacob B. Agus, "The Reform Movement," *Understanding American Judaism,* Vol. II, ed. Jacob Neusner (New York: KTAV Publishing House, Inc., 1975), pp. 7–8.

the inherent tensions between science and religion. In some ways our concerns seem infinitely more urgent and sophisticated than those of our nineteenth-century ancestors, because they bear upon the very survival of the planet as we know it and perhaps of humanity. We may, however, be indulging ourselves in an arrogance typical of many eras of human history: a conviction that our dilemmas are the worst and our fears for survival the best founded. Nonetheless, we ask our religious traditions to provide us with their wisdom and guidance regarding nuclear weapons, genetic engineering, and the prolonging of human life through medical advances. Whatever the subject of the discussion, the dialogue between science and religion in America, sometimes bitter but often fruitful, appears to be a continuing feature of the culture.

visible saints: biography in american religious history

Now that we have looked at two examples of general trends that have affected both religion in general and specific religions in particular in the course of American history, it is time to become acquainted with the lives and works of individuals who have served as interpreters of and for the times in which they lived: Jonathan Edwards (1703–1758), Harry Emerson Fosdick (1878–1969), Martin Luther King, Jr. (1929–1968), and Dorothy Day (1897–1980). What specific experiences moved them to devote their personal lives to interpreting and acting out their religious beliefs? What did they come to believe in the course of their lives about the nature of God, the way the universe works, and the obligations humans have toward God and one another? What were their fears and their doubts? All of them lived in times when old values were being replaced by new ones and people sought, sometimes desperately, help in sorting out what they must preserve of the old and what they must adopt of the new. To Edwards fell the task of undergirding the waning religious fervor of eighteenth-century America with theological creativity. Fosdick faced the difficulty of making religious doctrine compatible with the culture of a scientific age without losing its integrity. King raised up the vast problem of racism in America and called upon both Christians and Jews to combat it. Dorothy Day proclaimed the need for the Catholic Church in America to take a strong stand on social issues, and she lived a life of intentional poverty as her own statement. The three men, two white and one black, were all ordained, and they were famous preachers as well, illustrating the tremendous influence that male Protestant clergy have had on the public aspects of religion in American history. The ability to preach the Word in an articulate, even charismatic way has been one of the surest paths to fame in American religion. In spite of the success that they achieved, these men lived lives that society as a whole would characterize as traditional: They were married and had children; they experienced the patterns of education expected of ministers; and they spoke with the authority of the male minister in American culture. Women, on the other hand, were seldom ordained until recently and were almost never permitted to preach. Thus most women who have achieved historical prominence in America have done so outside the mainstream of institutional religion and middle-class American culture. Dorothy Day provides a good illustration of this pattern. By her lifestyle, which she lived in opposition to middle-class values, she provided leadership of one aspect of American Catholicism and in doing so set herself apart from most American Catholics. Gender patterns aside, all four of these leaders had to confront the implications of the times in which they lived for the religious beliefs they espoused. All four of them experienced fame and widespread approval during their lifetimes, but they also came face to face with bitter controversies, hostile opposition, and spiritual crises that engendered self-doubt.

JONATHAN EDWARDS

Jonathan Edwards lived more than half of his life in rural Massachusetts, first as pastor at Northampton for twenty-four years and then, after being dismissed by his congregation, at Stockbridge for six. He died from the effects of a smallpox vaccination within months of being called to the presidency of Princeton University, at that time known as the College of New Jersey. If pressed, many Americans could name Edwards as the author of that prototypical revival sermon "Sinners in the Hands of an Angry God," but most likely could not add much to that bit of information. And yet twentieth-century scholars see him as a man immensely talented in a variety of disciplines—not only theology, but philosophy and the psychology of religion as well. He is respected as one of the greatest interpreters of American Puritanism and of the First Great Awakening, as well as a highly creative thinker who moved away from the characteristics of English Puritanism to an articulation of a more American way of being religious.

Edwards lived out his life in an attempt to revitalize Puritan theology. He wanted to restore the theological system in which he believed and participated so fervently to its former power as a world view that kindled the heart and soul into loving divine things for their own sake, rather than deadening the spirit with an endless list of prescriptions to keep the individual from falling into sin. By the time Edwards came to his pastorate at Northampton in 1726, Puritanism had become for many a religion of empty forms. Ola Elizabeth Winslow, one of Edwards's biographers, describes it as having degenerated from emphasis on "inner satisfaction of the spirit" to a spiritless listing of "don'ts." "Through too frequent repetition condemnation failed to condemn. Young people went away from the very Assembly to sit out the remainder of the afternoon in the tavern, now a place of rendezvous in every village. Smoking in the street was no longer a family disgrace, and if a church member were caught taking his ease and chatting with friends under his own apple tree in time of divine service, the state might still put him in the stocks for 'ye horrible neglect and contempt of God's Ordinances,' but the week would not be long enough to give all offenders a due sitting.''[1]

The revitalization of Puritanism that Edwards undertook for his lifelong work was not just his nostalgic longing for times of glory that could never be again. Nor did he see in the revivals of the Great Awakening the simple solution to widespread lack of religious enthusiasm. Not even the living of a virtuous life was sufficient of itself to satisfy Edwards as a complete manifestation of one's religious beliefs, and certainly knowledge of and agreement to church doctrine was not enough. Edwards wanted it all: He wanted a religion of both heart and mind, not a religion of either heart or mind. As he tried to hold together both the intellectual and the emotional aspects of his own belief system, he seemed to anticipate the tendency that has plagued American culture and American religions: to break apart into that which is either too intellectual or too emotional.

To understand the implications of Edwards's life work for the study of American religion, we need to pay further attention to the historical context out of which he sought to make sense. As we know from brief mention in the chapter on revivalism, Edwards lived at a time in New England when Puritan theology had constituted the predominant world view for more than 100 years. To us who live in the late twentieth century and have experienced the optimism about human nature and potential that has been building up since the Enlightenment in the eighteenth century, the doctrines of Puritanism appear stark indeed. Puritan theology stressed the sovereignty and power of God and the depravity and helplessness of the human. Men and women were considered predestined from the dawn of time to heaven or to hell; and since all were, by their very human natures, deserving of hell it was only God's graciousness that afforded some the gift of salvation. Puritans were constantly reminded that they could not "earn" God's grace or salvation by their own actions—nothing they did could affect their already predestined souls—yet at the same time they were admonished to lead virtuous lives. Great emphasis was placed on the necessity of the conversion experience, an overwhelming conviction that one had experienced saving grace; yet to feel confident that one was among the elect, the saved, was a sin in itself. Puritan concerns and obligations were not confined to private matters of religion. Because the Puritans had agreed to live in covenant with one another and with God, those actions that might in another system have been considered matters for the individual conscience took on significance for the whole community. Church and state were not separate, and each shared responsibility for the rectification of private sin and public disorder as well.

The tensions that sprang from this theological system were numerous. How

---

[1] Ola Elizabeth Winslow, *Jonathan Edwards* (New York: The Macmillan Company, 1940), pp. 100–01.

was it possible to adore or to love a God who seemed so capricious and even vengeful in dealings with humans? How could either the individual or the church determine the validity of the conversion experience as a basis for church membership when it was possible that excess emotion or even self-deception might be involved? If salvation or damnation were already determined and did not depend upon how one lived one's life, what was the necessity for living virtuously? And was it not a travesty to speak of freedom of the will in such a situation? Exactly how far could the church go in making judgments about people's private lives and their worthiness for church membership? Within the framework of Puritan theology, Edwards derived answers to all of these questions with intellectual integrity and creativity combined with never-flagging religious belief. The answers to the first questions form the basis of some of his greatest written works. His putting into action his own answer to the last—that of the extent of ministerial and church authority—resulted in his dismissal from the pastoral post he had held for twenty-four years. Edwards's times are not our times, and his answers are not our answers, but we see in the working out of his theological system a rejection of easy answers and misleading dichotomies between reason and emotion, faith and works, freedom and bondage, individual and community. He combined this rejection with a faithful attention to what he considered the revealed truths of his religion, the reasoning powers of the human mind, and the experiences of the heart.

The beginnings of Edwards's answer to the questions of Puritanism emerged from his own conversion experience. In the *Personal Narrative* Edwards recounts that he was particularly interested in religion from the time he was a small child. He and his schoolmates built a "praying booth" in a swamp, and Edwards often retired alone to the woods to think and pray. "My affections," he said, "seemed to be lively and easily moved, and I seemed to be in my element when engaged in religious duties." These feelings were not long lasting, however, and from the time he was thirteen until he was seventeen, Edwards engaged in what he felt was a struggle for salvation. He tried to avoid sin and worldly temptations, but there was none of the joy in religious things that he had formerly experienced. Part of his pain came from his difficulty in accepting the doctrine of God's sovereignty or total power over all creation: "From my childhood up, my mind had been full of objections against the doctrine of God's sovereignty, in choosing whom he would to eternal life, and rejecting whom he pleased; leaving them eternally to perish, and be everlastingly tormented in hell. It used to appear like a horrible doctrine to me." The conversion experience that occurred after four years of anguish convinced him of the rightness of the doctrine of God's sovereignty, and he was able not only to accept it but to "delight" in it. It became for him a doctrine that "has very often appeared exceedingly pleasant, bright, and sweet. Absolute sovereignty is what I love to ascribe to God."[2]

---

[2] All the quotations in this paragraph are taken from the "Personal Narrative" in *Jonathan Edwards: Basic Writings*, ed. Ola Elizabeth Winslow (New York: Signet, 1966), pp. 81–84.

The fact that his conversion experience prompted intellectual assent to a doctrine that Edwards had previously "felt" to be intolerable was one of the effects of this incident. Edwards confessed that at the time he was not even aware that he had undergone conversion; that fact became apparent only in retrospect. Edwards speculated further that the religious "affections" he had experienced before this time were transitory and not very genuine, leading him to assume that one could be deceived about feelings that might appear to be religious in nature but in fact were not. Both of these realizations moved him to several conclusions about the nature of an emotional religious experience: first, that it could be of immense assistance in the acceptance of religious doctrine and in the living out of a life that was virtuous and filled with love for God and humanity; but, second, that the experience could not go unexamined in reference to the theological system of the believer and the context of the person's whole life. According to Edwards, one had to look beyond the temporary feelings of religious enthusiasm, such as those engendered by the revivals, and test their validity in their fruits. It simply was not possible to make an accurate assessment of a religious experience based on that one experience alone, for salvation to Edwards was a process, not a moment.

Edwards seemed to imply in his examination of the validity of religious feelings that individuals have some control over their eternal destiny, that there is freedom to choose a path of action leading to the transformation of a formerly sinful life. How does this fit in with the fact that Puritans were cautioned not to presume that they could earn salvation for themselves by thought or deed? What possible place could the concept of free will have in a system that seemed to deny its very possibility? Here is another instance of Edwards's wanting it all. He saw as his obligation in *On the Freedom of the Will* the reconciliation of the doctrine of God's sovereignty with that of human responsibility and dignity. He concluded the existence of a limited kind of freedom: people are free to carry out their own choices, Edwards claimed, and these choices are inclinations in one direction or another. Therein lies human freedom. The inclinations themselves, however, are directed by motives, and the motives lie outside human control—they are engendered by God. Therefore human freedom is conditional and must be understood within the theological framework Edwards espoused.

Edwards's analysis is not a particularly satisfying one to us of the twentieth century, although we certainly know that there are limitations on our freedom. If we are not compelled by the content of the argument, we need nonetheless to look at Edwards's phenomenal ability to maintain a tension between what appear to be two mutually exclusive concepts—God's sovereignty and human freedom—when one would think he would be absolutely forced, finally, to deny one or the other. He did not choose one, though; he chose both. And in doing so Edwards looks to the possibility of liberation from the "either/or" dichotomy so common in American religions and in the culture as a whole: faith or reason; head or heart; salvation or damnation. To say that Edwards "wanted it all" is not to accuse him of having his cake and eating it too but to recognize his ability to perceive reality in a comprehensive and holistic way and his refusal to accept easy answers.

A discussion of Edwards's skills in theology might give the impression that he functioned mostly on an abstract and theoretical level, that he did not much enter the fray of human interaction and controversy except through his writings. But this is not the case. It was Edwards's sermons at Northampton that along with those of George Whitefield sparked the First Great Awakening, and he was particularly gifted at painting the picture of God's wrath in so personal a way that his listeners were moved to terror. Edwards was not satisfied merely to elicit repentant cries and shrieks, and it was his insistence that the church and the pastor indeed have much to say about the social behavior of parishioners that led to his dismissal from the church at Northampton. Additional causes stemmed from an ongoing salary dispute, typical of that between many ministers of the day and their churches, and a tempest in a teapot called the "bad book" episode. Part of the rancor toward Edwards evolved from his attempt to make standards for church membership more rigorous than they had been since 1660, when his grandfather, Solomon Stoddard, initiated the Half-Way Covenant. Briefly, the Half-Way Covenant permitted church membership without a conversion experience; it was an effort to enlarge church membership. Edwards permitted it during twenty-three years of his pastorate, and then, because he considered it an invitation to hypocrisy, sought to reinstate the requirement of conversion experience. Anger and resentment, already bubbling because of the salary dispute, boiled over into a move to have him dismissed. The "bad book" episode only exacerbated an already unpleasant situation. Some teenage boys and girls got hold of a book on midwifery, which they passed around. Edwards and the congregation authorized a committee to investigate, after which Edwards read a list of both culprits and witnesses from the pulpit, apparently failing to distinguish between the two. This incident increased the feeling that Edwards was overstepping his bounds in overseeing private actions. In June 1750, the congregation asked him to leave his post.

It was a year before Edwards moved to Stockbridge, Massachusetts, to become a pastor to the Housatonnick Indians and then the Mohawks, but there he was not free from controversy either. He became embroiled in a disagreement over how to teach Christian doctrine to Indian students. In spite of the intensity and turmoil of this period at Stockbridge, Edwards was able to do a great deal of writing, including *On the Freedom of the Will*. He also began what would have been his most comprehensive work, *The History of Human Redemption*, in which he planned to interpret the whole of human history as the work of the Holy Spirit. It was with the hope that he might better be able to complete this work in an academic setting that in part prompted Edwards to accept the presidency of New Jersey College in late 1757. Edwards was inducted into office on February 6, 1758, received a smallpox inoculation on February 23, and was dead a month later.

Viewed from one perspective, Edwards appears to have spent his life in defense and explication of a theological system that was on the verge of obsolescence, in spite of its long-lasting effects on American culture. No matter how brilliant his insights or how persuasive his sermons, he was engaged in the overwhelming task of attempting to stem a tide of religious pluralism and indifference that had already washed over the American landscape. Looked at from a broader view, however, Edwards, we find, was concerned with universal matters more than those of one theological system: trying to understand the role of sensory and emotional experience for the conversion or transformation of the individual, as well as finding the means by which to judge the validity of the conversion experience. Finally, to conclude with an even more general application, we see Edwards facing a dilemma experienced by countless religious leaders in America: how to maintain the heart of a religious tradition and still not close off the possibility of the invigorating ideas of a new age.

HARRY EMERSON FOSDICK

Harry Emerson Fosdick was both a famous preacher and a well-known spokesperson for the liberal Protestant position in the debate between religious fundamentalism and liberalism that continues to hold a prominent place in American religious history. Fosdick's admirers perceived him as a preacher of tremendous power who spoke to the needs of the times and was able to accommodate Christian doctrine and tradition to the changes in American culture. His critics saw him as foolishly optimistic and dangerous in what they considered his much-too-willing attempts to dilute the Biblical basis of Christianity in order to make religion more respectable in an age of science. Fosdick's autobiography, *The Living of These Days,* as well as his many other books, provides us with his own interpretation of his life and ideas. The responses of his critics give us another view. Together these sources help us to understand some of the issues involved in the liberal/fundamentalist debate and to get some sense of how the debate affected the personal life and career of one of the participants.

Harry Emerson Fosdick's life spanned almost a century. He experienced two world wars and an economic depression, as well as tremendous changes in modes of communication, transportation, and the waging of war. He was born only fourteen years after the Civil War ended, when horse-drawn conveyances and trains were the chief means of transportation. By the time he died, the United States was already involved in Vietnam; the world had known for almost twenty-five years the devastation that could be wrought by nuclear weapons; and jet travel was commonplace. In 1878 Darwinian thought or evolution was still highly controversial; by 1969 popularized explanations of microphysics appeared in news magazines. During the late nineteenth century, when Fosdick was growing up, there was great confidence that ''science'' would save the world. By the time he died, science and the sciences had become immeasurably more complex, and the fear that the fruits of a post-mechanistic world view might ruin the world instead of saving it were becoming widespread among the American populace. If Jonathan Edwards saw his work as the revitalizing of a waning orthodoxy, Fosdick understood his mission to be the reconciling of religious truths with the discoveries of science and the vast changes they had brought about during his lifetime. Fosdick changed his mind about some very basic issues during his career, for example pacifism (greatly in favor of World War I, he became a pacifist after visiting the battlefields). What he persisted in was his notion that religion must be made "reasonable," such that its teachings did not fly in the face of contemporary understandings of both the powers and the limitations of humankind. If religion was to endure, Fosdick claimed, it must not take refuge in rigid orthodoxies of former times.

To sum up Fosdick's life very briefly, he was born a Baptist and educated in western New York state. After receiving a bachelor of divinity degree from Union Theological Seminary in 1904, he served as pastor of First Baptist Church in Montclair, New Jersey, until 1915. During those years he was already acquiring a reputation as a highly skilled preacher and had begun publishing books. Fosdick served Union Theological Seminary as a part-time faculty member during his years in New Jersey and in 1915 resigned his pastorate to become a full-time professor of practical theology there. In 1919, although he was a Baptist, Fosdick was asked to be a visiting preaching minister at First Presbyterian Church in New York. He served there until 1925, but the last two years were marked by constant controversy resulting from one of Fosdick's most famous sermons, "Shall the Fundamentalists Win?" which he preached in May, 1922. After two years of tension, Fosdick resigned from First Presbyterian rather than become a Presbyterian, as he was invited to do by the Presbyterian General Assembly if he would subscribe to the doctrines of Presbyterianism as they appeared in the Westminster Confession. He declined, he said, because he believed that insistence on a "definite creedal subscription, . . . is a practice dangerous to the welfare of the church and to the integrity of the individual conscience."[3]

Far from being the end of his pastoral career, Fosdick's resignation gave him the freedom to become minister at Park Avenue Baptist Church, known as "John D. Rockefeller's Church," which was to be rebuilt as Riverside Church. At first Fosdick resisted the offer, and during a meeting with Rockefeller gave as one of his reasons Rockefeller's wealth: "I do not want to be known as the pastor of the richest man in the country." Rockefeller responded, "I like your frankness, but do you think that more people will criticize you on account of my wealth than will criticize me on account of your theology?"[4] The new Riverside Church was completed in 1930 and Fosdick remained its senior minister until he retired in 1946. Riverside remains today as a nonsectarian church that has no creedal requirements for membership and that stresses a ministry that encompasses an interracial and international sense of mission.

Although this is only a skeletal portrayal of Fosdick's life, it provides us with a starting place from which to examine in more detail the controversy between

---

[3] Harry Emerson Fosdick, *The Living of These Days: An Autobiography* (New York: Harper and Brothers, 1956), p. 172.

[4] Ibid., p. 178.

liberals and fundamentalists in American religious history as it was carried on during the first half of the twentieth century. Fosdick's theological stance toward fundamentalism did not spring up in middle age but dates from his college years. As a boy he had never questioned the literal accuracy of the Bible or of church doctrines. He recalled in high school days "talking with a boy who doubted the doctrine of immortality and who argued with me against its truth. I was horrified that such an attitude was possible. The fundamentalists in later years have hated me plentifully, but I started as one of them."[5] In his autobiography Fosdick elaborated upon his struggles with religion during his college years, and his experiences echo those of Jonathan Edwards at about the same age. But, whereas Edwards turned to the structures of orthodoxy as he emerged from his years of questioning, Fosdick went the other way: "The more I was aware of an inner center of spiritual satisfaction and resource, the more independent I became of the outward formulas of religion in which I had been trained."[6] Fosdick saw his time of religious questioning as taking place chiefly on an abstract level, since he had not yet confronted the tragedies that come with the living of life, one of which for Fosdick was a nervous breakdown at the age of twenty-two. This was an experience, he said, that forever afterwards colored the way he treated the emotionally disturbed who were in need of pastoral care.

Fosdick's famous and controversial sermon "Shall the Fundamentalists Win?" is an expression of his maturity. It was delivered when he was forty-four and was based on his experiences as minister, teacher, and theologian. He said he considered the sermon to be conciliatory, that he meant it as a plea that the fundamentalists not try to push out of the churches those with whom they disagreed. Fosdick insisted that both liberals and fundamentalists could coexist within the same denomination, the fundamentalists keeping the liberals from succumbing to "a supine surrender to prevalent cultural ideas" and the liberals seeing to it that the fundamentalists did not give in to "hidebound obscurantism, denying the discoveries of science and insisting on the literal acceptance of every Biblical idea. . . ."[7] The sermon set off the two-year struggle that ended with Fosdick's resignation; and one of the quotes he cites from it in his autobiography provides a clue that perhaps the sermon was not quite so conciliatory as Fosdick considered it: "Just now the fundamentalists are giving us one of the worst exhibitions of bitter intolerance that the churches of this country have ever seen. As one watches them and listens to them, one remembers the remark of General Armstrong of Hampton Institute: 'Cantankerousness is worse than heterodoxy.'"[8]

What exactly was at the basis of the controversy between liberals and fundamentalists? And what was Fosdick's stand on the matter? One way to understand is to look at the theological differences involved. Fundamentalism urged an

---

[5] Ibid., p. 517.
[6] Ibid., p. 145.
[7] Ibid., p. 144.
[8] Ibid., p. 145.

acceptance of five essential points: (1) the inerrancy of Scripture; (2) the virgin birth of Christ; (3) Christ's substitutionary atonement, meaning that Christ died to redeem humankind from the sin of the Fall; (4) Christ's bodily resurrection; and (5) the authenticity of Christ's miracles.[9] Liberalism, on the other hand, as Fosdick saw it, maintained that asking Christians in the twentieth century to believe in these five points was asking them to set aside reasonableness and common sense and to reject the findings of science about the orderliness of a universe that proceeded without the kind of divine interference that belief in miracles presupposed. The liberals did not deny the truth of the Bible, nor the importance of Jesus Christ, although there were arguments among them about his actual divinity. But in contrast to the fundamentalists' tendency to hold fast to certain doctrines and to see cultural changes as potentially dangerous to basic Christianity, liberals were more likely to identify change with progress not only in culture but in religion as well. In *Christianity and Progress* Fosdick claimed that the human race had emerged from such stultifying world views as the "endless cosmic cycles of the Greeks or the apocalyptic expectations of the Hebrews." In his view, the concept of progress was liberating, not frightening: "We are committed to the hope of making progress, and the central problem of coming to intelligent terms with this dominant idea."[10]

What begins to emerge from this debate is the fact that liberals and fundamentalists disagreed not just on such doctrinal points as Biblical inerrancy, but also on such matters as how truth, religious or otherwise, could be known; how the divine is revealed in nature; how to interpret history; and how to view human nature. In a refutation of Fosdick's ideas called *The Failure of Modernism* (liberalism), John Horsch, a fundamentalist, accused Fosdick and liberals in general of placing too much pride in human ability to discern truth unaided by divine revelation and of being much too optimistic about human ability to bring about moral reform and affect the course of history. Specifically, Horsch was responding to an article by Fosdick, "What Are Christian Liberals Driving At?" which appeared in the January 1925 issue of *Ladies' Home Journal* (a source that gives us insight into the widespread and popular nature of this controversy), but in general *The Failure of Modernism* sums up Horsch's estimation of the fallacies inherent in liberalism. His conclusion assails liberalism as a "religion which is self-contradictory and irrational, insisting on the one hand on creedlessness, individualism, and sole personal authority, and realizing on the other hand that unless something taking the place of a Christian creed is produced (an impossibility where individualism reigns supreme) there is no chance for success."[11] Horsch and other fundamentalists saw the liberals with their looseness of doctrine as

---

[9] George Marsden, *Fundamentalism and American Culture: The Shaping of Twentieth-Century Evangelicalism, 1870-1925* (New York: Oxford University Press, 1980), p. 117.

[10] Harry Emerson Fosdick, *Christianity and Progress* (New York: Fleming W. Revell Company, 1922), pp. 41-42.

[11] John Horsch, *The Failure of Modernism: A Reply to Harry Emerson Fosdick* (Chicago: The Biblical Colportage Association, 1925), p. 61.

marking the end of a Christianity that bore any similarity to the revealed religion of apostolic times. Fosdick quoted another of his critics as calling him the "Jesse James of the theological world." Liberals like Fosdick feared that the fundamentalists would push "reasoning" Christians out of the churches with their insistence on doctrinal compliance.

Fosdick's articulation of the liberal Protestant viewpoint was not his only contribution to American religious life. His many books of an inspirational nature, such as *On Being a Real Person* (1943) and *A Faith for Tough Times* (1952), were read by millions; and as professor of homiletics at Union Seminary he influenced the preaching style of several generations of ministers from many denominations. Fosdick was active in such social issues as pacifism, and under his leadership Riverside Church became a model for interracial, interdenominational, and ecumenical congregations—a true celebration of diversity in American religion and culture. In his liberal religious beliefs Fosdick embodied a spirit of American optimism that extended beyond religion to the overall culture itself. He did not deny the prevalence of evil and sin in the world, but he expressed great confidence in the ability of human reason, aided by God, to overcome almost any obstacles to self-fulfillment, whether individual or national. Fosdick believed in free enterprise and in the validity of a capitalistic system—he specified that to be successful it must have love, not greed, as its motivating power. Fosdick called himself an "evangelical liberal," meaning that he chose to stay within the institutional church rather than seek out a meaning for his life in some other setting. In the arena he chose there is no doubt that his life is a success story, in terms of the immense numbers of people he influenced, his perfection of the form of the sermon almost as an art form, and his brave espousal of views that he knew would be controversial. Nonetheless, the most intense controversy of his long career, the debate between religious liberals and fundamentalists, is an illustration of the very thing that Jonathan Edwards feared: the potential for religions to break apart into those aspects that spoke either to reason or to the emotions. Edwards could not have seen the role that modern science would play in this coming apart, nor could he have anticipated the dilemmas that Fosdick and others of his time would have to sort through. But he seemed able to anticipate some of the divisive consequences for religion when the choice appeared for many people to be between what made sense to their heads and what appealed to their hearts.

MARTIN LUTHER KING, JR.

Harry Emerson Fosdick has been perceived as a social activist, but the Reverend Martin Luther King, Jr., gave the term *activist* new meaning as it applied to American religion in the 1950s and 1960s. Assassinated at the age of thirty-nine, he left us no autobiography composed of reflections in old age upon those influences and experiences that were the pivotal and motivating aspects of his life. We do know that as the son and grandson of black Baptist ministers and their wives he had a middle-class childhood in Atlanta, where he was born in 1929. We know, too, that having a financially secure existence among Atlanta's black middle class did not make a black child immune to the indignities suffered by all blacks in a segregated social system that took for granted separate schools and neighborhoods as well as public bathrooms and drinking fountains, restaurants and hotels that were off limits to blacks, and seating areas on buses and trains that were set apart.

King's biographers cite two or three incidents in his childhood that convey the need for constant watchfulness and apprehension on the part of blacks in their relationships with whites: in one case a shoe-store clerk's refusal to wait on King and his father unless they moved to seats farther back in the store (his father walked out), and in another a slap in the face in a department store by a white woman he had never seen before, who said, "The little nigger stepped on my toe."[12] King attended segregated grammar and high schools in Atlanta, and one of his memories of entering first grade was the end of his friendship with the sons of the white grocer in the neighborhood; the parents made it clear that friendship with black children was inappropriate beyond a certain age. At fifteen, King entered Morehouse College, a black men's school in Atlanta, and by graduation he had rejected a career in medicine in favor of the ministry. He entered Crozer Seminary in Chester, Pennsylvania, where he studied the writings of Washington Gladden and Walter Rauschenbusch, theologians of the Social Gospel Movement with its optimism about human ability to change social conditions. But he also encountered other theologians, such as H. Richard Neibuhr and Paul Tillich, who, having experienced two world wars and an economic depression, took a gloomier view of human nature. In 1951 King enrolled in a doctoral program at Boston University. He received a Ph.D. in systematic theology in 1955, by which time he and his wife, Coretta Scott King, lived in Montgomery, Alabama, where King was pastor of Dexter Avenue Baptist Church. It was in Montgomery, as leader of the famous bus boycott, that the activist phase of King's life began.

The bus boycott was sparked by Rosa Parks, a black seamstress who quietly but adamantly one day on the way home from work refused to move from a seat in the front of the bus reserved for whites to a rear section. She explained later, "I was tired." Rosa Parks was remanded into custody, and that incident catalyzed the black community into taking action. At a meeting of black community leaders Martin Luther King was elected leader of the Montgomery Improvement Association, the group that organized the bus boycott. In this position he became involved in a pattern of events that was to be repeated in many other cities in the South—Selma, Birmingham, and Atlanta among them—as blacks, and then whites, began to protest the racial separation that had been so much a part of American culture, enforced by both law and social custom. Through the boycott King became involved in a complex intertwining of events: further attempts at

---

[12] These stories appear in two biographies: Lerone Bennett, *What Manner of Man: A Biography of Martin Luther King, Jr.* (Chicago: Johnson Publishing Co., 1964), and David L. Lewis, *Martin Luther King: A Critical Biography* (New York: Praeger, 1970).

organization, confrontations with bus-company and city officials, nonviolent protest, time spent in jail, and finally violence when King's home and later other homes and churches were bombed. King's speech at the organizational phase of the boycott to an audience of 4,000 gives us an indication of the emotional state of the black community of Montgomery in 1954 as well as a sense of the rhetorical ability that was to become one of the marks of King's great power in the struggle for civil rights. He used as his theme Rosa Parks's straightforward statement that she was tired:

> But there comes a time when people get tired. We are here this evening to say to those who have mistreated us so long that we are tired—tired of being segregated and humiliated, tired of being kicked about by the brutal feet of oppression. We have no alternative but to protest. For many years we have shown amazing patience. We have sometimes given our white brothers the feeling that we liked the way we were being treated. But we come here tonight to be saved from that patience that makes us patient with anything less than freedom and justice.[13]

The Montgomery struggle ended in 1956 when the Supreme Court handed down a decision affirming that of a U.S. District Court that Alabama's state and local laws requiring segregation on buses were unconstitutional. King said that the spirit of the boycott had come from Jesus and that the technique had come from Mohandas K. Gandhi (who had been influenced in his own theories by reading the works of Henry David Thoreau while in jail).

There is a temptation to sum up Martin Luther King's significance for American religious history in terms of what he "did"—to give details of the civil rights marches he led; to quote at length from his speeches; to recount the attempts on his life; and to catalogue his awards, among which was the Nobel Peace Prize in 1964. But King did not just go from one march to another in the years from 1956 through 1968. He was also developing a theology and philosophy of nonviolent protest that was to form the basis of his actions as well as the organization of the Southern Christian Leadership Conference, founded by sixty blacks, mostly ministers, in 1957. King was president of SCLC until his death in 1968. King drew the theological and philosophical underpinnings of nonviolent protest from his own heritage of black Southern Christianity, as well as from his encounters with white European and American theologians: Rauschenbusch and Gladden; Tillich, Karl Barth, and Niebuhr. To this black-and-white mixture King added the understandings of Gandhi, the Hindu religious leader and social reformer who led his people in their rejection of British rule.

To begin with King's own heritage, the experience of slavery in America resulted in a black Christianity that saw those traits needed for survival—meekness, patience, and good nature—as embodying not subservience but the Christian ideal: "No race ever acted more like Jesus Christ, whose life was one long patient non-resistance to wrong,"[14] said Bishop W. H. Gaines of the

---

[13] Lewis, p. 58.

[14] S. P. Fullenwider, *The Mind and Mood of Black America* (Homewood, Illinois: The Dorsey Press, 1969), p. 30.

African Methodist Episcopal Church. When he published these words in 1897, Gaines was exhibiting the confidence of many black clergy that the blacks' Christ-like example would result, finally, in a reformation of white society that would bring about the racial equality that the thirteenth and fourteenth amendments had promised but that were nowhere in evidence in American life. Although King had this same understanding of blacks in American society—that of captives whose own virtues would eventually set them free—by the time of his first pastorate in Montgomery it was obvious that actual emancipation from the bonds of a racist society would not occur without action. S. P. Fullenwider, author of *The Mind and Mood of Black America,* gives us a picture of the racial situation in America in the mid–twentieth century:

> ...[O]nly the tiniest token of school integration has taken place since the Supreme Court decision [in 1954].... school integration was actually losing ground as whites in northern cities fled the spreading black ghettos.... [Y]oung civil rights workers were being beaten, jailed, and terrorized in Alabama and Mississippi.... churches were being bombed, crosses burned.... federally built housing was only one-tenth integrated;... politicians, union leaders, real estate dealers and bankers were combining to raise higher the walls that ring the ghettos;... and there was day to day police brutality that makes most Negroes feel that they are a conquered people within an alien land.[15]

King saw the goals of his leadership as combatting all the abuses of racism in America with what he called "the mighty army of love," rather than by other means, such as violence or black separatism. For King there was redemptive power in the example of those who endured undeserved suffering, but he also knew, as Gandhi had, that this power must be displayed in public ways—such as the marches, the strikes, the boycotts, and the lunch-counter sit-ins that became the marks of King's leadership. King realized, further, that these actions alone did not bring about change. Because the majority of bus riders in Montgomery were black, for example, the boycott of public transportation diminished the profits of the bus company, just as strikes and sit-ins had negative economic effects. Nor was King oblivious to the disagreement among blacks as to whether nonviolent tactics might not be just an extension of the knuckling under to white domination that had characterized black culture since the first slaves arrived in 1619. For example, the black novelist John Killens observed that "the Negro has always been non-violent—by necessity. I see no reason now to make a philosophy out of it."[16] Those who participated in protests that were meant to be peaceful were constantly exposed to the violence of others, and King realized that one of his most formidable tasks was to head off the violence that would discredit the whole civil rights movement and that finally did erupt with great force during the summers of the late 1960s and at the time of King's assassination.

It is possible to see Martin Luther King, Jr., chiefly within the context of

---

[15] Fullenwider, p. 230.
[16] Bennett, p. 207.

black religion and culture in America with its emphasis on the experiential over the doctrinal and its roots in the religions of Africa and the long years of slavery. But King also participated deeply in the traditions of American revivalism with its optimism about humankind's capacity to repent of its sins and then to apply the grace of redemption to the reform of all the ills of American society, racism among the worst. In spite of the great sufferings of his race, King could say with the greatest optimism on the steps of the Lincoln Memorial in 1963, "I have a dream that my four little children will one day live in a nation where they will not be judged by the color of their skin but by the content of their character." What King did more than anything else was to assess American culture as inherently racist and to explicate by nonviolent protest as clearly as he could all of the consequences of that racism—economic, social, political, educational, and spiritual—and the kind of brutalization, not just of the oppressed but of the oppressors, that resulted from it. He called to account the churches and synagogues, temples and mosques of America, clergy and laity alike, to refuse any longer to tolerate racism as an acceptable undergirding for the structure of American society.

DOROTHY DAY

Neither Dorothy Day's early life nor the controversial work she engaged in during her middle years gave much indication that upon her death in 1980 she would be eulogized as a kind of saint by American culture at large and as a prophetic and welcome voice in American Catholicism. There was very little of organized religion in her childhood; she was not a "cradle Catholic." As a child she had only minimal contact with religion in the form of Episcopalianism, although she mentions in her autobiography, *The Long Loneliness,* that the family had a Catholic maid who took her to Mass once: "I slept in the same room with Mary and I must have seen her saying her prayers, but I do not remember it."[17] Day's father was a journalist, and her mother was one of the first women trained as a stenographer. The family was mobile, moving from Brooklyn, Dorothy's birthplace, to California and Chicago. When it came time for college Dorothy received a Hearst scholarship in journalism to the University of Illinois. She was there for two years, living in great poverty, until she was befriended by a wealthy young woman, Rayna Simons Prohme, who sought in communism an understanding of life's meaning and later died in Moscow as she was about to enter the Lenin Institute. Day, in fact, had many friends who were socialists and joined a socialist club at the university; she thought the meetings dull and didn't go very often. It was not until she left school and returned to New York, where her family then lived, that she became more actively involved in socialism. She took a job on *The Call,* a daily socialist newspaper, partly because no other paper would hire her. She speculated

---

17 Dorothy Day, *The Long Loneliness* (New York: Harper and Row, Publishers, Inc., 1952), p. 305.

that her lack of success might have been the result of her father's asking his city-editor friends to tell her that journalism was not suitable work for a woman.

As Day tells it in *The Long Loneliness*, the years between her work on *The Call* and her meeting in 1932 with Peter Maurin, her co-founder of the Catholic Worker Movement, were years of disorder and searching. After leaving *The Call*, she became a nurse in a Brooklyn hospital until the end of World War I, went back to Chicago to write, and left Chicago for New Orleans, where she worked on a newspaper and wrote a series of articles on taxi-dancers. She left New Orleans when she sold the movie rights to a novel she had written and returned to New York to buy a little beach house on Staten Island. During these years she twice spent time in jail, once in Washington for participating in a march for women's rights and then in Chicago when she was mistakenly arrested as a prostitute while caring for a sick friend in a Wobblies' (International Workers of the World) boarding house. Upon her return to New York, Day entered into a common-law marriage with Forster Batterham, a biologist and anarchist, with whom she lived for four years and who was the father of her daughter, Tamar Theresa, born in 1927.

There are threads that run through the apparent randomness of these fifteen years: Day's ongoing life as a journalist; her contact with and attraction for Catholicism; her continuing association with socialists, communists, anarchists, and "bohemians." During all those years, Dorothy Day saw herself as seeking not only a religious system, but social justice. She became a Catholic a year after her daughter was baptized (at the time she felt insufficiently certain to become a Catholic herself), knowing that she would forfeit her relationship with Batterham, who was intensely antagonistic to organized religion; and fearful also that Catholicism would provide her no outlet for her socialist activities. She knew nothing of the social teachings of the church at the time of her conversion:

> I had never heard of the encyclicals. I felt that the Church was the Church of the poor, that St. Patrick's had been built from the pennies of servant girls, that it cared for the emigrant, it established hospitals, orphanages, day nurseries, houses of the Good Shepherd, homes for the aged, but at the same time I felt that it did not set its face against a social order which made so much charity in the present sense of the word necessary. I felt that charity was a word to choke on. Who wanted charity?[18]

By her account, Day was drawn almost irresistibly into the Catholic church, but at the same time she expected that "one must live in a state of permanent dissatisfaction with the Church." She was to live as a writer in California and Mexico before her encounter with Peter Maurin would help to bring the various threads in her life together into one cloth.

Dorothy Day always gave Peter Maurin credit for the founding of the Catholic Worker Movement. Actually, it was a joint effort, each bringing to the

---

[18] Ibid., p. 172.

enterprise talents that the other lacked. In spite of eccentricities of dress and manner (he didn't bathe often, change his clothes, or carry money—in order not to
"excite envy," Day once said), Peter Maurin was a creative and compelling
theological thinker. He deplored the secularism of contemporary society and
wanted to restore unity between the material and the spiritual. Maurin preached
the doctrine of "personalism," which insisted on the responsibility of the individual to take action that would better the condition of humanity. For him the essential foundation of the virtuous and Christian life was voluntary poverty. Maurin,
for example, was opposed to the wage system; he gave his own labor freely and
received in return "gifts" of food, clothing, and housing. What Peter Maurin
provided for Dorothy Day was a theological and philosophical framework within
which to combine her desire for a life of socialism and social action, both rooted in
religious practice. He allayed her previous fears that she could not be both a
socialist and a practitioner of religion. What Day provided for Maurin was the in-
itiative along with the organizational skills to put his ideas to work.

Basing it on a combination of Maurin's ideas and her own, Day founded a
newspaper, the *Catholic Worker,* which from the time of its origin until the present
has maintained a stance that is pro-labor, pacifist, and opposed to racism and anti-
Semitism and has as a constant theme the need for sharing of wealth. It still sells
for a penny a copy, just as it did when the first issue was sold on May Day in 1933.
Day's second undertaking, beginning with the Worker headquarters in the
Bowery, was the setting up of hospitality houses, which began to appear in cities
all over the country and that persist to this day. Next, she carried out the purchase
of a communal farm in Pennsylvania. Both the houses and the farm practiced
"open hospitality"—that is, they fed and sheltered anyone who came. A description of the residents of Maryfarm during its first summer gives a good indication
of the varied types the Worker movement attracted and took care of. In addition to
Day, her daughter, Maurin, and some student Workers, "there was a man just
out of Sing Sing who planted flowers, a seminarian who brought six pigs, a group
of children from Harlem, some striking seamen, and an ex–circus performer who
would do cartwheels down the hill in back of the house when the moon was full."[19]

Perhaps the clearest measure of the success of Dorothy Day's enterprises is
that they are still in existence; and the greatest indication of her own personal success is to say that she lived the life she preached—one of self-sacrifice and poverty.
Once her search for constant values was ended, she was amazingly consistent in
putting those values into action, whether in support of a grave diggers' strike
against St. Patrick's Cathedral or the peace movement during the Vietnam war.
She was tireless in her work of traveling and speaking on behalf of the Worker
movement, and her efforts involved not only trying to raise money but also
refereeing the various fights and factionalisms that were inevitable among the independent types who made up the movement all over the country. Day was a

[19] William D. Miller, *A Harsh and Dreadful Love: Dorothy Day and the Catholic Worker Movement* (New York: Loveright, 1973), p. 124.

religious and political radical. In her radicalism she and her followers went against the mainstream of American culture in general, particularly in its economic and nationalistic aspects. In addition she antagonized many American Catholics. Many first- and second-generation immigrants of the post-Depression years were just beginning to make financial gains. Her insistence on poverty annoyed some who were anxious to become members of the American middle class. Further, Day's sympathies for socialism made American Catholics nervous. Finally, because the Workers stressed that the laity must take action against poverty and injustice regardless of whether the American Catholic hierarchy provided leadership, there was an anti-clerical aspect to the Worker movement that antagonized church leaders.

Given all these ways in which Dorothy Day, Peter Maurin, and the Catholic Worker movement departed from mainstream values in the culture, it is important to stress that their spirit of optimism about the individual's power to effect social change fit perfectly into the American ethos. And if the Workers spoke of community in the more "Catholic" terms of the Mystical Body of Christ, there was nonetheless much in their system of the American millenial impulse that pervades both the religions and the culture of the United States—an expectation that, finally, their efforts combined with God's grace would result in a time of peace and justice. In the meantime, Dorothy Day knew that that time would not come soon. She completed her autobiography in 1952, but the questions she asked herself at its conclusion have not lost their poignancy or their relevance for Americans who value both the individual and the community:

> Can there be a just war? . . . What about the morality of the use of the atom bomb? What does God want me to do? And what am I capable of doing? Can I stand out against state and church? Is it pride, presumption, to think I have the spiritual capacity to use spiritual weapons in the face of the most gigantic tyranny the world has ever seen? Am I capable of enduring suffering, facing martyrdom? And alone?
>
> Again the long loneliness to be faced.[20]

---

[20] Day, p. 305.

6

"the law knows no heresy": dissent in american religion

Religious dissent in America is not the dangerous business that it is in Ireland, Lebanon, or Iran. Although we can point to incidents of violence over religion in our history since freedom of religion was established in 1791—the burning of a convent in Massachusetts; President James Buchanan's readying of troops to send against the Mormons; attacks on Jehovah's Witnesses who refused to salute the flag—as a general pattern what Martin Marty has said is true: "Religious dissent and conflict left few dead bodies" in the course of American religious history.[1] That religious disputes, however acrimonious, have not led us into armed conflict results from the fact that the very nature of dissent is necessarily different in a culture that upholds religious pluralism as an inherent good. Traditionally, *dissent* has referred to a protest against or a departure from an established church. In England, for example, a Dissenter is one specifically opposed to the Church of England. Since in America there is no established church against which to rail, the question that looms largest in a discussion of religious dissent is "dissent against what"?

In attempting to answer what seems at first to be a fairly simple question we come face to face with the immense variety of forms that religious dissent has taken in America. To avoid being overwhelmed by the many examples of religious activity that could accurately be described as "dissenting," common sense dictates at least a preliminary division into three categories. First, there is strife

---

[1] Edwin Gaustad, *Dissent in American Religion,* Introduction by Martin Marty (Chicago: University of Chicago Press, 1973), p. xii.

that begins internally within a denomination or religious group, often over doctrinal matters, such as the literal interpretation of the Bible, the ordination of women, or the authority of leaders. Frequently, these disputes can be resolved within the guidelines of the particular denomination. Sometimes resolution does not come so easily, and the result is the splitting off of one group from another—for example, the division of the Presbyterian Church into North and South during the Civil War that lasted until 1983, or the formation of Seminex, a ''seminary in exile'' that came about in the 1970s over the question of Biblical interpretation in the Missouri Synod Lutheran Church.

A second manifestation of religious dissent is the formation of new religious movements, examples being Shakerism in the eighteenth century, Mormonism and Christian Science in the nineteenth century, and the Church of Scientology in the twentieth century. New religions frequently arouse fear and suspicion in the American population, not so much because they are unorthodox but because they appear to be in revolt against dominant cultural values. That has been the case with all four of these religions. The Shakers preached a belief in a Mother/Father God, the practice of celibacy, and separatism from the prevailing culture. The Mormons, too, appeared to want to live separately from the rest of American society, and the relatively few years during which they practiced polygamy has had a much longer-lasting effect on how Americans in general have viewed Mormonism. The doctrines of Christian Science radically questioned the reality of matter during a time when American culture was growing ever more materialist and decried the use of doctors just when medicine was showing obvious signs of the professionalism it exhibits today. Scientology draws its teachings from electronics, psychotherapy, and science fiction, which would seem to fit right in with current tastes in American culture, but these are not the traditional sources for religious truth in a Judaeo-Christian culture.

Third, there are the imported religions, usually from the East, movements like Zen Buddhism, Baháí, the Unification Church, Meher Baba, and Hare Krishna. They, too, preach doctrines and practices that do not fit in very well with the general American conception of what a religion should be. Whether or not they excite hostility or merely curiosity often depends upon their recruiting and fund-raising techniques. Whereas Zen Buddhism and Baháí are often perceived as appealingly exotic and a healthy alternative to Western religious traditions, some of the others—among them Hare Krishna, Meher Baba, and Unificationism—have been labeled as ''cults,'' and that designation in American culture has strong connotations of something dangerous to American values. The Unification Church, for example, arouses suspicion partly because of its foreign origin, but also because its intensely hierarchical system of organization and what appear to be high-pressure recruiting methods fly in the face of an American understanding of the voluntary nature of religion.

Edwin Gaustad, an American religious historian who has written on dissent, uses a different system of categorizing. He speaks of schismatics, ''sinners against love"; heretics, "sinners against faith"; and misfits, "sinners against society."[2] Schismatics are those who break away from existing groups, some because they disapprove of the decline in fervor from other times; others because they chafe at restrictive rules of organization; still others because of ethnic and racial considerations. Among these have been New Light Baptists, members of the Polish National Catholic Church in America, and Black Methodist and Baptist groups. The heretics departed from Judaeo-Christian orthodoxy, generally in the direction of a more optimistic view of human nature with a corresponding decline in emphasis on a sovereign deity. Gaustad cites as examples Deists, Transcendentalists, humanists, and skeptics. The so-called misfits have dissented not only against existing religions but against American culture as well. Among these, Gaustad numbers the Ghost Dance religion of the American Plains Indians, the Mormons, the Black Muslims, the Amish, and the Quakers. Considered a greater threat to American society than either schismatics or heretics, these social dissenters are likely to arouse fear especially if they preach separatism. Gaustad makes the assessment, however, that in addition to fear the misfits are as likely to excite other emotions that have rendered their criticisms of American society ineffective: Millennialists have been ridiculed; Buddhists and Hindus patronized; and the Amish and Mennonites sentimentalized.[3]

By now it is obvious that there are many different answers to the question "Dissent against what?" Nonetheless, common patterns exist in the relationships among mainstream religions, religious dissent, and American culture, no matter how varied the forms and results of protest might be. One of the most important points to understand in getting at the nature of religious dissent in America is the fact that there is an extremely high tolerance for dissenting "ideas," but when these ideas are acted upon in ways that seem to threaten the American value system, tolerance disappears. Dissent that stays within the realm of doctrine does not often become a matter of public concern. The Missouri Synod Lutheran conflict mentioned previously is of intense interest to members of that denomination and to theologians, historians, and sociologists as well; but there is no fear that the controversy will have adverse effects on American society in general. Let the doctrinal dispute erupt beyond the confines of a denomination, however, or even a coalition of several denominations, and news of the friction moves from the "religious news" section of the newspaper to the front page. One example is the battle to have creationism taught in public-school science classes in Arkansas on an equal basis with evolutionary theory. The law passed by the legislature of Arkansas was declared unconstitutional in a federal court because it appeared to establish one religious view over others in public education. Or, take an incident that occurred in Minneapolis in 1981, when a religious group called the Church

---

[2] Ibid. Gaustad's book is an elaboration of these three categories with a chapter devoted to each one.
[3] Ibid.

Universal and Triumphant purchased a mansion as a study center in a very desirable residential neighborhood. Those in the neighborhood who protested the purchase cited as objections problems with parking, disregard of zoning laws, and potential proselytizing in the neighborhood. There was no mention in newspaper articles of the actual "beliefs" of the group; their doctrines, even though unorthodox, were not the issue.

Whereas church leaders and theologians may be apprehensive about the consequences of doctrinal dissent and the general public may be fearful of religious movements that foster separatism, departures from traditional family structure and economic systems different from capitalism, the student of religion can afford to be more detached in an analysis of religious dissent. Looked at in one way, a study of religious dissent reveals points of tension in American culture, points past which diversity becomes too intense to be incorporated into the whole. The tension may arise from racial, economic, gender-based, or social inequalities that then find expression in religious dissent. Looked at in another way, patterns in the history of religious dissent may illuminate the creativity of the human spirit inherent in the formation, particularly, of new religious movements. Robert Ellwood used the expression "alternative altars" to refer to religious movements in America that have departed in doctrine and practice from more mainstream expressions of religious faith and that have contributed their own kinds of spirituality to American religion and culture.[4]

Both of these approaches are useful in looking at three examples of religious dissent in America: the Quakers, the Christian Scientists, and the Black Muslims. We need to ask not only what they were "against" but also what they were "for" in the context of the different historical periods that gave rise to them. How did they express their concept of the deity, and what relationship did that deity have to human persons? What objections did they have to a variety of aspects of American culture—not just the prevailing religious beliefs, but economic and social conditions as well? What did the members of these three religious movements see as their unique contributions to religion in America? And, finally, what has been the history of their relationships with the mainstream religions and American culture in general?

THE QUAKERS

The Quakers, or the Religious Society of Friends, were active in England at least ten years before the first of their members arrived in America.[5] Quakerism,

---

[4] Robert Ellwood, *Alternative Altars: Unconventional and Eastern Spirituality in America* (Chicago: University of Chicago Press, 1979).

[5] Whether apocryphal or not, the following story is told about the origin of the name "Quaker": When George Fox appeared before officials on the charge of refusing to remove his hat to an authority, he told the officials that they ought "to tremble before the word of God." The response to Fox was, "You are the Quaker, not I." Margaret H. Bacon, *The Quiet Rebels: The Story of the Quakers in America* (New York: Basic Books, 1969), p. 17.

founded primarily by George Fox (1624–1691), was an attempt to push religion even further away than had Puritanism from medieval Catholicism and the Anglicanism that had taken its place in England, and in a new direction. If the Puritans wanted to rid religion of elaborate liturgies, sacraments, and hierarchy, the Quakers were even more inclined in the direction of simplification. Far from being admired by the Puritans, however, for their strenuous efforts at reform, the Quakers (who wanted to purify the Puritans) represented a threat both to religious doctrine and social stability. Margaret H. Bacon, an historian of American Quakerism, recounted the coming of two Quaker women, Mary Fisher and Ann Austin, to Boston in 1656:

> The women were held on shipboard while their boxes were searched for "blasphemous" documents. One hundred such books found in their possession were burned in the marketplace by the common hangman. The women were then transferred to prison, stripped naked and searched for tokens of witchcraft, and kept for five weeks without light or writing materials. The master of the *Swallow* was finally ordered to transport them to Barbados and to let no person in the American colonies speak to them enroute.[6]

Nonetheless, other Quakers came to take their place, and word of the new belief spread. Rhode Island and Pennsylvania became strongholds of Quakerism. By the time of the Revolution there were 50,000 Quakers in America in a population of a little more than a million and a half.

What was it about Quakerism that made it appear so insidiously dangerous to the Puritans? Why, if the Quakers saw themselves as reformers in the same tradition as the Puritans, did Quaker doctrine appear to have within it the potential to destroy Puritanism? At its very basis the disagreement was theological. In spite of their common impulse toward reform, the Quakers and the Puritans espoused radically different theologies of the divine and the human. Whereas the Puritans preached a depraved humanity and an omnipotent sovereign God who had revealed himself through the Bible, the Quakers believed in the possibility of human perfection and in a deity who was made known through the religious experience of the individual. For the Quakers there were no creedal prerequisites, no clergy, no sacraments through which the experience of the divine would be mediated—at the heart of Quakerism there was just the individual experience of the Inner Light—the Quaker term for the in-dwelling presence of God.

This Quaker belief led to their insistence on the equality of each person. To reflect and emphasize that equality, the Quakers radically simplified their lives in every aspect—from worship to dress and speech. They wanted to eliminate all those manifestations of rank which appeared to indicate that some people were better than others. Quaker worship took the form of a *meeting,* the word also used as the equivalent of *congregation.* The meeting was regulated by no set ritual, nor was it celebrated by a member of the clergy. Members of the meeting sat in silence

---

6 Ibid., pp. 3–4.

together, opening themselves to the experience of the Inner Light. When a member was moved to speak, he or she did so. Further, it was the Quakers, not the Puritans, who wore plain, unadorned clothing; and their use of *thee* and *thou* instead of *you,* which today seems merely quaint, served the same purpose as simple dress—to minimize rank and social status. According to Margaret Bacon, common people in the seventeenth century were expected to address their betters as *you* whereas *thee* and *thou* were more intimate forms, and the Quakers refused to comply with this linguistic form of ranking. For this same reason of equality, Quakers did not remove their hats to authorities nor did they take oaths, since that custom seemed to imply two standards of truth, the oath being for special occasions.

Far from being merely irritating to the Puritans, Quaker beliefs and practices appeared to threaten the very foundation on which society was built: the acknowledgment of and submission to authority and leadership, whether it be in the government, the church, or the family. Thus, the Puritans perceived Quakerism not only as a competing religious system but as a threat to the entire social order. But in spite of Puritan efforts to stop it—in some cases going so far as execution—Quaker membership grew steadily during the seventeenth and eighteenth centuries, and one might have guessed that Quakerism today would be among the mainstream churches in America. On the contrary, Quakers now number about 120,000 in a population of more than 230 million.

There are several factors that account for this. One is the series of divisions and schisms that occurred in American Quakerism during the late eighteenth and nineteenth centuries, which resulted from disagreements over rigidity of doctrines, evangelical forms of worship, abolition, and the establishment of foreign missions. Another theory is that of Rufus Jones, Quaker historian, teacher, humanitarian, and mystic, who speculates in his history of Quakerism in the American colonies that as long as the "tragic collisions" with Puritanism persisted, the Quakers experienced a dynamism and unity that resulted from their need to establish their identity and resist persecution. When freedom of religion was established, fervor diminished. Even more telling, according to Jones, was the Quaker predilection, developed early, to see themselves as a "peculiar people," a people set apart to preserve a universal truth that the rest of the world refused to accept. As a result, the Quakers turned in upon themselves, paralleling the trap that many other dissenting religious groups had fallen into: "The living *idea* organizes a definite society for the propagation of it, and lo, the Society unconsciously smothers the original idea and becomes absorbed in itself!"[7]

The small number of Quakers in America, however, belies the influence they have had on social action, and their activism has consistently encompassed the rights of women, blacks, Indians, and pacifists. From the beginning women fared better in Quakerism, because there was no gender requirement for experi-

---

[7]Rufus Jones, *The Quakers in the American Colonies,* first published in 1911 (New York: Norton, 1966), p. xxiii.

encing and proclaiming the Inner Light. The divine made itself known to women as well as to men, and Quaker women shared influence in the movement in a way that their sisters in the mainstream churches did not. Lucretia Mott, a nineteenth-century Quaker, was among the organizers of the Women's Rights Conference at Seneca Falls, New York, in 1848, and her activities in the abolition, temperance, and peace movements reveal the interweaving of these causes in the lives of many Quakers. Early in their history the Quakers also took up the cause of Indians deprived of their lands, and that cause has prevailed into the twentieth century. The Quakers' long history of efforts on behalf of the rights of black Americans began with John Woolman, an eighteenth-century Quaker, who was asked by his employer to write a bill of sale to another Quaker for a slave. "But," he said, "at the executing of it I was so afflicted in my mind that I said before my master and the Friend that I believed slave-keeping to be a practice inconsistent with the Christian religion."[8] A revolutionary insight for its time, Woolman's understanding began a pattern that emerged strongly during the abolition movement of the nineteenth century and again in the civil rights movement of the 1960s. Finally, the Quakers have had a long history of opposition to war, believing that the non-violence and peacemaking taught in the Sermon on the Mount can be made to work in the real world.

Quaker historians caution that it is an error to assume that all Friends have the same opinions on social issues—the various divisions in Quakerism give evidence to the contrary—or that it is possible to walk into a Quaker meeting anywhere in the country and encounter a similar scene. Some Quaker groups have adopted a more typically Protestant form of worship with hymn singing and Scripture reading; some groups have pastors, as well, and refer to their groups as "churches." But running through American Quakerism in all its varieties is a consciousness of Quaker history in America with its insistence that equal, unmediated access to the Inner Light makes all persons likewise deserving of equal social treatment. The Quakers began their history as an actively persecuted minority, feared because of their theological beliefs and the social implications of those beliefs. In spite of their small numbers, Quakers have been disproportionately active in the areas of human rights and social justice in America and, in fact, might be said to hold a position of "established dissent" within the culture. Quakers embody what theologians call a prophetic stance toward American society, urging that its citizens put issues of social justice and equality before economic and nationalistic concerns.

THE CHRISTIAN SCIENTISTS

If some knowledge of religious conflict in seventeenth-century America is essential to understand the place of Quakerism in American religious dissent, then Chris-

---

[8] John Woolman, *The Journal of John Woolman and a Plea for the Poor* (New York: Corinth Books), 1961, pp. 14–15.

tian Science is illuminated by a study of its founder, Mary Baker Eddy, and of the conflict between science and religion in nineteenth-century America. "In the year 1866, I discovered the Christ Science or divine laws of Life, Truth, and Love, and named my discovery Christian Science," wrote Eddy in *Science and Health with Key to the Scriptures*. What she claimed to have discovered during yet another episode of a chronic illness was that matter was illusory and only spirit was real, "a conviction antagonistic to the testimony of the physical senses."[9] It followed, then, according to Eddy, that all those manifestations of belief in matter—"error, sin, sickness, disease, and death"—were likewise unreal. Basing it on this radical, ontological premise, the unreality of matter, Mary Baker Eddy propagated her Christian Science method of healing in classes beginning in 1867 in Lynn, Massachusetts. In 1875 she published *Science and Health,* the book that has remained the chief repository of Eddy's ideas for Christian Scientists. By 1885 the movement was known as far west as Denver and had attracted enough attention from the Boston clergy that Mary Baker Eddy spoke in its defense at Tremont Temple in Boston. And, by 1910, the year in which Eddy died, Christian Science was established in American culture as an unusual and controversial yet nonetheless accepted religious movement.[10] In the 1980s most Americans perceive Christian Science as one among many religions, unusual only in that Christian Scientists do not consult doctors. That this practice is based on a denial of the reality of the material world is probably not generally understood.

When Mary Baker Eddy came to the conclusion at the age of forty-five that matter had no basis in reality, she was operating very much within the tensions of her own personal life and those of the culture in which she lived. She had had a Calvinist upbringing and rejected the emphasis on a stern and angry God. She had suffered early widowhood and an unhappy second marriage (her third marriage, to Asa Gilbert Eddy, did not occur until 1876). Poverty, emotional instability, and illness had made her unable to care for her son. To tie the development of Christian Science totally to facts in Eddy's life would be misleading and inappropriate, just as it would be to try to comprehend Quakerism solely within the context of George Fox's biography. On the other hand, it is possible to look at Mary Baker Eddy as an example of one whose life in all its aspects seemed beyond her control; further, she did not find the potential for either consolation or transformation in the prevailing orthodoxies of her times. Add to this the fact that she lived in nineteenth-century America at a time when the age-old dualism of Western civilization, the battle between spirit and matter, was in one of its most acute phases. For many the growing preeminence of science and the scientific method based on analysis of physical data seemed to signal the inevitable abandonment of belief in a spiritual reality. It was the genious and the appeal of Mary

[9] Mary Baker Eddy, *Science and Health with Key to the Scriptures* (Boston: The Christian Science Board of Directors, 1971), pp. 107–8.

[10] Stephen Gottschalk chronicles the history of Christian Science's development as a religious movement in *The Emergence of Christian Science in American Religious Life* (Berkeley: University of California Press, 1973).

Baker Eddy's new religious movement that it insisted on the reality of the spiritual—the spiritual as the only reality, in fact—and at the same time incorporated the notion of "scientific proof." For Eddy, the healing brought about by the Christian Science method constituted demonstrable evidence of the reality of the spiritual.

Mrs. Eddy was very articulate in *Science and Health* as to her quarrel with traditional Christianity. Instead of God the Father, creator of a sinful humanity, she preached an impersonal God that was Spirit and manifested itself as both Mother and Father. She decried the fact that orthodox religion had chained God in an erroneous image of an imperfect humanity: "Human philosophy," she said, "has made God manlike. Christian Science makes man Godlike."[11] Eddy claimed that a perfect and beneficent God had created likewise a perfect humanity. All the talk of traditional religions about sinfulness, sickness, and death served only to perpetuate a false belief in the reality of matter and to withhold from humanity the knowledge of its own perfection. There would be no sin or sickness or even death, if the human race, finally, refused to believe in their reality. To "understand," then, that cancer, for example, was the result of a false understanding of the nature of God's creation was to deprive cancer of its existence. In Eddy's system Jesus came not to redeem humanity from Original Sin—that, of course, was unnecessary—but to heal the human race of errors in understanding. The Bible, according to Christian Scientists, is a chronicle of that healing process.

Mary Baker Eddy's theological insights produced a church organization that, like the Quakers, has minimized liturgy and ritual. Christian Science Sunday services consist of readings from *Science and Health* and the Bible. Wednesday meetings are for testimonials from those who have been healed. Christian Science has no clergy, but it elects from the congregation readers who serve for three years. Christian Scientists also consult Practitioners who must be approved by the Mother Church in Boston. Practitioners are listed in the Yellow Pages just as are other professionals, and a survey of their names usually reveals that half or so are women. From its beginnings Christian Science attracted a large number of women because it provided the example of a woman religious leader, referred to the female as well as the male attributes of the divine, promised women power over their lives that came from mental rather than physical strength, and made available positions of authority denied women in the mainstream religions. In spite of various episodes of inner turmoil in Christian Science, the influence of Mary Baker Eddy has remained the predominant one, and the tight structure of the Christian Science organization ensures that documents which emerge as church publications will be congruent with her teachings.

The interaction of Christian Science with American culture must be looked at on at least two different levels: first, its place within the histories of theological and intellectual thought; and, secondly, its development from a new and sometimes threatening religious movement to its present place as an accepted part

---

11 Eddy, *Science and Health,* p. 269.

of American religious life. Theologically, Christian Science did not come out of a void. Mary Baker Eddy was familiar, for example, with the Transcendentalism of Emerson, which emphasized an optimistic view of human nature, a monistic understanding of the universe that denied the reality of evil, and a Jesus who was perceived as being fully human rather than divine. In fact, Mary Baker Eddy had behind her the whole tradition of idealism in Western philosophy, which saw mind as more real than matter. Further, Mary Baker Eddy had herself consulted a mental healer. The unique quality of Christian Science, however, came from Mary Baker Eddy's combining of radical idealism and mental healing into a religious movement that insisted it was possible to have ''scientific proof'' of what she called the ''spiritual fact'' of the exclusive reality of mind or spirit. Mrs. Eddy seemed to understand instinctively the emphasis that her own culture was beginning to place on the need for proof in religion as well as in science, even though at the same time she denied the very reality of the sensory data that formed the basis of scientific proof.

The relationship of Christian Science to American culture has not always been smooth. It is not hard to imagine that clergy and doctors would see the new religion not only as fallacious, but also as impinging on their areas of expertise. Stephen Gottschalk quotes *The Journal of the American Medical Association* for November 18, 1899, in its urging that steps be taken ''to restrain the rabid utterances and irrational practices of such ignorant and irresponsible persons'' as the Christian Scientists. In other ways, however, Christian Science fit in very well with American cultural values. In spite of their denial of matter and the physical body, Christian Scientists did not turn to asceticism. Instead they embodied what came to be called ''the power of positive thinking,'' a conviction that one could better one's own lot with the right thinking and understanding. They wrought what the Epicureans had recommended in another age and time: a body free from pain and a mind free from fear. In spite of a radically dissenting theology, then, the acting out of Christian Science beliefs were in conflict with American middle-class values only in the area of medical treatment; and although that fact has occasioned some harsh criticism of Christian Science, it has not prevented the movement from being assimilated into American culture. Because the Christian Science organization does not release membership figures, it is not possible to determine the extent of that assimilation by making numerical comparisons with other religious groups.

THE BLACK MUSLIMS

Assimilation into American culture has never been one of the stated goals of the Black Muslims, members of the Lost Found Nation of Islam in the Wilderness of North America. It was not until the late 1950s and 1960s that the movement came into national prominence, but it had its beginnings in the ghettoes of Detroit and Chicago in the 1930s, and its origins go back to early-twentieth-century black leaders such as Marcus Garvey (1887–1940), who advocated that blacks return to Africa. Founded by W. D. Fard, the Nation of Islam had among its best-known leaders Elijah Muhammad (1897–1975) and Malcolm X (1925–1965), born Malcolm Little, who broke away from Elijah Muhammad during the last year of his life. Theologically, Black Muslims reject Christianity in favor of Islam, a religious system that Muslim leaders feel is better suited to the "Moorish" or "Asiatic" origins of the black race and that is untainted by the compliance of American Christianity with the institution of slavery. Socially, Black Muslims have rejected the attempts of black Christian Americans to become a part of white Christian culture, and have until recently affirmed black separatism.

Martin Luther King, Jr., represents one line of the history of black religion in America, which has remained within the Christian tradition and has sought an understanding and redress of racial discrimination through its symbols. The Nation of Islam has a different ancestry that centered on black separatism as the only remedy for the pervasive racism of American culture and which has fostered a religious system that affirms blackness and negates whiteness. Growing out of a despair of black Americans' achieving human dignity and political and social economy in America itself, movements such as Marcus Garvey's Universal Negro Improvement Association, the African Communities League, and the African Orthodox Church tried to raise black self-esteem and to promote a back-to-Africa movement. Garvey was deported for fraud in 1927, but Sydney Ahlstrom sees him as particularly effective in awakening the spirit of black nationalism in urban ghettoes and also in exposing the degree to which black Americans were alienated from the mainstream culture.[12] Another contribution to the complexities of the Black Muslim movement came from the Moorish Science Temple of America, founded by Timothy Drew. Drew was convinced that American blacks must abandon the appellation *Negro* with its connotations of slavery and inferiority and assert their "Asiatic" origins as a race much older than the white race.[13] In *The Fire Next Time,* the black novelist James Baldwin gives an eloquent description of the theology of the Nation of Islam that arose from these two different sources and that was given impetus by the growing disillusionment of black Americans that came during the years after World War II:

> God is black. All black men belong to Islam; they have been chosen. And Islam shall rule the world. The dream, the sentiment is old; only the color is new. And it is this dream, this sweet possibility, that thousands of oppressed black men and women in this country now carry with them after the Muslim minister has spoken, through the dark, noisome ghetto streets, into the hovels where so many have perished. The white God has not delivered them; perhaps the Black God will.[14]

---

[12] Sydney Ahlstrom, *A Religious History of the American People* (New Haven: Yale University Press, 1972), pp. 1066–67.

[13] C. Eric Lincoln, *The Black Muslims in America* (Boston: Beacon Press, 1961), p. 50. Lincoln postulates that all black nationalist movements have three common characteristics: a disparagement of the white man and his culture, a repudiation of Negro identity, and an appropriation of "asiatic" culture symbols.

[14] James Baldwin, *The Fire Next Time* (New York: Dial Press, 1963), p. 71.

One way to understand the implications of Black Muslim theology and the internal dissent over how it was to be implemented in American culture is to examine the relationship between Elijah Muhammad and Malcolm X, whose departure from the Black Muslim movement signalled the presence of assumptions between the two so different that they could not be resolved within the organization. Muhammad's interpretation of the Black Muslims was a harsh one that left no room for dialogue with the mainstream culture. He and his followers considered the whites ''devils'' and did not tolerate any mixing of the races; they advocated a separate economic system for blacks and demanded that nine or ten states be given over to black Americans in payment for slave labor. James Baldwin quotes Muhammad as having said, ''Return to your true religion; throw off the chains of the slavemaster, the devil, and return to the fold. Stop drinking his alcohol, using his dope—protect your women—and forsake the filthy swine.''[15] Malcolm X (the ''X'' represents the African name he never knew) was converted to the Nation of Islam in prison, often the site of successful Black Muslim recruiting, and his correspondence with Elijah Muhammad led to his adopting and then very effectively preaching Black Muslim beliefs: that Allah was the one true God and that Elijah Muhammad as Allah's messenger was the only leader capable of saving blacks from God's wrath when the world of white supremacy collapsed. Malcolm X was one of the Black Muslims' most effective spokespersons for more than ten years, but when he left the movement in 1964 he began to deemphasize both the separatist, and, finally, the religious aspects of the movement. Nonetheless, it was a trip to Mecca, in the nature of a pilgrimage, that seemed to convince him that separation of the races was not the answer to racism and that his concerns and those of other black Americans must become more international in scope and include the liberation of all oppressed peoples. One can only guess where Malcolm X's new understandings would have led him had he not been shot to death a year after leaving Elijah Muhammad's organization. But the Nation of Islam, too, experienced a moving away from the separatist stance. When Elijah Muhammad died in 1975, his son Wallace became leader of the Black Muslims. He has opened membership to whites and has lifted prohibitions against voting and serving in the armed forces. He has also given the organization a new name: the American Muslim Mission.

The relationship of the Nation of Islam to the overall American culture is complex. The movement has been marked by violence, both internal and external: W. D. Fard disappeared mysteriously in 1933, and Malcolm X was assassinated in 1965. Black Muslimism has engendered fear in black and white Americans alike because of its policy of separatism, and some of its members were associated with the race riots of the 1960s. Although there has not been a Black Muslim case in the Supreme Court, lower courts have upheld the legitimacy of the movement as a bona fide religious organization rather than a group of racial extremists—mostly through decisions upholding the rights of members to practice

---

[15] Ibid., p. 90.

their religion while in prison. Despite public fears of violence from the Black Muslims there are personal standards that members are expected to maintain. Religious practices, highly patriarchal in nature, are very demanding and include abstinence from pork, alcohol, tobacco, and premarital sex; members are expected to hold steady jobs and to center their religious and social lives on temple activities. This combination of requirements has led to the kind of stability that enjoys a great deal in common with mainstream American values regarding family life and hard work. When Malcolm X and then Wallace D. Muhammad began to move away from the separatism that had for so long been a part of the identity of Black Muslims, their intention was not to say that Elijah Muhammad or his predecessors had exaggerated the suffering of blacks in America. But they had come to a realization at which so many other religious dissenters had arrived: that American society does not tolerate religious dissent past the point of violence. Perhaps even more compelling was the growing understanding among black nationalists that whatever changes occurred in the lives of American blacks, they would have to take place not in Africa but in America itself. James Baldwin, who had to go to Paris to discover that he was as American as "any Texas G.I.," articulated that conclusion after a meeting with Elijah Muhammad: ". . . in order to change a situation one has first to see it for what it is: in the present case to accept the fact, whatever one does with it thereafter, that the Negro has been formed by this nation, for better or for worse, and does not belong to any other, not to Africa and certainly not to Islam."[16] To say that American blacks do not "belong" to Africa or Islam does not mean that these concepts cannot be used fruitfully as a basis for religious and social dissent against the values of the prevailing culture—only that African origins and the Islamic religion most likely will not function as creatively if they are used to blot out the 400-year history of blacks on the American continent.

---

[16] Ibid., p. 95.

7

sacred and secular images of the eternal: religion and art in america

To put it bluntly, there is no glorious tradition of religious painting, music, architecture, or literature in American culture. This is not to say that religions in America have never given rise to distinctive or good or even great works of art, but our very diversity of religious expression has worked against the composition of art that speaks for the beliefs of the whole culture. In fact, beginning with the Puritans, who avoided "church" architecture for their meeting houses and the use of elaborate music for their services out of moral conviction that worship must be simple, the relationship between religion and the arts in America has often been uneasy. Frequently, our greatest works, no matter how much they speak to questions of ultimate meaning, are not labeled "religious." Nineteenth-century American literary classics provide a good example of this phenomenon. As much as the works of writers such as Ralph Waldo Emerson, Nathaniel Hawthorne, Walt Whitman, Emily Dickinson, and Herman Melville have had to say about matters of a religious nature, most of us encountered them for the first time in high school literature classes, not in courses on religious studies. We never realized that these authors and their works had a great deal to tell us about religious belief systems. What we need to do, then, to study religion and the arts in American culture is to look not only in the obvious places for examples—churches, synagogues, hymn books, and paintings with religious content—but beyond them as well.

There are at least three general perspectives from which to look at the relationships between religion and the arts in American culture. The first is the most obvious and it is to concentrate on the music, literature, painting, architecture, and dance that would be called "religious" by most people's definition—that is, it has obvious religious content or is characterized by use in a specifically religious context and is meant to instruct about and to celebrate the religious understandings of a particular group of believers. Into this category would fall church and synagogue architecture, music and dance, devotional poetry and fiction, paintings and stained-glass windows, and artifacts such as vestments, statues, and communion vessels. It is possible and helpful to make general statements about religion and art in America on such topics as church architecture in the nineteenth century or religious best-sellers of the 1940s, but if the discussion is not to gloss over the differences inherent in the phrase "American religion," it is necessary to speak about various art forms as they emerge from specific groups: Puritan meeting-house architecture, Moravian music, Shaker dance rituals and spirit drawings, Protestant gospel hymns of the nineteenth century, Catholic liturgical music since Vatican II, synagogue architecture after World War II. There is a kind of implicit assumption in American culture that religious art forms of this obvious kind may be so overwhelmed with ideological content that the aesthetic considerations are a secondary matter, and the question arises, "Is this really art?" or has the artistic imagination been too fettered by the demands of the belief system imposed upon it? The question seems ludicrous when applied as it might be, for example, to the ceiling of the Sistine Chapel, but in American culture, where pluralism of religious belief has tended to compartmentalize the religious from the aesthetic, the question is asked with seriousness.

The second perspective arises out of looking at the works of artists who are identified in terms of their religious beliefs as they interpret various aspects of American culture. They are attempting the difficult dual task of speaking from within a particular religious framework and at the same time producing a work of art that has universal significance and whose value and meaning are perceived by a wider audience than that of one's fellow believers. It is interesting to note that the artists who fall into this category are usually Jewish, whether practicing or not, or Catholic. This is testimony to the fact that in the arts, as in many other areas, mainstream Protestantism is perceived as "American" and its artists presumed to be speaking for American culture in general, whereas Catholics and Jews are understood as operating from within a narrower tradition. Among writers, for example, Flannery O'Connor and Walker Percy are seldom mentioned without reference to their Catholicism, but the subject of the religious beliefs of Robert Penn Warren or Robert Frost seldom comes up. That bit of information aside, what might we learn about the relationship between religion and the arts from this approach? From Henry Roth or Chaim Potok we might derive an understanding of how orthodox Judaism in America provides the raw material for literature; or how the fact of the authors' Judaism has equipped them with a particular understanding of American culture in general and the pressures it exerts on the members of a particular religious group. The chief difficulty with this means of looking at religion and art in America comes from the tendency to emphasize the religion too greatly at the expense of the artist and the content over the form, thereby posing two dangers: that the work of art will be regarded from the outside as a textbook might be, as simply a source of information about a particular group of believers, or else that it will be regarded by insiders, members of the artist's religious group, as needing to reflect accurately the beliefs of that group and even to defend them. As a Catholic writer, Flannery O'Connor was aware of both dangers, as we shall see later in the chapter.

A third method of looking at religion and the arts in America is to examine the works of those artists who do not write, paint, or compose from an obviously religious point of view but who nonetheless produce works that elicit from the observer or listener a response that compels a confrontation with ultimate reality, a need to assess what it might be that the artist has understood and tried to convey about the essence of life and death, what it means to be human, and the inevitability of suffering and death. What can we learn of these ultimately religious subjects from the stories and novels of Nathaniel Hawthorne, who writes so often of the Unpardonable Sin, or from the poetry of Emily Dickinson, so frequently concerned with the subject of death, or from the works of Wallace Stevens, for whom the obligation "to find what will suffice" in the most ultimate sense falls not to organized religion but to poetry? What can we learn about the nature of life and death from Georgia O'Keeffe, who juxtaposes dried animal bones with flowers in her paintings? One of the obvious dangers of this approach, analyzing so-called secular works of art for religious meaning, lies in an overenthusiasm to impose too much meaning upon the work of art from without, to push and pull and manipulate so that the poem or painting or building or piece of music says what we want it to say, to deprive the work of a multiplicity of meaning levels in our need to have it say one thing that the artist may never have intended at all. This is not to say, of course, that we exhaust our rights of interpretation if we go beyond what the artist may have intended originally. A good or great work of art has inherent in it a depth and multiplicity of meanings that accrue over time as it is encountered, analyzed, and appreciated by many persons, meanings that even the artist may only have intuited when the work was produced.

This chapter will make use of all three methods of looking at religion and the arts in America. As an illustration of the first, a work of art brought into being through the specific intentions of a particular religious group, architecture provides an excellent example. Church architecture is usually "talking architecture"; it is meant to give flesh and bones to the theology of a group of believers, to display what is most central in their worship and to illuminate what they consider to be the most appropriate surroundings in which to conduct that worship.

The second example is derived from literature, specifically the fiction of Flannery O'Connor (1925–1964), an American Catholic writer whose subject was the Protestant evangelicalism of the rural South in which she was raised. O'Connor affirmed her Catholicism as the basis of her world view but denied that it fettered her imagination in such a way that her integrity as an artist was diminished. In her struggles to come to terms with what it meant to be a Catholic writer, struggles imposed both from without and from within, we derive some knowledge of how the fact of one's religious beliefs influences artistic creativity.

The third example is that of Grant Wood (1892–1942), an American painter of the Regionalist school. Wood was not an overtly religious painter, but in his portrayal of rural America, Iowa in particular, he conveyed over and over his own conception of one of the most dominant myths of American culture: that of the sacred and unchanging aspects of the land and of the natural nobility of those who till the soil.

The three places of worship I've selected to illustrate a direct relationship between religion and architecture are all contemporary in design. They incorporate the traditional symbols of Congregational Protestantism, Roman Catholicism, and Judaism transplanted to American soil and embodied in what modern architecture has to offer. In all three cases, both the congregations and the architects they commissioned were able to be highly articulate about what they wanted, and thus these buildings are set apart from churches and synagogues that were built to conform to architectural fashions of a particular time—for example, synagogues or churches built in Greek Revival not because that style suited the theological traditions of the congregation it was to house but because Greek Revival was considered suitable for buildings of worship in general. The buildings I've chosen as a means of illustration cause us to answer in the affirmative the question as to whether they are both "religious" and "art."

Colonial Church of Edina, a Congregational Church that has just recently joined the United Church of Christ, reflects the congregation's wish to emphasize the Puritan heritage of Congregationalism. Built in a suburb of Minneapolis in 1979 and designed by a local firm of architects, the church is actually a complex of buildings joined together and meant to convey the impression of a New England village and meeting house. The outside of the building is gray-stained clapboard with painted white trim. The free-standing bell tower and steeple reflect the influence of Anglican church architecture on Puritan meeting houses, particularly in the eighteenth century (seventeenth-century meeting houses eschewed the bell tower and steeple, because they were reminders of the very religious traditions—Roman Catholicism and Anglicanism—against which Puritans had rebelled). The interior rooms have open ceilings, and the trusses, posts, and beams are visible as they would have been in an early colonial barn. In addition to the large room in which worship takes place, there is a parlor–seminar room and a "great hall," both with massive fireplaces. There is also space to house the offices of a large staff and a room for younger church members. The congregation of Colonial Church sees its facility not only as a place of worship, but as the site of a religious community that provides its members with education and a forum from which to deal with social issues.

Colonial Church represents an effort to make use of modern architectural principles and materials in such a way that they will be useful for the needs of a Protestant congregation in contemporary society and that will at the same time make a statement about the theological traditions from which the congregation draws its self-understanding. The seventeenth-century meeting house, which Colonial Church emulates, was a multi-purpose building; it was not meant to be a "church," which to the Puritans signified not a building but a covenanted body of people. For Puritans the meeting house was a place for public assembly as well as worship. Meeting-house architects expressed the Reformation point of view that the house of God was not a mysterious, sacred place set apart, and the building itself was often the site of "a number of secular buildings; powder house, court house, school house, meeting hall, town house, parsonage, and fort."[1] Because there was no separation of church and state in colonial New England, the construction of the meeting house was financed through taxes.

In a study of New England meeting houses, Peter Bemes and Phillip D. Zimmerman distinguish between two different definitions of meeting house. One we derive from the architectural historian, who defines it by the short-side alignment of the main entrance and the pulpit as opposed to the church in which the entrance and altar face each other across the length. The other comes from the social historian, who sees the essence of the meeting house in its combining of religious and secular activities and support by public taxation. The interior arrangement of the meeting house reflected the Reform belief that the preaching of the Word took precedence over the sacramental aspects of worship. Thus it was the pulpit, not the altar, that dominated. Instead of an altar, meeting houses made use of communion tables that resembled the domestic variety—another attempt by the Puritans to demystify the act of worship and to dissociate themselves from Catholicism, either Roman or Anglican. Communion vessels, too, were likely to resemble household dishes, rather than to look like special ecclesiastical artifacts.[2]

In its attempt to derive its identity from the traditions of Puritanism and the meeting house, Colonial Church congregation could not, of course, duplicate the social milieu of seventeenth-century New England; for one thing, there was no tax money to pay for construction. But the congregation's desire to convey the sense of a small village that could supply a variety of its members' religious, social, educational, and even recreational needs is obvious. The interior, particularly of the "meeting" room, reflects Puritan theology. The pulpit, across the short dimension of the room from the entries, dominates; it is huge. The communion table, which would be perfectly suitable in a home, stands in front of the pulpit, dwarfed by it, its only adornment two plain candlesticks.

Colonial Church took what it could of Puritan architectural, social, and ecclesiastical traditions and combined those with modern architecture to fit its needs as a congregation in contemporary America with a strong attachment to its origins. The Abbey and University Church of St. John the Baptist, built in 1953 in Collegeville, Minnesota, represents a very different tradition from that of Colonial Church. It looks back not to seventeenth-century America for its origins but to the founding of the Benedictine Order in the sixth century. The Abbey Church was designed by Marcel Breuer, a Hungarian-born Bauhaus architect whose

---

[1] Peter Bemes and Phillip D. Zimmerman, *New England Meeting House and Church: 1630–1850* (Boston: Boston University and the Currier Gallery of Art, 1979), p. 1.

[2] Ibid., pp. 73–75.

practice in the United States became known after World War II. Breuer belonged to no church, but that was not a bar to his being selected as the designer not only of the Abbey Church but of the monastery as well. In a letter written to twelve architects, among them Gropius and Saarinen, Abbot Baldwin Dworschock, O.S.B., expressed a desire for a building that would reflect Benedictine tradition and at the same time make an architectural statement about Catholicism in America:

> The Benedictine tradition at its best challenges us to think boldly and to cast our ideals in forms which will be valid for centuries to come, shaping them with all the genius of present-day materials and techniques. We feel that the modern architect with his orientation toward functionalism and honest use of materials is uniquely qualified to produce a Catholic work. In our position it would, we think, be deplorable to build anything less, particularly since our age and our country have thus far produced so little truly significant architecture.[3]

The monks at St. John's selected Breuer at least in part because they were impressed by his willingness to work with them. Of the church Breuer said, "You will have to tell me how you use the floor and I will put a sacred shell around that space."[4] His work, in collaboration with that of Frank Kacmarcik, an authority on liturgical design, produced a church that preceded by a decade Vatican Council II's emphasis on eliminating irrelevant and obsolete trappings that had come to dog Catholic architecture. The result was a church that incorporated the traditions of an ancient monastic order and the Catholic theological emphasis on the sacramental aspects of worship.

Because it is not the typical parish church but part of a complex that contains a university, a monastery, and a preparatory school, St. John's needed to be designed in such a way that it would serve these various constituents and parish members from the surrounding countryside as well. Because of the large number of priests in residence, there had to be provisions for a large number of daily masses. Further, because the canonical hours of the Divine Office are sung or recited within the Benedictine community, a large number of choir stalls were needed.

Within the interior of the church, it would be difficult to find a more striking contrast of theological traditions articulated than with the Colonial Church of Edina. In this building it is the altar, not the pulpit, that predominates: "Immediately the converging of folded concrete walls, the pitch of ceilings and balcony, the position of choir stalls and pews point to the altar, the place of the Holy Sacrifice and the Eucharist." The two monks who wrote the booklet that describes the theological significance of the church could not have made it any plainer: "The altar which represents Christ is the most sacred place, the magnetic

---
[3] "One Great Architect's Legacy to Minnesota" *Architecture Minnesota* (December–January 1981–82), p. 24.

[4] Ibid.

and architectural center of the congregation."[5] Designed by Breuer and made of white Vermont marble, the altar is meant to be a large rock and this to represent the stability of the Church. The pews and the monks' choir stalls are arranged so that the altar is visible to all. The pulpit is off to the right side of the congregation, easily visible, but not a focal point until someone stands in it. The exterior of the church dominates the countryside of the rural Minnesota setting. Although they are very different in structure, the bell tower of Colonial Church in Edina and the massive banner and bell tower of St. John's, 112 feet high and 90 feet wide, serve the same purpose: They are meant to symbolize the presence of the worshiping community. The five bells in the St. John's tower were originally cast for the first abbey church built in 1897.

St. John's Abbey and University Church leaves no doubt in the observer's mind that although it is a place of worship and as such an articulation of the Roman Catholic emphasis on the sacramental tradition, it is also a statement about Catholicism's European origins, its flowering within the monastic tradition, and its implantation in and adaptation to the soil of America. Abbot Baldwin and his monks wanted a church that would be Benedictine and Catholic and American. Marcel Breuer, a transplanted European himself who could make use of what the monks told him about their traditions and their lives, was able to give them just that.

Mount Zion Temple in St. Paul, Minnesota, is the home of a Reform Jewish congregation that has also chosen to symbolize its traditions in contemporary architecture. The temple was designed by Eric Mendelsohn, another European-born architect, and completed after his death in 1953. The present temple is not the first building to house the congregation. The history of the buildings that have housed the Mount Zion congregation, culminating in the present temple, provide not only an architectural pattern, but a theological one as well as to the assimilation of Jews into the overall American culture. Mount Zion had its origins in 1856 in St. Paul when eight families formed an Orthodox community that met in a third-floor rented room downtown. In fewer then twenty years the congregation had moved to a white clapboard structure and had begun the movement toward Reform. By 1903 the building that had replaced the wooden structure was outgrown, and the downtown neighborhood no longer seemed suitable. The congregation moved to a residential area, the famous Summit Avenue in St. Paul, where such people as James J. Hill and F. Scott Fitzgerald had had their homes. The new building was a blend of Byzantine and Greek architecture, typical of synagogue architecture early in the twentieth century.[6] Theologically, by this time the congregation had incorporated most of the changes of Reform Judaism: for example, less and less Hebrew in the services, men and women sit-

---

[5] Ronald Roloff, O. S. B., and Brice Howard, O. S. B., "Abbey and University Church of Saint John the Baptist, Collegeville, Minnesota." No date and no page numbers.

[6] A history of the buildings of Mount Zion congregation appears in Lori Rotenberk, "Reform Wrestles with Tradition at Mt. Zion," *Twin Cities* (September 1981), pp. 68–73, 112–18.

ting together, deemphasis on dietary laws—changes that eventually brought about a crisis of identity on the part of many American Jews.

The need to come to terms with American Jewish identity was very much a part of the decision as to what kind of building would suitably house the Mount Zion congregation when they decided on a new temple in the early 1950s. More in keeping with Puritanism and less like Roman Catholicism, Reform Jews had come to view the synagogue not as sacred space that housed the Deity but as a place of assembly: "God is no longer conceived of as dwelling in a particular place. He is everywhere. . . . Prayer, which had been attached to the sacrificial ceremony in the temple, emancipated itself in the synagogue, joining with instruction and discussions. The magical elements in the sacrifice and the unconditioned submission to God through the mediation of the priest were abandoned and gave way to symbolic rituals and the rational elements of study and discourse."[7] In spite of these changes in ritual and emphasis, American Jews—and the people of Mount Zion were no different—came to realize in the time since World War II that there was a strong need to incorporate traditional Jewish symbols into their synagogues and temples. They would do so through the medium of contemporary architecture, which one critic, Avram Kampf, claims is a style particularly suited to Jews: "It held the promise of efficiency, rationality, economy, order, and a fresh start."[8]

In the case of Mount Zion, Kampf sees both the exterior and the interior as articulating the traditions and symbols of Judaism. The two high, rectangular roofs that are painted black remind Kampf of "a pair of monumental phylacteries," the two small leather cubes containing Bible verses that Orthodox Jewish men attach to the left arm and forehead when praying. The interior compels one to contemplate the all-powerful Yahweh of the Old Testament, "the One Mighty God of Israel, Who has created heaven and earth, Who is powerful in battle and awesome in His Judgment."[9] Even if one might wish for a more humble depiction of the Deity, Kampf claims, there is no denying the power of this architectural statement of a vast space that "unites and dwarfs both those who conduct and those who participate in the service." In Mount Zion Temple it is not the altar or pulpit that is central but the Ark, which contains the Torah scrolls (the Pentateuch, or first five books of the Old Testament) and whose importance is accentuated by the series of steps leading up to it. Present on the *bimah*, the platform on which the Ark rests and from which services are conducted, but lower, are the pulpits of the rabbi and the cantor as well as an Eternal Light that shines on a metal sphere shaped like the hub of a wheel and suspended from the ceiling on a thirty-foot chain. Mendelsohn used this symbol in other synagogues that he designed: "For the architect it was symbolic of the world. The wheel is divided

---

[7] Avram Kampf, *Contemporary Synagogue Art: Developments in the United States, 1945-1965* (Philadelphia: The Jewish Publication Society of America, 1966), pp. 3-4.

[8] Ibid., p. 27.

[9] Ibid., pp. 177-78

into four-fold repetitions of the Hebrew letter *shin,* which stands for God, and which points to the four directions of the compass. The omnipresence of God in the universe is thus indicated."[10]

For many in St. Paul, Mount Zion represents a departure from traditional Jewish ways. Its rabbi (at the time of his appointment in 1975 he was the youngest senior rabbi in the country) is the only one in Minnesota who will marry a Christian to a Jew, although he does it reluctantly, and he speaks out on social issues and urges his congregation to do likewise. Mount Zion also has one of the few woman cantors in the country. But the temple itself is a monument to the traditional symbols of Judaism as they have found a home in America and to the struggles and success of its assimilation into American culture. Prized by the people of the Twin Cities as an architectural asset, the Temple has also been the target of anti-Semitism. In 1979 vandals defaced its outside with swastikas. The Council of Churches of St. Paul, an interdenominational organization, contributed money and volunteers to restore the building. What better incident to underline what can be the sometimes schizophrenic nature of religious pluralism in a society that insists on the right of all its members to the free practice of religion but that has still not come to terms with all its realities?

If architecture provides us with the opportunity to see direct connections between religion and the arts, literature can often reveal relationships that are more subtle. Flannery O'Connor was an American Catholic fiction writer whose chief subject was Southern Protestant evangelicalism, many of her characters extreme manifestations of that way of being religious. She was identified by critics and by herself as a "Catholic writer" (a phrase that, she joked, always appeared within quotation marks), in spite of the fact that she wrote chiefly about Protestants. What that phrase actually meant in terms of the way she saw herself and for the ways her works have been interpreted by others is a source of continuing discussion. O'Connor herself was ambivalent on the subject, at least insofar as she answered the question "Are you a Catholic writer?" In a letter to John Hawkes, also a fiction writer, O'Connor said, "People are always asking me if I am a Catholic writer, and I am afraid that I sometimes say no and sometimes say yes, depending on who the visitor is. Actually, the question seems so remote from what I am doing when I am doing it that it doesn't bother me at all."[11]

The question may not have bothered her while she was actually writing, but we know from the evidence of her letters and speeches that it was of great concern to her in other contexts. O'Connor pinpointed over and over again the double-edged implication of the question. First was the assumption that if she were indeed a Catholic writer, her beliefs would interfere with her artistic integrity, her ability to write good fiction: "Although I am a Catholic writer, I don't care to get labeled as such in the popular sense of it, as it is then assumed that you have some religious

---

[10] Ibid., p. 179.

[11] Flannery O'Connor, *The Habit of Being: Letters of Flannery O'Connor,* ed. Sally Fitzgerald (New York: Farrar, Straus & Giroux, 1979), p. 353.

axe to grind. However, since the review in *Time,* my mail has been full of attempts to save me from the Church . . . and I have received an anonymous message in a shaky hand to the effect that my religion is phony.''[12] The second assumption was usually made by other Catholics: that O'Connor either must be or should be using her fiction in order to put forth and defend the beliefs of Roman Catholicism. O'Connor resisted that interpretation of her work even more strenuously than she did the first, expressing an aversion for such motivation and claiming that an attempt to mold reality in the interests of abstract truth could result only in bad writing:

> It is generally supposed, and not least by Catholics, that the Catholic who writes fiction is out to use fiction to prove the truth of the Faith. He may be. No one certainly can be aware of his low motives except as they suggest themselves in his finished work, but when the finished work suggests that pertinent actions have been manipulated or overlooked or smothered, what purposes the writer started out with have already been defeated.[13]

As an example of the kind of didactic fiction she meant, O'Connor cited a novel written by Cardinal Spellman of New York, *The Foundling:* ''You do have the satisfaction of knowing that if you buy a copy of *The Foundling,* you are helping the orphans to whom the proceeds go; and afterwards you can always use the book as a doorstop. But what you owe yourself here is to know that what you are helping are the orphans and not the standards of Catholic letters in this country.''[14] O'Connor's humor does not disguise her lack of respect for those fictional works whose literary merits are secondary to their preaching function.

How, then, did O'Connor see her own works in relation to the question of how they were affected by her Catholicism? As an American and as a Catholic, what vision did she bring to her task as a writer whose intention it was to illuminate the world and humanity according to her own lights? Flannery O'Connor saw herself as a writer who was Catholic, in that she wrote fiction from within the framework of what Catholicism taught and she espoused. She believed implicitly in the Incarnation, the Word made flesh in Jesus Christ in a creation that was good but flawed by human sin, and in a sacramental system that had as its source of divine grace Jesus' redemption of the sins of humanity. Since she died before the reforms of Vatican II had taken much effect with their emphasis on ecumenism, her tendency was to emphasize the differences between Catholic and Protestant understandings of such things as the doctrines of grace or of the Eucharist—not, as she insisted, to show that Catholics were right and Protestants were wrong, but to point out how her understanding of the divine and the human

---

[12] Ibid., letter to Elizabeth Bishop, p. 391.

[13] Flannery O'Connor, "The Church and the Fiction Writer," in *Mystery and Manners* (New York: Farrar, Straus & Giroux, 1962), p. 145.

[14] Ibid., "Catholic Novelists and Their Readers," p. 175.

from a Catholic viewpoint provided the undergirding for the motivations of her characters.

O'Connor was frequently asked to give readings of her stories to audiences, after which she answered questions about the stories, so we don't have to guess as to how she herself understood what was going on. O'Connor's fiction, which consists of two novels and many short stories, is filled with violence and with characters that many critics have called grotesque. In *Wise Blood*, her first novel, Hazel Motes, a self-styled prophet who is desperate to escape his insistent knowledge of God's existence and presence, goes to the city to preach of the Church Without Christ. At the end of the novel Motes has blinded himself and is finally clubbed to death by a policeman. O'Connor's second novel, *The Violent Bear It Away*, depicts the life of Tarwater, another reluctant prophet, who cannot escape the double destiny his great-uncle has thrust upon him: to go to the city and proclaim its sinfulness and imminent destruction and to baptize the uncle's small grandson. This novel, like the first, ends in violence and tragedy. The short stories are no less filled with bizarre characters and events. In "A Good Man Is Hard to Find," an escaped convict, The Misfit, encounters a family whose car is broken down while they are on vacation; he kills all of them, including the grandmother. In "Good Country People" a con man masquerading as a Bible salesman lures an arrogant and nihilistic young woman into the hayloft of a barn where he seduces her and then steals her wooden leg. In "The Displaced Person" a woman farm owner and her hired man fail to prevent a Polish refugee from being run over by a tractor, because he has failed to understand the intricate social balance between the races upon which that rural Southern community depends for its stability.

What does this list of horrors have to do with Catholicism? Or with any kind of religion, for that matter? In spite of the violence and the profusion of bizarre characters, each of O'Connor's works offers a moment with potential for redemption from self-delusion and sin, a point at which a central character finally "sees" and makes a choice based on that grace-inspired revelation. We have as an illustration of this pattern one story, "A Good Man Is Hard to Find," that O'Connor discussed in some detail in her letters and in some of her lectures, so we have the advantage of knowing both how she interpreted it and what others thought it meant as well. The story line itself is not very complex: a family—mother, father, three children, grandmother, and cat—sets out on a driving trip to Florida. The grandmother insists on looking for a plantation she had seen as a child, but her memory is vague and the search takes the family onto a dirt road where the car runs into a ditch. While they are stuck, The Misfit, an escaped convict about whom the family had heard rumors, and his two partners come upon them. In spite of much pleading the partners take the family members into the woods and shoot them. The grandmother is the last and even though she sees that her begging is having no effect she cries to The Misfit, " 'Why you're one of my own babies. You're one of my own children.' She reached out and touched him on the shoulder. The Misfit sprang back as if a snake had bitten him and shot her three times in the chest.''[15] The Misfit, O'Connor said, had recoiled in ''horror at her humanness, but after he has done it and cleans his glasses, the Grace has worked in him. . . .''[16] The story concludes in the following way:

> "She would of been a good woman," The Misfit said, "If it had been somebody there to shoot her every minute of her life."
>
> "Some fun!" Bobby Lee said.
>
> "Shut up, Bobby Lee," The Misfit said. "It's no real pleasure in life."[17]

Throughout the story the grandmother was depicted as shallow, superficial, and self-serving. Nonetheless, O'Connor meant her to be the medium of divine grace for The Misfit. O'Connor saw her depiction of the old lady as a vehicle for grace as reflective of her Catholic viewpoint: ''Grace, to the Catholic way of thinking, can and does use as its medium the imperfect, purely human, and even hypocritical.'' She contrasted that understanding with what she considered to be a Protestant interpretation: ''In the Protestant view I think Grace and nature don't have much to do with each other. The old lady, because of her hypocrisy and humanness and banality, couldn't be a medium for Grace. In the sense that I see things the other way, I'm a Catholic writer.''[18] Being a Catholic, then, influenced the way O'Connor depicted human relationships as well as the way in which she described the divine as revealing itself to men and women. But her Catholicism never tempted her to manipulate a happy ending that would have necessitated characters' making choices not consonant with her description of them. The Misfit did not suddenly fall to his knees, ask forgiveness for his sins, and spare the old lady; and O'Connor did not take kindly to advice that she should have strung out the story long enough for the police to rescue the grandmother. Nor did she have much patience for the kind of tortured literary exercise that involved squeezing meaning out of every small detail in the story. When asked why The Misfit wore a black hat, she explained that it was merely the kind of hat that a man of his type in the South was likely to wear; it had no ''religious'' significance. Along those same lines, when she received a letter from three English professors asking for her opinion of their interpretation that The Misfit was not real but only imagined by the other characters, O'Connor responded tersely: ''If teachers are in the habit of approaching a story as if it were a research problem for which any answer is believable so long as it is not obvious, then I think students will never learn to enjoy fiction.''[19]

---

[15] Flannery O'Connor, *Three by Flannery O'Connor* (New York: Signet, various copyright dates for works included), p. 143.

[16] O'Connor, *Letters*, p. 389.

[17] *Three by Flannery O'Connor*, p. 143.

[18] *Letters*, p. 390.

[19] Ibid., p. 437.

As an American Catholic writer, Flannery O'Connor produced a body of literature that proceeded, as she insisted, not from her Catholicism but from her own particular talents—she wrote because she was good at it, she once told a group of students. On the other hand, her Catholicism was not by-the-way. She acknowledged its influence on the way she understood the world she knew best, rural Georgia, and that she sought to record in her fiction. But if she claimed loyalty to a set of standards, it was to the dictates of the artistic process that in her view had to take precedence over ideological or theological considerations—if not, one produced tracts, not literature. O'Connor refuted those who insisted that a Catholic was too thoroughly brainwashed by the teachings of the Church to produce great art. She was equally unsympathetic toward those who would saddle her with the obligation to write fiction that upheld Catholic doctrine and lifted the heart as well, as one critic pleaded with her to do. She depicted one way of being religious in America, that of the intensely evangelical Protestant in the rural South, from the perspective of another viewpoint, that of the Southern Catholic, and her desire was that "the Catholic fiction writer, as fiction writer, will look for the will of God first in the laws and limitations of his art and will hope that if he obeys these, other blessings will be added to his work."[20]

Up to this point the examples of the relationships between religion and the arts have been revealing of specific religious traditions. The final example has a different focus—the farm paintings of Grant Wood (1892–1942), an artist whose works were not explicitly religious but whose paintings help us to understand that the terms *religious* or *religion* can be used not only in a specific way to refer to the doctrines, rituals, and moral codes of a particular denomination, but in a broader sense, as Paul Tillich has pointed out, to indicate matters of ultimate concern in a culture, that is, assumptions about reality accepted so unquestioningly by even the most diverse members of a culture that they take on connotations of the sacred. Among those symbols that have about them the aspect of the sacred and the inviolable in American culture has been that of "the land"—its abundance, its availability, its everlastingness, its saving and ennobling powers. Wood achieved his greatest popularity as an artist with what one critic called his "fantasy farmscapes" in the 1930s, a time during which neither he nor his public could have been ignorant of the dust bowl or the Depression or the foreclosures on farm mortgages or the ways in which unceasing labor with little yield could grind down farm men and women.[21] Yet he chose to portray the farm as unblemished by poverty and exhausting, never-ending work, and the public affirmed his portrayals.[22] A

---

[20] O'Connor, *Mystery and Manners*, p. 152.

[21] James Dennis, *Grant Wood: A Study in American Art and Culture* (New York: Viking Press, 1975), p. 75.

[22] An interesting contrast with the popularity of Wood's paintings is the photographic and journalistic account of the daily life of tenant farmers in Alabama put together in 1936 by James Agee and Walker Evans. The work was rejected by *Fortune* magazine, which had commissioned it in the first place, and finally published by Houghton Mifflin in 1941, at which time it sold only 600 copies. A stark account of the poverty and hopelessness of Southern tenant farming, *Let Us Now Praise Famous Men* has become a classic since a new edition was brought out in 1960.

short history of Wood during the decade of the 1930s and a close look at some of his paintings can help us understand the power that the idea of the land itself has exerted in Americans of many different eras and also of very different religious persuasions.

Along with Thomas Hart Benton and John Steuart Curry, Wood belonged to the American school of painting known as Regionalism, whose credo was based on a belief that the artist's region, one's native territory, provided the most appropriate subject matter for painting. Wood's early years as a painter provided little indication that he would return to Iowa to paint farm scenes and to decorate government buildings with murals of rural life. Most of his paintings had European subjects as their inspiration. But when he returned to Iowa in 1928 from his last trip to Europe, Wood began to paint the farms and the people of his native Iowa, finding, he said, "to my great joy . . . that in the very commonplace, in my native surroundings, were decorative adventures and that my only difficulty had been in taking them too much for granted."[23] For Wood, the subject of his paintings took on moral as well as aesthetic considerations. He was deeply involved in the effort to promote regional painting and to counter the European influences on American painting of academicism and modernism. Wood became caught up in the American myth of the land itself as the catalyst that called forth true American virtues in contrast with the sophistication and even the corruption of the Eastern seaboard, which had never moved beyond its dependence on European culture. Eden imagery, which stressed endless abundance, was typically used in the nineteenth century to describe the seemingly endless lands of the West and Midwest, and even though the frontier had officially been closed by the federal government in 1890 (by which time it was far west of Iowa), two years before Wood was born, he, too, was heir to an understanding of the land as filled with power to give not only food but spiritual sustenance as well to those who would work it with simplicity and good will. Like many others of this time, and ours as well, Wood feared the encroachment of the city and the machine on the countryside in a way that would desecrate the authentic nature and virtue of the Americans who lived there.

Looking at some of Wood's paintings in chronological order, we discover that the more idyllic farm scenes, those with no machinery in them, no bad weather or bugs or sweating workers or blighted crops, come later in the decade. His most famous painting, *American Gothic*, finished in 1931 and bought immediately by the Chicago Museum of Art, tells us that he was well aware of the ambiguities of rural life. If ever a painting sent mixed signals, *American Gothic* is the one. On the one hand we have the glory of Gothic architecture transplanted from the castles and cathedrals of Europe to the small frame Iowa house. We perceive the simplicity of the house, the attempts at adornment in the window and the lace curtain and the plant on the porch; we notice the corner of the neat red barn on the right and the church steeple on the left horizon—all of which constitute a neat and

---

23 Dennis, p. 75.

peaceful, under control, scene of country life. Then we are confronted by the people: a man and a woman (Wood maintained that they were townsfolk—a father and daughter—but most Americans probably see them as a farm husband and wife) who have been described by critics as grim, bewildered, even menacing, with several suggesting that the man may be the devil. The pitchfork, which was a garden rake in an early sketch for the picture, and the snake-like tendril of hair escaping the woman's bun help to bolster this interpretation. Is the painting meant to be a satire of country life—to say that what appears to be simple, unsophisticated, virtuous living really leads to a grimness and an aggressive closing off of outside influences? Are we meant to have pity for the man and woman who seem to have so little to protect and yet appear to be fending off outsiders with a kind of ferocity? Are we meant to be afraid of them? There is, of course, no one ''answer'' to what *American Gothic* means, and speculation requires the offices of the art historian as well as the social historian. But we are left to wonder why, after a painting that seems to offer so many different possibilities for an interpretation of American rural living, Wood turned to painting much less ambiguous scenes of farm life, especially at a time in American history when the farm was so economically unstable.

There is not much ambiguity in another painting, *The Appraisal,* also done in 1931 and originally called *Clothes.* In *The Appraisal* we come upon an encounter between city and country in the persons of two women. One, the farm woman, dressed in warm, sensible, and unfashionable clothes, is the provider who holds a fat chicken that we assume she will sell to the other woman, whose double chin, fashionable hat and earrings, and fur-collared coat and brocade purse mark her as both the city dweller and consumer. The farm, the painting seems to say, is life-giving, whereas the city is death-dealing: The city woman who already wears the fur of a dead animal around her neck will take the chicken home, have it butchered, and eat it, without expending more effort than it takes to open her brocade purse. I don't think we are going too far to speculate that Wood is asking us to contemplate through his painting something as basic and ultimate as the sources of life and virtue as well as of death and corruption, as they are acted out in American culture of the 1930s, the decade after the Depression when the land took on an even more concentrated burden as the symbol of abundance in a nation terrified by the instability of ''artificial'' sources of wealth such as banks and stocks.[24] In another painting, *Dinner for Threshers* (1934), we find the same celebration of the fruitfulness of the farm, although this time without the contrast to the city. If Wood did not speak of his paintings in specifically religious terms, there are critics who have done so. One of them, James Dennis, author of a volume that places Wood in the context of American culture, sees *Dinner for Threshers,* a rectangular work in which farm laborers come into the kitchen for a noonday meal served by the women, as portraying ''a ritual celebration of mythical self-sufficiency and of

---

[24] I owe this interpretation to James Dennis.

Colonial Church of Edina

The Abbey and
University Church
of St. John the Baptist

Mt. Zion Temple

American Gothic by Grant Wood
Collection of the Art Institute of Chicago.

Appraisal by Grant Wood
Anonymous collection.

Dinner for Threshers by Grant Wood
The Fine Arts Museums of San Francisco; gift of Mr. and Mrs. John D. Rockefeller 3rd.

perennial plenty gained through cooperative labor.'' Dennis goes on to elaborate
further upon what he sees as the religious implications of the scene:

> Outside, where no heavy threshing machinery may be seen, the pristine yeoman,
> after his morning of field work, symbolically cleanses himself with the holy water
> of the barnyard before entering the sacred interior. Once seated, he will wait for
> the bowl of plenty ceremoniously carried by an archaically stylized woman in an
> immaculate early-American costume.... Heavy with sentiment, Wood's painting
> represents the sacramental last supper of an allegedly independent community of
> cooperative labor on the American "Middle Border," consecrated by the high
> priestess of the family farm who tends an elaborate altar of the vanishing past.[25]

Dennis's descriptive language about *Dinner for Threshers* is heavy with irony
and the knowledge that in the 1930s the farm was no longer a safe haven from
economic difficulties or the corruption of civilization, as Grant himself very well
knew. He was not trying to "fool" anyone—his farm scenes were decorative in
style rather than realistic, and they idealized working the land beyond what even
the most naïve city dweller could accept as accurate. Wood would probably not
have agreed to Dennis's blatant use of religious terminology to describe his painting. He himself was not a religious person in the traditional sense of that word.
When he died, his friend and colleague Thomas Hart Benton said, ''So far as I
know Grant had no God to whom he could offer a soul with memories.''[26] But he
must have sensed how deeply Americans were drawn to the idea of the farm and
the land as the "garden," whose transformational powers could instill virtue in
the most dissipated and sinful, and whose magical properties could keep
technology at bay. Wood's "fantasy farmscapes" called forth all the power of land
perceived as sacred in America, and not only sacred, but unchanging, always
there to be tapped for its life-giving abundance for both body and spirit. By 1940
Wood's popularity both as a painter and as a promoter of regionalism had waned,
and he died convinced that neither his art nor his theories were appreciated any
longer. Perhaps it was the threat of World War II that caused Americans to turn
away from the land and toward what they saw as the saving qualities of technology
as well as to a more global perspective than regionalism offered. But in little more
than twenty years after Wood's death, American culture was gripped by the revolt
against technology that characterized the turbulence of the 1960s, indicating
forcefully that the myth of the land as sacred is such an essential component of
American self-identity that it can be put aside only temporarily, whether as a
catalyst for artistic or for political expression.

---

[25] Ibid., p. 218.

[26] Joseph S. Czestochowske, *John Steuart Curry and Grant Wood: A Portrait of Rural America*
(Columbia: University of Missouri Press, 1981), p. 217.

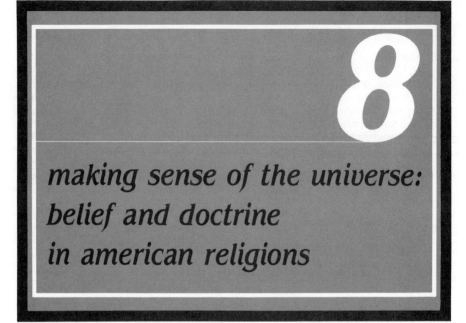

8

making sense of the universe: belief and doctrine in american religions

In 1965 Georgia Harkness, a Methodist theologian, published a little book called *What Christians Believe* in which she asked some questions that are highly pertinent for Americans, the majority of whom appear to be religious believers but not very introspective or knowledgeable about their beliefs: "Why is it important for Christians—or for anyone else—to know what Christians believe? Why is it not enough to live decently, treat other people fairly, and not bother about such questions? In short, if one is to be a Christian, why not just try to live by the Golden Rule and let it go at that?"[1] Why not, indeed? According to a Gallup Poll Opinion Index on Religion in America published in 1981, that's exactly what most Americans are doing. Although 94 percent professed a belief in God, very few were able to indicate *why* they believed in God. Similarly, the vast majority of Christian Americans claimed a belief in the divinity of Jesus Christ but had not come to terms with what this belief meant for their lives. Again, according to the Gallup survey, almost every home in the United States has at least one Bible, but only 12 percent of the population reads the Bible daily. Fewer than half those asked in a survey conducted by Gallup for *Christianity Today* could name more than four of the Ten Commandments. Most Americans say that they pray often, but they do so in an unstructured and superficial manner—and most of the prayers are prayers of petition. Americans overwhelmingly want religious training for their

---

[1]Georgia Harkness, *What Christians Believe* (Nashville, Tennessee: Abingdon Press, 1965), p. 9.

children and at least half would be pleased if their son became a member of the clergy (there was no mention of daughters), but these strong feelings of approbation toward religion are not translated into other areas of life: "One would likely assume that when persons are truly sincere in their faith, religious belief would be the most important influence in their lives. Yet only about 3 in 10 say this is the case."[2] From the evidence presented, America would seem to be a nation of fervent believers who have compartmentalized their religion: They consider themselves highly religious and at the same time lead very secular lives without much demonstrated ability to explain their beliefs or to see their broader significance.

What accounts for this situation? Will Herberg noted in 1955 that most Americans "believe" in religion—they think it is a good idea to go to religious services and be members of a congregation. Thus, there is a national tendency to support religion in general, and Herberg quotes then-President Eisenhower as saying, "Our government makes no sense unless it is founded in a deeply religious faith—and I don't care what it is."[3] This general approval of religion seems to foster an indifference to specifics, and when it comes to a knowledge of actual doctrine, whether their own or others, Americans are not very interested. Certainly this lack of interest stems in part from the realities of life in a religiously plural society. For the very reason mentioned in the chapter on dissent, that "the law knows no heresy," not only the legal system but the culture in general looks not at religious beliefs but at the actions that proceed from those beliefs. Too great an emphasis on doctrinal differences among religious groups might cause an unrest that would be intolerable in the United States. But that is not the whole story. There is a strong anti-intellectual streak in American culture that fosters an impatience with the kind of abstract speculation that doctrinal discussions necessitate. This shows itself in several ways: a concern that "knowing" too much about the history and development of doctrine might diminish one's ability to believe; a tendency for American clergy to see themselves as pastors concerned for the good of their flocks rather than as theologians who hide in seminaries and universities and think esoteric thoughts; and the kind of natural bent toward action characteristic of Americans who prefer to get on with the business of living a good life and forget about lengthy theorizing. Ironically, it may be this very lack of interest in the actual beliefs of themselves and others that impedes the progress of greater religious understanding and tolerance among members of various religious groups, for it is among theologians that discussions of interfaith unity proceed more profitably than they do among churchgoers in general who may cling to long-outmoded stereotypes of what Catholics or Methodists or Jews or Baptists "are really like."

Whatever the inclinations of the American public, no student of religion can

---

[2] *Religion in America*, The Gallup Opinion Index, Report No. 184, January 1981 (Princeton, New Jersey: The Gallup Organization, Inc., and the Princeton Religious Research Center, Inc.), pp. 3–4.

[3] Will Herberg, *Protestant, Catholic, Jew: An Essay in American Religious Sociology* (New York: Anchor Books, 1960), p. 84.

afford to omit a study of belief systems in the attempt to understand the intricacies of American religion in general and specific religions as well. A study of beliefs that constitute the heart of a particular religion not only provides us with factual information, but just as important gives us insights into the world view that informs the members of the group as they come to terms with life's most basic questions. Further, an attempt to learn about and understand the actual beliefs of religious groups fosters that kind of "critical empathy" mentioned in Chapter 1 that prevents an easy dismissal of religious systems that at first appear to be unappealing, incomprehensible, or even bizarre. To use a somewhat extreme example, the religious sects that engage in snake handling strike most people as deserving of immediate rejection rather than serious consideration. But when one begins to understand that the handling of snakes is perceived as a sacrament somewhat akin to the Eucharist and is looked upon as a sign of God's presence among them as well as a test of faith that God has commanded through the Bible, then one is not so likely to turn away from the phenomenon with cries of disgust. We may not take up snake handling, but neither are we so inclined to look upon its proponents as sick or crazy. The question "How can they believe that?" becomes, then, not a question of rejection uttered in recoil, but the beginning of serious investigation.

Before beginning a discussion of actual religious beliefs, it may be helpful to make two points. The first is almost too obvious to state: the fact that even within the same religious group there is often widespread disagreement as to essential beliefs and their interpretations. The second is the following: although every religious group has a discernible belief system, some are much more elaborate and all-encompassing than others and are seen as more compelling. Roman Catholicism has a massive compendium of normative and binding beliefs derived from Scripture and Tradition, covering everything from metaphysics to ethics to social justice. Those teachings set forth as *dogma*, that is, "a doctrine that is taught with the fullest solemnity . . . so that its rejection is heresy," must be adhered to by Catholics or they place themselves outside the Church.[4] It is not all so clear cut as it seems, however, since, surprisingly, there is no official list of dogmas to which all theologians and clergy would agree. Nonetheless, the Catholic doctrinal system includes an immense amount of territory and is binding on its members. By contrast, the United Church of Christ, whose membership is generally liberal Protestant, is constituted as a noncreedal church, that is, its members do not have to espouse a certain set of doctrines to stay in the church, although they most likely share agreement about the centrality of the life of Jesus Christ for their understanding of what it means to be Christian. Even farther from the doctrinal emphasis of Roman Catholicism are the Unitarian Universalists, who believe that all persons must decide for themselves about the existence of God and whose basis for belief has sometimes been described as an agreement on all the tenets they do not subscribe to in other religions. Judaism, too, is a relatively creedless faith that emphasizes *orthopraxis* rather than *orthodoxy;* in other words, Jewish religious identity

---

[4] Richard P. McBrien, *Catholicism* (Minneapolis, Minnesota: Winston Press, 1981), p. 67.

is not so tied up in espousing a set of beliefs as it is concerned with living out "the way of Torah." Christian Science provides another way to look at a belief system. In fact, this is a religious movement that speaks not of a set of beliefs at all, but of the availability of religious knowledge that is not dependent upon an act of faith. Like Spiritualism and Theosophy, Christian Science speaks to the modern hunger to know rather than to have to believe, and Mary Baker Eddy meant the term *science* to connote the certainty with which she felt the Christian Science method of healing could demonstrate the power and presence of God.

No matter the different roles that belief systems and doctrine play for members of various religious organizations—or for those outside organized religion—they share the common function of imposing meaning upon reality, of attempting to make sense out of the collection of paradoxes that we as humans experience as we live out our short lives, always dogged by the knowledge that our deaths are inevitable. Meaning systems, of course, do not necessarily have a religious basis—they can be economic or psychological or anthropological in nature—but those that have as their basis belief in a reality that transcends the obviously physical generally deal with the following questions: What is the nature of the divine? How does it make itself known to humans? What does it mean to be human? What is the meaning of life—a question that implies a need to reflect on how we are to conduct ourselves, how we are to perceive the world, or, more theologically, what we must do to be saved. What happens to us after the death of the body? In spite of the immense variety of answers to these questiosn, as well as the questions within questions that they contain, I am going to suggest the possibility of providing some general answers to these questions to which most Americans who profess a belief in God would subscribe. In addition I will mention some of the variations on these beliefs that have developed in the course of American religious history.

A majority of Americans who claim to believe in God, and that is 94 percent of 230 million people, are likely to describe the divine being as personal in nature, just and merciful, loving and demanding, and concerned with human affairs. This is the God of the Old and New Testaments, omnipotent and omniscient, who created the universe and its creatures from nothing. Evidence to be found in such places as Fourth of July sermons and speeches, presidential inaugural addresses, and campaign speeches suggests a widespread belief among Americans that this is also a God who is particularly interested in America, specifically the United States, and who has set it aside as a special land of great abundance to be both an example to and a resource for other nations of the world. This continuing and widespread belief in a personal God is often a source of great astonishment to European visitors, who assume that religious belief will most likely be confined to the uneducated and the naïve and are amazed to find that it cuts across social, economic, racial, educational, and denominational divisions. A study of theological trends in American religious history tells us that there are many alternative beliefs about the divine from the Deists of the eighteenth century who affirmed God as creator but not as concerned with the workings of the world (the watchmaker theory), to the Freethinkers of the nineteenth century and the "God is Dead" theologians of the twentieth, and these movements would seem to indicate a diminished number of believers in the God of the Bible. But, as important as they have been in theological and intellectual history, they have apparently not affected in any large numbers the belief of Americans about the nature of the divine.

In what way do Americans believe that the divine reveals itself to humans? Most would give as a basic answer their thought that God is revealed through the Bible, through creation, and for Christians through the person of Jesus Christ (to repeat the Gallup information, the "vast majority" of Americans believe in the divinity of Jesus Christ). This rather straightforward-sounding statement on some general beliefs about revelation and its sources is accurate as far as it goes, but it masks the immense potential for disagreement inherent in the various subtopics. For example, the general consensus about Judaeo-Christian revelation is that it has ended, at least in a formal way—that there are no more essential truths about the nature of the divine and of reality to be revealed beyond those made known during Biblical times. Members of newer religions would not assent to this, and often a new religion's claim to authenticity, such as Mormonism, Spiritualism, Christian Science, or Unificationism, is based on the very fact that its founder and his or her followers see it as a "new revelation." Secondly, one has only to read the headlines to know that, although the Bible may be regarded as the word of God by most Americans, the understanding of what "word of God" actually means is the subject not only of theological dispute but of court battles as well, with interpretations ranging from a view of the Bible as inspired by God and true, word for word, in the most literal sense to understanding of the Bible as "containing" the word of God in a more general and figurative way. Third, in spite of the "vast majority" agreeing about the divinity of Jesus Christ, many who profess to be believers may not be able to articulate very well what they understand by that divinity other than some kind of connection with God—while millions of other Americans see Jesus not as divine but as the greatest example who ever lived of what humanity can attain. Members of some groups see Jesus even more specifically as an example of the attributes their particular religion considers most important: thus, Christian Scientists are inclined to look upon Jesus as the greatest of all healers and Spiritualists to see him as the most accomplished of all mediums. There is a kind of internal consistency in most belief systems as to a correlation between their view of human nature and their interpretation of Jesus: the higher the view of human nature, the less emphasis on the divinity of Christ, on the theory that a humanity that is not depraved by sin is not in need of a divine redeemer, but instead an example of the potential each person might achieve.

The actual interpretation of the limits of human potential, of what it means to be human, is no longer the sole province of religion, and twentieth-century Americans are probably as likely to turn to psychology, psychiatry, anthropology, and the natural sciences for such speculation as they are to look to religion. Nonetheless, the question of essential humanity is one of the most important in religious belief systems, and any theology of human nature has to take into account those paradoxes of human existence with which we are only too familiar: We are both bound and free, and we have the capacity for great good and for great evil. We experience the finiteness of our own bodies and we know the inevitability of our own deaths, yet at the same time we find it almost impossible to imagine that we, as individuals, might some day cease to exist. We are often overwhelmed by great anxiety, even despair, but are also visited by hope. We are intensely alone, finally, yet we know also that we are members of various human communities and perhaps much more like our fellow humans than unlike them.

Most Americans who espouse religious beliefs are Christian and are therefore familiar with a theological interpretation of these paradoxes and polarities that uses such terms as "Fall," "redemption," and "grace" to describe the human condition. The Christian framework tells us that we are sinners and that our only hope for salvation from sin and from death is to depend upon God's saving grace, made available to us through Jesus Christ's death on Calvary. There, unfortunately, agreement ends, and various interpretations of how one receives grace, whether as a freely given gift from God or whether through the work and cooperation of the individual, has occasioned many a bitter theological dispute, to say nothing of the Reformation. Judaism, too, has an understanding of a divided human nature, and although Jewish Talmudic and rabbinical tradition does not stress the paradigm of the Fall as does Christianity, it nonetheless teaches that each person is possessed of *yetzer tov,* good, and *yetzer ra,* evil—that each person is capable of fulfilling the Law but at the same time feels the pull to avoid obligations. There is another strain in American religion that denies human nature as being in any sense fallen, that looks upon evil and sin not as inevitable parts of human existence but as the absence of good. Ralph Waldo Emerson is probably the most famous exponent of this view in American culture, but the fruits of his ideas have been popularized in the "positive thinking" religions such as Christian Science, Divine Science, Religious Science, and the Unity School of Christianity. It is a common stance among many religions that stress physical and mental healing.

Thus far much of the discussion has centered on the theoretical aspects of meaning systems, but a system also carries with it answers to the question "How shall I live my life?" Some religions are much more detailed in their expectations for members. Catholicism imposes more obligations on its members than most churches, particularly in the area of church attendance and sexual behavior, but far fewer than it did before Vatican II in such areas as fasting and abstinence from meat. Orthodox Jews have many more rituals to fulfill that are concerned with clothing, food, and prayer than do Conservative or Reform Jews. Some of the newer religions of both the nineteenth and twentieth centuries have more to say about particular aspects of their members' lifestyles than do the more mainstream churches: Mormons, Jehovah's Witnesses, and Seventh Day Adventists all have strictures on diet; and religious movements who have some members living in community, from Catholicism to Buddhism to the Church Universal and Triumphant (founded in 1958), expect their members to order their days according to the rules of the community.

All of these specific beliefs aside, if asked to distill their understanding of religious obligations apart from practices particular to individual groups, most Americans would no doubt echo Georgia Harkness's statement of what she perceived as the typical American way to be religious: "live decently . . . treat other people fairly . . . just try to live by the Golden Rule."

It is at this point, however, that the discrepancy between Americans' widespread religious beliefs of a general nature and their inability to articulate those beliefs and apply them to their lives becomes most obvious. What does it mean to "live decently"? When it comes to questions of poverty, war, nuclear arms, sexual behavior, capital punishment, political or business or medical ethics, what exactly does it mean to "live decently" and "treat other people fairly"? Most Americans are not very well able to interpret their religious beliefs—although they can mouth them—as they might apply to the dilemmas of modern existence. Currently only 65 percent of those interviewed by Gallup say that "religion can answer all or most of our present problems. . . ." In fact, there is a widespread fear that specific religions may exert too much influence in trying to solve various problems in America, and there certainly seems to be as much strong feeling in favor of keeping "politics out of the pulpit" as there is to seek out theological interpretations for contemporary anxieties with accompanying calls to action. Obviously, then, membership in a group that provides answers to questions of life's meaning cannot by itself guarantee an understanding of how to proceed. For this reason theological interpreters who take into account the contemporary situations in which they live have been particularly important in American culture, people capable of saying not just "This is what we believe" but "This is what we must do, because these are the things we believe." These interpreters establish correlations between the abstract concepts that form the basis of a religious system and the obligations that follow from these beliefs as they must be acted out within the culture. There is no intention here to say that these theological interpreters—mostly members of the clergy—are correct or incorrect in what they have expressed. In the history of America they have displayed great diversity of opinion: for and against the American Revolution; for and against the abolition of slavery; for and against welfare; for and against the war in Vietnam. The emphasis here is on the task they have set for themselves of defining for their followers how they are to conduct themselves both as Americans and as members of a particular religious group.

The three representatives I've selected all performed that task of interpretation, but in different settings and from different theological perspectives: Rabbi Isaac Meyer Wise, Georgia Harkness, and Bishop Fulton J. Sheen. They are not the great theorists of American religion and culture, such as Jonathan Edwards, Ralph Waldo Emerson, or H. Richard Niebuhr. By that statement I do not mean to say in any way that they are lacking in intellectual capabilities—very much the contrary—but that their task was not so much the generation of paradigmatic and abstract insights but instead the interpretation of both doctrine and social obligations for the general public.

Rabbi Isaac Meyer Wise (1819–1900), one of the strongest influences of Reform Judaism in America and the founder of Hebrew Union College, wanted to bring about ritual reform in Judaism, to unite different factions of American Judaism, and to incorporate it into the American social structure. At the same time and in spite of criticism to the contrary, he maintained an intense interest in fostering Jewish tradition and identity. Georgia Harkness (1891–1974) was a Methodist theologian, an academic, who felt an obligation to interpret Protestant Christian doctrine for the average person without being either simplistic or condescending. She was a prolific writer, her published volumes totaling thirty-six, and the titles of her books, from *The Church and the Immigrant* (1921) to *Women in Church and Society* (1972), reveal her propensity for dealing with contemporary issues. Fulton J. Sheen (1895–1979) a Roman Catholic Bishop, may be the best-known American Catholic after John F. Kennedy. Sheen reached millions of listeners as a radio preacher on "The Catholic Hour" in the 1930s and 1940s and then an even greater audience through his television show, "Life Is Worth Living," which was broadcast during the 1950s. In many ways Sheen's message did not differ greatly from those of some of the other positive-thinking preachers of the 1950s, notably Norman Vincent Peale, even though what he (Sheen) said had its foundation in Catholic doctrine. What he did do that was unique, however, standing before a huge audience in the robes of a Catholic bishop, was to make American Catholicism more accessible and comprehensible, more "American" and respectable in the eyes of Protestants and Jews (and Catholics as well) than it had ever been up to that time.

ISAAC MEYER WISE

When Rabbi Isaac Meyer Wise arrived in New York from Bohemia in 1846 with his wife and small daughter, he encountered not only the freedoms that life in American promised for Jews, which were considerable in contrast with conditions in Europe, but also the more deleterious effects that those same freedoms brought with them. Not confined to ghettoes by European law and social custom, the Jews of America in the mid-nineteenth century had much greater choices of occupations and dwelling places, but they were also experiencing a loss in identity and community as they grappled with what it meant to be Jewish in America. There were fewer than 100,000 Jews in the New World when Wise arrived, and apart from synagogues they had no institutions to hold them together. They were separated from one another by ethnic differences brought about by different patterns of immigration: Sephardic Jews of Spanish and Portuguese descent were the earliest arrivals in America; the German Jews, Wise among them, began arriving in great numbers during the middle of the century; and the Jews of Eastern Europe were yet to come at the close of the century. And they were separated from other Americans by customs of worship that seemed strange and foreign. Wise learned very quickly from Gentiles that Jews were largely an unknown entity in the United States, and his fellow Jews informed him that the climate of freedom and materialism in his newfound home had the effect of diminishing the spiritual qualities of Jewish life. In *Reminiscences,* an autobiographical account of his life from 1846 to 1857, Wise recounted his experiences of both of these truths. During a train ride to Syracuse his first year in America, Wise was questioned by an ''inquisitive Yankee'' as he sat reading the Pentateuch in Hebrew with commentaries in Aramaic and rabbinical Hebrew. Upon learning of Wise's recent arrival in America, the man ventured a guess as to his identity: ''Ah, now I know who you are; you are a Jewish bishop.'' No amount of explaining convinced the man that ''bishop'' was not a term applicable to Jewish rabbis, since there was no hierarchy in Judaism, and he continued to treat Wise in a ''princely manner.''[5] It was from a fellow Jew that Wise began to learn what life in America often meant for Jewish spirituality and religious practice. The man, a merchant, explained to Wise some of the economic realities of America, all based on commercial exchange, and he categorized the Jews in America either as peddlers of various sorts or members of the ''aristocracy,'' such as jewelry sellers or store owners. ''But what about people of intelligence?'' asked Wise. The answer was startling to him: ''In America a man must be either all head or all back.'' Intellectual pursuits were not of great benefit in America because ''the foreigner must either become rich, or go to the wall; he has no alternative. The end and aim of all striving in this country is to become rich; everything else is secondary.'' When Wise asked why, if the situation was this extreme, Jews still formed congregations and built synagogues, he was informed, ''O, they do this from inherited habit. . . . There is no earnestness, no spirit, no idealism in the whole proceeding.''[6]

Such a bleak assessment of Jewish life in America might logically have elicited one of two responses in Wise: either to seek refuge in stringent Orthodoxy and build a wall around himself, his family, and any congregations he might serve to keep out the secular forces of American culture; or else to give up his rabbinic career and pursue another profession such as that of law, a step that he nearly took at a time in his life when he was particularly discouraged. Instead, Wise went in another direction. He chose as his task the accommodation of Judaism to life in America in such a way that he could help his fellow Jews retain the essence of Judaism and still enable them to adjust to the realities of life in America. This choice involved advocating Reform Judaism, which already had a following in Germany and was not unknown among American Jews.

Because of the great stress in Jewish identity on living within the Mosaic Law in contrast with insistence on doctrinal purity, Wise could not have functioned as an interpreter for American Judaism without a great deal of attention to ritual and organization. In fact, he was more practically than theologically oriented. Wise's vision of Reform Judaism had many facets: a Jewish identity

---

[5] Isaac Meyer Wise, *Reminiscences,* ed. David Phillipson (Cincinnati, Ohio: Leo Wise and Company), pp. 34–35.

[6] Ibid.

centered on "historic Judaism," rather than a longing for the return to Jerusalem; a theology that deemphasized supernaturalism; changes in rituals to make Jewish services conform more closely to what one might encounter in a Protestant church; and a Synod, or organization of congregations, and a conference of rabbis that would transcend ethnic barriers and provide a kind of unity for American Jews that they had not yet experienced. He preached the need for organization, but he also wanted to assure his listeners that he supported to a great extent the congregational autonomy that was part of the Jewish tradition. Underlying all these plans for change was Wise's emphasis on the rational and reasonable. As one might guess, what seems rational and reasonable to one person can be perceived as reprehensible to another. Thus, Wise's efforts met with both great success and great resistance.

During his tenure as rabbi of Beth El Synagogue in Albany, New York, Wise encountered as much opposition from members of his own congregation as he did from the outside. The majority of its members were Orthodox, and the tension fermented by Wise's changes in rituals finally became strong enough to produce a split in the congregation.[7] Wise became rabbi of the new synagogue, Anshe Emeth. In spite of the controversies in Albany, Wise was called to serve as rabbi of Bene Yeshurun congregation in Cincinnati on the strength of his reputation as a reformer, and he served there from 1854 until his death in 1900. This was a synagogue with strong leanings toward Reform Judaism, and Wise was able to put his ritual reforms into practice without opposition from the congregation. His life, however, was never without controversy, and his *Reminiscences* reveals that the role of a reformer is not an easy one; the temptations to forsake the cause are often many and overwhelming. At one point during his troubles in Albany, which included the death of his small daughter from cholera, Wise expressed the fear that "I shall never be happy. A terrible fate has condemned me to be the scapegoat of an era in contradiction with itself. I grew terrified. The future looked blank."[8]

In spite of Wise's occasional feelings of futility, the future was not by any means a blank. The reforms he accomplished, although those in ritual have been modified, endure to this day. To begin with the theological beliefs, Wise found, to his surprise, that he often had more in common with liberal Protestants, such as Theodore Parker, than he did with the Orthodox Jews. He had been affected strongly by studies in Higher Criticism (a scientific approach to Biblical studies), and he no longer espoused a belief in miracles, in a personal Messiah who would emerge as king and savior of the Jews, or in the resurrection of the body. Because of his stance, he antagonized both Orthodox Jews and traditional Christians: "I attacked Christianity critically from the rationalistic standpoint; hence I had to administer orthodox Judaism almost as many blows as orthodox Christianity. Miracles were not wonderful nor marvelous for me, and the Messiah was dismissed as a poetical fiction. The ascension of Jesus and the ascension of Elijah

---

[7] It is interesting to note that in 1885 the two congregations were reunited.

[8] *Reminiscences*, p. 196.

were equally important, or, rather, equally unimportant for me; therefore the orthodox became bitterly incensed at me."[9] In spite of what seems to be an all-encompassing dismissal of traditional religion, Wise did not reject all of what would be considered traditional Jewish beliefs. According to one of his biographers, James G. Heller, he maintained a strong sense of the historical reality of God's revelation to Moses at Mt. Sinai. For Wise, there could be no Jewish religion apart from this belief, even though he considered that human understanding of what the Sinaitic revelation actually meant for Jews could change and evolve according to different times and cultures.[10] Another biographer, Israel Knox, sums up Wise's beliefs as Wise expressed them in *Judaism: Its Doctrines and Duties* (1872): "the Oneness of God; the uniqueness of man as bearer of the divine image; man's capacity to choose between good and evil and hence his accountability to God; Israel's election as 'a light of the nations' in behalf of these eternal truths."[11]

Some of the changes put forth by Wise and other reformers have been mentioned briefly in Chapter 4 on religion and science in America. Wise's objective in making changes was to bring Jewish services closer to Protestant worship and thus make them seem more American. To this end he instituted the use of an organ and a choir, made the sermon the central focus of the service, began to speak of confirmation for both boys and girls instead of just Bar Mitzvah for boys, and permitted families to sit together rather than separating men and women. The result was *Minhag America,* a ritual Wise considered appropriate to life in America.

It is interesting to look at two of the changes in a little more detail: the use of a choir and the seating of men and women together. In his formation of choirs, Wise seems to have been motivated by a love of music, a conviction that good music would draw people to services, and a desire to introduce "decorum" into Jewish services. When he introduced the choir to his congregation in Albany, he made disparaging remarks about the *chazan,* the cantor, to the effect that "it made no difference to our *chazan* whether he began or ended a few notes lower or higher; he passed with surprising ease from one key to another and the choir was expected to keep up with him."[12] The choir was a source of great controversy and bitterness in Albany, and it disbanded after Wise's departure, but the choir Wise began in Cincinnati was successful and accepted from the beginning.

On the status of women in synagogues, Wise was especially forward-looking for his time. Many of the reforms he urged were not put into practice during his lifetime—women's suffrage, ordination of women to the rabbinate, women sitting on congregational boards—but he insisted that men and women must sit together in the synagogue in order that women might be full members of the congregation. Although he acknowledged her as "queen of the home," in traditional Jewish fashion, Wise claimed that "The Jewish woman had been treated almost as a

---

[9] Ibid., pp. 122–23.

[10] James G. Heller, *Isaac M. Wise: His Life, Work and Thought* (New York: The Union of American Hebrew Congregations, 1965), p. 526.

[11] Israel Knox, *Rabbi in America: The Story of Isaac M. Wise* (Boston: Little, Brown and Company, 1957), p. 57.

[12] *Reminiscences,* p. 53.

stranger in the synagogue; she had been kept at a distance and had been excluded from all participation in the life of the congregation, had been relegated to the gallery, even as was the negro in Southern churches.''[13]

Wise did not see ritual and theological changes in themselves as sufficient to bring about the assimilation of Judaism into American culture. He also saw the need for organizational unity both of congregations and of rabbis. Wise was very disappointed in 1848 when he and his supporters failed to institute a Synod of congregations, and he knew what kind of opposition he faced. In *Reminiscences* he speculated that, given the choice between anarchy and anything that hinted of hierarchy, Jews would choose anarchy. But he was convinced that in order for reforms to proceed in a regular way and to have some semblance of widespread approval, they would have to be enacted not congregation by congregation but through a constituted body with at least minimal powers of enforcement. Through this body Wise hoped to unite both Orthodox and Reform congregations. Although he was never successful to that extent, he did see the fruition of part of his dream of unification in the Reformed Union of American Congregations, the Central Conference of American Rabbis, and the founding in 1875 of Hebrew Union College of which Wise was president until his death.

Wise never wavered in his concept of America as the ideal homeland for a universal, rational kind of Judaism that would fit into a democratic and pluralistic culture without the loss of its essential identity. To scholars of the twentieth century he seems almost prescient in his conviction that the religious pluralism of American culture would change the very nature of Judaism. His critics accused him of trying to deprive American Jews of any sense of their own uniqueness as a religious people, although his writings give evidence that he was always acutely aware of the need to retain Judaism's essential elements. The disagreements arose out of the effort to discern exactly what those essential elements might be. If Wise had a blind spot, it was in his failure to understand the pull of the old ways, his inability to value sufficiently the nonrational aspects of Judaism that arose from adherence to rituals practiced through many centuries. Wise was wrong in his prediction that Orthodox Judaism would not long remain on the American religious scene, and he did not seem to anticipate the formation of a third branch of American Judaism in 1887, the Conservative, which has provided a choice for American Jews other than Reform or Orthodox. Wise lived in an age when the rational was becoming the arbiter of every truth, and like many of his fellow American clergy, he saw no other way for religion to survive without accommodating itself to the demand that it be reasonable.

GEORGIA HARKNESS

Georgia Harkness had a long and fruitful career as a teacher, a theologian, and a writer. She was working on a manuscript for a book, *Biblical Backgrounds of the Mid-*

---

[13] Ibid., p. 212.

dle East Conflict (a colleague completed the last four chapters), until a few days before her death at eighty-three in 1974. If she had been a man, her life's work would certainly have been judged prodigious in both amount and quality, but not atypical. For a woman born in 1891, her accomplishments were remarkable, and Harkness holds many "firsts," among them being the first woman to hold a professorship of theology at a theological seminary and the first woman elected to the American Theological Society. She gave credit to her father for instilling in her a curiosity about "persons, places, books" and for seeing to it that she had a better education than was usual for "country girls" in upstate New York at the turn of the century. With family encouragement and the impetus of her own talents and interests, Harkness was graduated from Cornell University in 1912 and received a Ph.D. from Boston University in 1923. She taught high-school Latin for six years, was a college professor for another seventeen at Elmira College for Women and Mount Holyoke, and was a seminary professor at Garrett Evangelical Theological Seminary in Evanston, Illinois, and the Pacific School of Religion in Berkeley until her retirement in 1961. There is a chair of theology at Garrett Seminary named in honor of Georgia Harkness, a position held at present by Rosemary Radford Ruether, a feminist theologian.

Harkness was a highly active lifelong Methodist. She was taken to church by her parents from her earliest memory, and during her professional career she represented Methodism at conferences all over the world. She was ordained a local deacon in 1926 and is generally referred to—and referred to herself—as a Methodist minister. But Methodist ordination is a two-step process, and until 1956 Methodist women were not permitted the second step to full ordination. At that time, although she had worked for women's ordination and was greatly influential in putting an end to male domination in the Methodist church, she did not choose full ordination for herself, deciding instead to maintain an identification with the laity.[14] Outside Methodist circles she was best known as an interpreter of Protestant doctrine for the laity. The form of that interpretation varied: she wrote Bible studies, devotional poetry, hymns, and examinations of social and economic issues in light of church doctrine. In her first interpretive volume, *Conflicts in Religious Thought* (1929), Harkness very clearly articulated her task in the preface: to make religious thought comprehensible to lay people and applicable to their lives. She seems highly American in her assessment that doctrines and ideas couched in abstract and esoteric language are not very useful to most people. The book, she said, dealt "with the profoundest questions and conflicts of human thinking, and in the argument here presented the author's main objective, aside from the desire to state it truly, has been to avoid stating it profoundly."[15]

If Isaac Meyer Wise found his life's work in the assimilation of a virtually

---

[14]*Dictionary of American Religious Biography,* ed. Henry Warner Bowden (Westport, Connecticut: Greenwood Press, 1977), pp. 191–92.

[15] Georgia Harkness, *Conflicts in Religious Thought* (New York: Henry Holt and Company, 1929), p. xi.

unknown religious tradition into American culture, Harkness faced a very different task. As a Methodist she belonged to the Protestant mainstream, and so her struggle was not assimilation. Instead, she feared that the truths of Protestant Christianity were more and more perceived as irrelevant, not only for daily life but also in overcoming such problems of global magnitude as war and poverty. She sensed that the truths in which she believed very deeply and the institutions responsible for their propagation had become *too* assimilated into the culture and that they served to uphold the status quo rather than to make prophetic judgments upon it. She intuited early what the Gallup polls of recent years have indicated so clearly—that no matter how fervently people may say they believe in the doctrines of a particular religion, they probably do not understand their beliefs well and cannot easily put them into practice.

Although she herself was a committed Christian when she wrote *Conflicts in Religious Thought,* that book is not a defense of Christianity but of religion in general, and it is interesting to follow Harkness's development from a defender and interpreter of "religion" to a spokesperson for a specific kind of Christianity that she, along with Harry Emerson Fosdick, called evangelical liberalism. Much of Harkness's education and teaching were in philosophy, and *Conflicts in Religious Thought* is a good illustration of that interest. It is a defense of the reasonableness of religious belief, proceeding from Harkness's underlying Christian assumptions about the nature of God, the universe, and the human but not blatantly Christian (for example, the book has no chapter on Jesus Christ). One could speculate that in *Conflicts* Harkness was not so much trying to explain the actual doctrines of Christianity as she was attempting to convey the logic of espousing a religious world view over an irreligious one: that it simply made more sense to believe in God, in an ordered universe, in the worthwhile nature of the human struggle, and in life after death than not to believe these things. In the book she covered a wide range of religious and philosophical questions: Why have religion? Is there a God? What is truth? Why do men suffer? Why do men sin? Throughout, however, she made it clear that she intended more than an appeal to the intellect: "To carve it [religion] up in intellectual analysis and leave it dismembered is to miss its meaning. We must walk by faith, if we walk at all. And hope and love must be conjoined with faith, if we would see."[16]

An examination of one chapter—"Why Do Men Suffer?"—illustrates Harkness's method of posing a series of alternative ways to look at a question, culminating in the argument that she herself found most compelling. She began with questions that plague all humanity: Why do we have to suffer? If there is a God who is good, why can't or doesn't this divine being put an end to suffering? She affirms that human suffering is not illusory or minimal and that its constant presence and seemingly arbitrary distribution among the undeserving pose great problems for religious believers. She continued by putting forth four points of view from which the reader might interpret both the nature of the universe and the

---

[16] Ibid., p. 47.

presence of suffering—atheism, pessimism, optimism, or meliorism. She rejected, although not in a bludgeoning way, atheism ("Atheism more than once has rendered good service to religion by jolting it out of its smug complacency!''), which she found lacking intellectually because it does not take into account the goodness and order in the universe and lacking emotionally because it gives humanity nothing to rely on outside ourselves. She rejected pessimism because it asserts that life has no goals worthy of our suffering and religious pessimism in particular because of its emphasis on a cataclysmic and all-too-soon end of the world. Finally, Harkness rejected optimism as a reasonable way of looking at the universe, the kind of cosmic optimism that sees evil as a negative rather than an absolute and posits that everything happens for the best. This stance is unreasonable, she said, because it forces one to ignore the reality of suffering and evil and always to play the "glad game." Harkness elected the fourth option, which she called *meliorism,* saying that "the truest theories are often the simplest." She interpreted meliorism as based on common sense and in her explanation of it one can see her talent for appealing to the realities of human existence in combination with a religious belief system, as well as her American penchant for practicality even in matters of religion and philosophy. "Meliorism," she said, "recognizes some truth in both optimism and pessimism, but says that neither can give us the whole truth. It challenges the human effort to make the world better by eradicating as much as possible of its sin and suffering. Its incentive to betterment is compatible with a wide variety of religious views; for whether there be no God, or a God limited in power, or an omnipotent God, we still can 'carry on.' ''[17]

Ten years after completing *Conflicts in Religious Thought,* Georgia Harkness wrote an autobiographical article for the *Christian Century,* part of a series by theologians called "How My Mind Has Changed in This Decade." In it Harkness makes clear her position in four fields: theology, worship, social action, and the church. These positions seemed to remain constant for her for the rest of her life, whether she was writing devotional works, protesting the use of the atom bomb for defense or retaliation (as she did in 1950), or advocating the ordination of women. During the ten years between 1929 and 1939 Harkness saw herself as becoming more Christ-centered theologically, more convinced of the value of liturgical worship, more emphatically a pacifist and a socialist, and more committed to the institutional church. She did not repudiate any of what she had said in *Conflicts,* but there was much in 1939 that she wished she could add. Harkness attributed the changes partly to her contact with other theologians but more directly to influences in her personal life, thereby reaffirming her conviction that the intellectual and the experiential must be taken together to form the basis of theology. During those ten years she had experienced the loss of both of her parents, but also the growth of her professional life in the publishing of six books, the move from a department of philosophy at Elmira College to a department of religion at Mount Holyoke, the writing of poetry for the first time, and the attending of two world

---

[17] Ibid., p. 198.

conferences of religion in England and India. "If these experiences had not affected my religion," she said, "nothing would." [18]

The books Harkness wrote after 1939 and what she called the "second blessing" of her middle years left no doubt that for her the answers to the questions she posed in *Conflicts* lay in Christianity and particularly in adherence to what she considered the most distinctive of Christian doctrines, the belief in and devotion to Jesus Christ. For Harkness, Jesus was the ultimate revealer of God and the redeemer of humankind. She stressed the cross and its suffering as the central symbol of Christianity, the sign of Jesus' vicarious atonement for the sins of humanity. In *Our Christian Hope* Harkness imparted her understanding of Jesus' significance for Christians and for the world:

> . . . Jesus *is* the hope of the world. Through him above all other agencies and channels we find God or—to speak more accurately—we are led to that openness of life with ego barrriers down whereby God can find us. Christianity is not the only avenue to hope or to strength of character; yet without the message embedded in the words and the ministry, the death, the resurrection, and the living presence of Jesus Christ, neither an individual nor a civilization can have its most buoyant hope or its most enduring strength.[19]

Harkness's conviction of the centrality of Jesus' life and message formed her interpretation of what actions Christians must take in their lives in order to imitate Jesus. Thoroughly Protestant herself, Harkness nonetheless was inclusive enough in her theology to speak for a wide range of Christians. She was careful to avoid dogmatic pronouncements concerning matters of doctrine on which all Christians do not agree, such as the Virgin Birth and the divine/human nature of Jesus. Harkness was a "Christian Optimist," although not a foolish one. She believed that there was meaning in history, founded on God's providence, and she denied that history was "just one damn thing after another." In spite of the obvious evils in the world she perceived an increase over the centuries in human goodness.

Harkness may have been her own worst critic. In *Women in Church and Society* (written when she was eighty-one), in which she advocated the ordination of women to the ministry on the theological conviction that in Christ there is no male or female, Harkness confessed to a reserve and caution in advocating changes in the church. She had never participated in a protest march, a fact that she attributed to the possibility of "cowardice" or "deep-seated conformism."[20] A critic observing her from the outside world would judge that her ministry took the form of writing and preaching rather than marching. She certainly never minced words in her books, and those she wrote in her seventies and eighties displayed the same common-sense interpretations as her earlier works. Life is not perfect, she

---

[18] Georgia Harkness, "A Spiritual Pilgrimage," *The Christian Century* 56 (March 15, 1939), 348.

[19] Georgia Harkness, *Our Christian Hope* (Nashville, Tennessee: Abingdon Press, 1964), p. 154.

[20] Georgia Harkness, *Women in Church and Society: A Historical and Theological Inquiry* (Nashville, Tennessee: Abingdon Press, 1972), p. 31.

said, but neither is it hopeless; by means of a deep Christian faith combined with God's grace, and effort based on common sense, people must do the best they can. It was this kind of practical advice combined with her obviously sincere faith that made Georgia Harkness such an appealing interpreter of Christian belief for millions of Americans.

FULTON J. SHEEN

During the 1950s it was the ecumenical thing to do to watch Bishop Fulton J. Sheen's television program, "Life Is Worth Living," on Tuesday nights. Sheen was engaged in showing Americans that Catholics, even Catholic bishops, were just like anyone else, that they experienced the same problems of faith and personal dilemmas, and that "Catholic" answers to these difficulties were highly palatable to an audience of many faiths as well as to those who espoused no specific religious beliefs at all. In his bishop's robes Sheen displayed on network television just how American Catholicism could be, and yet he undergirded his messages with a world view that stemmed from a thirteenth-century philosopher-theologian, Thomas Aquinas. A great part of Sheen's appeal lay in his anecdotal style, his telling of jokes and stories; in contrast with the earnestness of many Protestant radio and television preachers, Sheen was funny. He spoke on a great variety of topics that included both personal and global concerns: nervous anxiety and the rat race of "making it;" the dangers of communism; the sustaining of a good marriage; the endurance of pain and suffering; even the psychology of the Irish and the Russians. Perhaps Sheen's ultimate appeal lay in his expressed conviction that life still made sense, that there was indeed a divine plan for the universe (one of his books was entitled *The Moral Universe*) and for America, and that human beings had the power to discern this plan and had not lost control over their own destinies. Sheen was at the peak of his popularity in the years before Vatican II, which brought with it the changes that plunged Catholics into the same uncertainties about the divine order of things that many Jews and Protestants had experienced since the nineteenth century. Sheen offered his audiences the certainties of the whole institution of Roman Catholicism on the nature of the divine, the human, and the world. By the 1960s, however, the certainties of Catholicism had begun to waver from the same pressures of cultural encounter that Protestantism had experienced earlier, and Sheen's last years were marked by the strain of living at the end of an era—in this case, the era of pre–Vatican II American Catholicism. As a theological interpreter, Sheen serves as an interesting contrast to both Wise and Harkness, whose early convictions seemed to develop and be confirmed as they grew older. For Sheen, the hard questions about the relationship between religion and culture came during his later years.

Fulton Sheen's early life was typical enough of an Irish American Catholic boy destined for the priesthood. Born in the small town of El Paso, Illinois, Sheen attended a Catholic boys' high school in Peoria and seminaries in Illinois and

Minnesota. His oratorical skills apparently were not obvious until his seminary career, and he was considered no great asset to his high-school debating team. But he showed great intellectual promise and after ordination was sent first to the University of Louvain, Belgium, where he received a Ph.D. in 1923. Sheen's doctoral dissertation was published as *God and Intelligence,* which he called an attempt "to suggest solutions of modern problems in light of the philosophy of St. Thomas." It received the Cardinal Mercier Prize for International Philosophy, the first American dissertation to do so. It was at this point in his life that Sheen might have elected to remain within the Catholic Church's corps of clergy-intellectuals, more at home in Europe than in America, but after teaching briefly in England, he returned to the United States. He was still under obedience to the bishop of Peoria in whose diocese he had been ordained, and the bishop sent him to serve a parish in Illinois for a year in order to ensure his humility before permitting him to take a teaching position at Catholic University. (It was regular practice for successful clergy to be relegated to a lesser role now and then to make sure that they did not develop excessive pride in their own abilities—for example, a university president might be sent to teach high-school Latin for a year between terms.) Sheen remained a professor at Catholic University for twenty-five years, although his teaching duties were minimal. In 1930 he began radio broadcasts of "The Catholic Hour," sponsored by the National Council of Catholic Men, on NBC, and it continued until 1952. By this time Sheen had acquired a reputation for a golden voice and an excellent dramatic presence, along with the ability, as *Time* once put it, to make religion sound "sensible" and "attractive." It was these gifts, no doubt, that led Sheen from a life of scholarship to one of public fame; and although he wrote many books and articles after *God and Intelligence*—the best-known being *Peace of Soul* (1949)—they were never marked by the same extensive research and reserved weighing of opinion. Instead, although supported by scholarly knowledge, they were meant for a popular audience.

Along with his media successes—including the winning of an Emmy Award in 1952—Sheen also achieved prominence within the institutional church. He was appointed national director of the Society for the Propagation of the Faith, the mission organization of the Catholic Church, in 1950, and a year later was consecrated a bishop. He was the friend of popes and royalty and consecrated missionary bishops at the side of Pope John XXIII in Rome in 1960 and 1961. Given all these honors, both secular and religious, it would not have been presumptuous for Sheen to have expected the cardinal's hat, but that privilege never came to him—because of, it was rumored, disagreements with Francis Cardinal Spellman of New York. In 1966 Sheen was appointed bishop of Rochester, New York, a position that did not appear to be much of a plum. Rochester turned out to be Sheen's "Calvary," as one biographer, D. P. Noonan, put it.[21] He resigned in

---

[21] D. P. Noonan, *The Passion of Fulton Sheen* (New York: Dodd, Mead & Company, 1972), p. 160. This is a peculiar book about Sheen written by an Irish priest who had served as his assistant. It is a jarring combination of the adulatory and the vindictive, but it does provide some anecdotes about Sheen that are unavailable elsewhere.

1969 after a contretemps in which he announced that the church would give the property of a particular parish to the government for low-income housing. Unfortunately, he had not consulted the pastor or parishioners before making the announcement; their reaction was one of rage, and under pressure Sheen reversed the decision.

This incident illustrates something of the dichotomy between Sheen's conservative theology and his more liberal social activism. It can only be praiseworthy that Sheen recognized the need for the church to share what it had with the poor, but his insensitivity in failing to consult with those most directly affected gives testimony to his failure to come to terms with a changing conception of the role of the hierarchy. This blow-up also provides some information about and illustrates something of the paradoxical character of Sheen, who was immensely charming and charismatic on television but apparently not so well able to sustain individual personal relationships. Noonan, for example, claimed that Sheen's classes at Catholic University were extremely popular but that he kept himself aloof from the students. On the other hand, Sheen had a long-standing friendship with a man who had been disfigured by leprosy; he frequently invited "Paul" to dinner and even cut his meat for him because his hands were disfigured. Further, Sheen seems to have been very skilled in "giving instructions" in the Catholic faith to those who wished to join, among them Clare Booth Luce, Henry Ford II, Fritz Kreisler, and Louis Budenz, a former communist.

As mixed as the reactions to Sheen may have been personally, there is no disputing the fact that millions of people watched his television program. What accounts for that appeal? On a superficial level one could say that Sheen was simply quite entertaining, but more than that he was accomplishing a three-fold task: giving American Catholics a pride in their religious heritage and diminishing their need for defensiveness; demonstrating to non-Catholic Americans that it was possible to be intensely Catholic, intellectual, and very patriotic all at the same time; and delivering a religious message of hope and confidence in human powers to prevail over chaos—a message that was very welcome in the 1950s. Sheen made no attempt to dilute his image as a member of the Catholic hierarchy. He wore his cassock with red piping, his red cape and cap, and his pectoral cross. He spoke frequently of his veneration for the Virgin Mary, the mother of Jesus, and in fact dedicated most of his books to her. The dedication to *Life Is Worth Living,* an interesting blend of Catholic tradition and modern electronics, reads as follows: "Dedicated to our Heavenly Mother who stands behind me at every telecast and before whom I kneel in filial love that these words borne on waves of light may bring readers to the Word and the Light of the World."[22] In addition to his obvious Catholicism, Sheen was also highly patriotic. He called Americans to task for secularism and for lack of zeal in spreading the gospels of Christ and democracy, but he was equally strong in his conviction that, troubled as it might be by the difficulties of contemporary society, America was particularly blessed by

---

[22] Fulton J. Sheen, *Life Is Worth Living* (Garden City, New York: Garden City Books, 1953).

God for its Constitutional guarantee of divinely ordained human rights. Sheen frequently contrasted the rights Americans enjoyed with those denied the Russian people, a topic of consuming public interest during the Cold War years of the 1950s, and he maintained that Russian communism will not prevail in the end but serves as a warning to American society that it must not lose its faith in God.

American Catholicism of the 1950s had not yet lost what the historian William M. Halsey called the "innocence" of earlier times in American history, and Sheen offered his audiences all the certainties of a church that had survived almost 2,000 years of changing times and differing cultures and had not yet come to terms, at least in America, with its lack of immunity to cultural pressures. Sheen preached belief in an omnipotent God who was both transcendent and imminent, not a God who had withdrawn from concern for the world or who, according to some contemporary theologies, was not omnipotent but limited in power. Sheen spoke of the human person as characterized by free will, able to make moral decisions, and the dominant creature of all creation, not just a bit of matter in an indifferent universe. Halsey speaks of Sheen's appeal to the American desire for "control and mastery."[23]

Sheen's views of psychoanalysis provide a good illustration of this emphasis on control. In a chapter in *Peace of Soul* titled "Psychoanalysis and Confession," Sheen compares psychoanalysis to the Catholic sacrament of Penance, the confessing of one's sins to a priest. The opening paragraph gives a sense of Sheen's typical certainty of tone and his conviction that many of society's secular rituals were empty forms if they had no religious foundations:

> A few decades ago, nobody believed in the confession of sins except the Church. Today everyone believes in confession, with this difference: some believe in confessing their own sins; others believe in confessing other people's sins. The popularity of psychoanalysis has nearly convinced everyone of the necessity of some kind of confession for peace of mind. This is another instance of how the world, which threw Christian truths into the wastebasket in the nineteenth century, is pulling them out in isolated, secularized form in the twentieth century, meanwhile deluding itself that it has made a great discovery. The world found out it could not get along without some release for its inner unhappiness. Once it had rejected confession and denied both God and guilt, it had to find a substitute.[24]

To Sheen, psychoanalysis was the perfect example of the secularization of religion: it treated sin as "mental disease" and in its talk of integration of personality put forth no model of health and wholeness as could be found in Jesus Christ. Psychoanalysis, according to Sheen, stopped short of what the confessional offered. In psychoanalysis the patient merely "tells secrets," but "a soul that has confessed its guilt wants an ideal to strive toward—and an ideal more inspiring than 'what everyone approves' in our society. This the confessional offers in the

---

[23] William M. Halsey, *The Survival of American Innocence: Catholicism in an Era of Disillusionment, 1920–1940* (Notre Dame, Indiana: University of Notre Dame Press, 1980), p. 158.

[24] Fulton J. Sheen, *Peace of Soul* (New York: McGraw-Hill Book Company, Inc., 1949), p. 124.

Supreme Example of the Person of Our Lord, Who gives us His grace to amend our lives through sorrow and repentance.''[25] Sheen saw in psychoanalysis the handing over of the individual's responsibility for his or her own life to an authority who did not have the power to make a moral judgment, to forgive and to reconcile, and finally to help effect spiritual transformation. By 1969, however, Sheen seemed to have changed his mind about the pitfalls of psychiatry and he spoke of instituting periodic psychiatric examinations for candidates to the priesthood in the diocese of Rochester.

Fulton Sheen's change of mind about the value of psychoanalysis over a period of twenty years gives us a small clue to other changes that were beginning to take place in the American Catholic church and among its clergy and laity. When he began his radio career in 1930, Sheen was confident of the respect and automatic hearing he would receive from the American Catholic laity. And when the broadcasts of ''Life Is Worth Living'' began in 1951, he could certainly still count on that same respect, as well as the pride that American Catholics felt in his popularity. During these years the greater task was not to convince Catholics of the world view he espoused, but rather to alleviate suspicions that had always lurked in American culture about the theology and the political intentions of the Catholic Church. By 1969, when Sheen resigned as bishop of Rochester, the rumblings were coming from within. Had he offered the parish buildings to the government in 1950, it is difficult to imagine that there would have been such an outcry against the authority of a bishop and there certainly would have been little expectation of previous consultation on the matter on the part of either pastor or parishioners. However, by the late 1960s American Catholics were beginning to question the authority of the church that previously they had accepted with only occasional protests.

Sheen's autobiography, *Treasure in Clay,* which was written shortly before his death, gives us some insights into his last years and how he judged his own life. Sheen could certainly not have been ignorant of the criticisms of him—that he was overly dramatic, impressed with himself, and lived too well—and perhaps it was a knowledge of these things that prompted him to find himself lacking in his willingness to suffer, to be a victim for Christ. He had dressed well, had enjoyed a very comfortable life, and had experienced the adulation and respect of literally millions. ''I loved creature comforts,'' he said. He interpreted the physical suffering (extended illness and open-heart surgery) and the great concern he experienced over the meaning of his life during his last years as a merciful opportunity from God:

> Since I would not take up the Cross, the Lord would lay it on my back as He laid it on Simon of Cyrene, who later came to love it. The cross took two forms: trials *inside* the church and *outside* the Church. Eventually I came to see that the Lord was teaching me not only to be a priest, but also to be a victim.[26]

---

[25] Ibid., p. 140.

[26] Fulton J. Sheen, *Treasure in Clay* (Garden City, New York: Image Books, 1982), p. 339.

Whatever Sheen's personal foibles may have been or his own final assessment of himself, the message he had for Americans was one they wanted to hear. Sheen projected a kind of serenity that had as its basis the certitudes of Neo-Thomism, its view of the universe derived from the tightly reasoned theology of Aquinas. This was not an anti-intellectual kind of certitude that thrived on ignorance; it had its own kind of profundity, but one that required the acceptance of basic premises about the nature of the divine and the human that became more difficult to maintain as the twentieth century wore on. Sheen's understanding of the human was an optimistic one, although not the kind of optimism about human capability that fueled the Social Gospel movement. Sheen saw each human person as sinful but not totally depraved. As William Halsey explains, ''In this system God necessitated man's own perfection. This had the effect of placing man at the center of the universe but not of making him self-centered.''[27] By 1969, and who could have guessed it in 1950, most of the certainties of Catholicism that Sheen had preached appeared to be gone or at least submerged in the chaos of those years, dissipated by the murders of the Kennedys and Martin Luther King, Jr., the bitter disagreement among Americans of all beliefs over our involvement in Vietnam, and the changing understanding of sexual mores with the advent of the Pill. In 1969 Fulton Sheen was seventy-four years old. Both he and his church were in the process of painful changes. But when he died ten years later he was best remembered for the years of certainty, the years of ''Life Is Worth Living.''

◆

[27] Halsey, p. 158.

9

ritual responses to the eternal: worship in american religions

If fifty Americans were asked to set aside for a moment their own particular beliefs and experiences and describe what they thought might be the most typical example of religious worship in America, my guess is that there would be a great deal of agreement about the following: the time, a Sunday morning, and the scene a small white Protestant church with a steeple, set, perhaps, in a small town or in the countryside. The minister conducting the service would be dressed simply, probably in a black robe, possibly adorned with a white cassock and a stole around the neck. The service would open with the singing of hymns, followed by readings from the Old and New Testaments and then the minister's sermon, which would draw upon the Scripture readings for the day. After more hymn singing, the members of the congregation would file out the door, shake the minister's hand, and climb into their cars for the drive home to Sunday dinner. No matter that the population of rural areas and small towns has been declining for years, so that of the 40 percent of Americans who worship weekly the majority are likely to be found in city churches or synagogues. No matter that many Americans, among them Jews and Seventh Day Adventists, do not worship on Sunday. No matter that the religious rituals of millions of Americans are not nearly so simple as that just described above and may not even be conducted in English. The image that persists in the American imagination of the typical religious service is that of a straightforward Sunday-morning Protestant service, conducted in English and focused on the preaching of the Word. It is the picture of American worship that dominates greeting cards and calendars, its only rival for widespread inculcation in the overall culture the heads bowed in prayer around the dinner table that holds the Thanksgiving turkey. And it is the form that has exerted a tremendous pull on American ways of worship, whether European Protestant in origin or not, arising from the impulse to simplify that came from the Reformation conviction that both services and church buildings themselves should be purified of music, words, gestures, and iconic trappings that might distract the worshiper from hearing the Word of God.

No matter how many examples there are to the contrary, the "American" style of worship has long favored a simple, not very ceremonial service conducted on a weekly basis and on special occasions and in which there is no evidence of the "smells and bells" associated with the more complicated and more frequently celebrated rituals of such denominations as Roman Catholicism, high church Episcopalianism, and Eastern churches such as the Greek and Russian Orthodox. There is not much room in the American Protestant tradition of public worship for elaborate vestments, ornate trappings for the altar, processions and pilgrimages, or lengthy liturgies conducted in foreign languages. Nor is the Protestant way of private worship in America one that generally encourages personal aesceticism in the form of fasting and doing penance or rigorously structured forms of prayer that manifest themselves in meditation, "spiritual exercises," or physical exercises designed to quiet the body and the mind in preparation for communion with the divine. American worship in this general sense tends to be an uncomplicated affair, robust and celebrative in nature and goal-oriented, intended to accomplish such things as encouragement for the living of a good moral life and—if the Gallup poll is correct in its findings that most prayers are prayers of petition—the acquiring of material goods, the maintenance of good health, and the sustenance of happy relationships. Even that most volatile and emotion-filled ritual of American religious life, the revival experience, has not been elaborate in nature or characterized by complicated procedures and special garments.

The forms of worship in America have been highly influenced by Protestantism, but worship's place in the life of Americans has also been a product of the separation of church and state. Religious rituals and prayer do not penetrate the fabric of life; they are kept private, that is, confined to the individual or to the celebrations of particular groups. The occasions when public prayer is rendered, such as the opening of Congress or the inauguration of a president, are kept to a minimum, and the prayers offered are usually utterances meant to be as general as possible and acceptable to most Americans, no matter what their specific beliefs might be. The blatant display of one's religious beliefs is not considered appropriate in American culture. The sight of a "prophet" walking the streets is likely to make people laugh or to make them nervous and annoyed; they do not take it as typical and reasonable behavior. Religious groups whose members go door to door proselytizing or who sing in the streets or sell things in airports are more likely to meet a hostile response than a friendly or encouraging one. The controversy over whether prayers can be said in public schools is a good example of the very high value that Americans place on not imposing particular beliefs on other people and not putting anyone in a situation where they are forced to participate in prayer or worship rituals that they would not choose to participate in on their own. This virtual exclusion of any forms of worship from the public arena assures Americans that neither the government nor any particular religious group will foster one way of being religious over another; it is a product of the "disestablishment" clause of the First Amendment. But this same privatization of worship also means that we don't know very much about one another's ways of worshiping. There is no religious ritual, outside of such exercises, perhaps, as prayers before meals and bedtime, that is common knowledge to all Americans, unless it be the rituals of the civil religion, the religion of Americanness, which emerge through the celebrations of national holidays such as Memorial Day, the Fourth of July, Labor Day, and Thanksgiving. Most people, however, would not recognize these celebrations as religious rituals and, in fact, would be inclined to deny that they are.

Having said all of these things that make it sound as though religious worship must certainly play a very minimal part in the lives of Americans, it is necessary to repeat that almost half attend religious services on a regular basis, and, whether they participate or not, most consider private prayer and communal worship "a good thing." Just as Dwight Eisenhower admonished that it didn't matter what religious faith Americans espoused as long as they believed something, so, too, Americans are reminded in spot ads broadcast by radio and television stations throughout the country that they should "worship at the church or synagogue of your choice." Of the Americans who do not worship on a regular basis, we need not conclude that they never attend services or that they do not worship in some way on their own. Some go irregularly and others attend on Christian feasts such as Christmas and Easter or the Jewish high holy days, Rosh Hashanah, the New Year, and Yom Kippur, the Day of Atonement (Eric Mendelsohn, the architect of Mount Zion Temple in St. Paul, allowed for this reality and designed his synagogues so that partitioned-off spaces could be easily put into use for days of heavy attendance). Leo Rosten identifies another group of Americans who call themselves the "unchurched" and who choose not to identify themselves with any organized religion. They do so out of conviction, not indifference, and prefer to give expression to their beliefs about ultimate reality in a private, nonritualistic way rather than through communal worship. Two such groups are the Society for Ethical Culture and the American Humanist Association.[1]

With these general statements about the form and the place of worship in the overall American culture, it is time to look briefly at the nature of worship itself, as well as those occasions that are considered appropriate for a ritualized expression of belief. Evelyn Underhill, a British scholar, called worship "the response of the creature to the Eternal," which implies that worship and the ritual behavior that accompanies it have a great deal to say about how human beings understand the relationship between the human and the divine, the temporal and the eternal, the

---

[1] *Religions of America,* ed. Leo Rosten (New York: Simon and Schuster, 1975), pp. 255–62.

profane and the sacred, the material and the spiritual, or, to put it very generally, between two different levels of reality.[2] We are correct in assuming, then, a direct and illuminating connection between religious beliefs and the various forms of worship that proceed from them. The rituals associated with worship provide a graphic illustration, in words and actions, of the acting out of the beliefs of a religion, those basic understandings a group of people hold about "the way things are."

What, specifically, are some of the things we can learn about the worship practices of religious groups by studying their patterns of communal celebration and the forms that their rituals take? First, if we know the occasions upon which and the frequency with which communal worship takes place—daily or more often, weekly, on special feasts or at particular times of the year, or to mark rites of passage such as birth, the achieving of adulthood, marriage, and death—we have a good idea of what aspects of life and which times a group holds to be so important that its connections with the sacred and the eternal must be celebrated. Once we know that in most Protestant denominations worship takes place once a week, that Mass is celebrated daily or more often in Catholic churches, that Jews seek a daily *minyan,* or quorum of ten for worship in the synagogue, that Muslims pray five times a day, we begin to realize that the frequency with which worship is held varies greatly among religions.

We also need to look at what constitutes the central focus of the worship. It may be the celebration of the Eucharist or "communion," as is the case with the Roman Catholic or Episcopalian Mass. Among Catholics the Eucharist is celebrated daily and in most urban Episcopal churches at least twice weekly. In other Christian denominations the Eucharist might not be so central to worship. Many Presbyterians have communion once a month, and many Baptists only quarterly. In these churches and many others in America, the Scripture readings and particularly the sermon are the most important part of the ritual. In some denominations there may be no obvious focus in the service, no one central point. For example, many Quaker meetings appear highly unstructured to the outside observer. Generally speaking, those traditions that emphasize the Eucharist are referred to as "sacramental" or "liturgical," and those that stress a simpler service with emphasis on preaching the Word instead of celebration of a sacred meal are called "nonliturgical."

Through a study of worship patterns, we develop an appreciation for the fact that ritual behavior is heavy with theological and metaphysical meaning. The words that are said and the actions that are performed at a weekly service, a baptism, funeral, or wedding tell us not only how the members of a religious group behave on a particular occasion, what they say and do, but they also give us a glimpse of the world view that the group espouses. Take funeral rituals as a specific example. In America, the actual preparation and disposal of the body of the deceased is, of course, not only a matter for religious concern, but of interest to

---

[2] Quoted in Lionel L. Mitchell, *The Meaning of Ritual* (New York: Paulist Press, 1977), p. 1.

health departments as well. Thus, not all of those preparations for burial or cremation have a religious significance, as they once had in other times and cultures
when death was totally the concern of the family. Nonetheless, those rituals
associated with death and carried out by various religious groups tell us a great
deal—what the believers hold to be true about the nature of the human; whether
or not the dead person is assumed to continue in another existence; what relationship that person will have to the divine; what might be the obligations of those still
living to the one who has died in order to ensure eternal rest; what is appropriately
done with the body. We're not just finding out about funeral customs; we are getting some sense of the world view that underlies the entire belief system.

An examination of most Protestant funeral rituals would reveal the assumption that the dead person has been united with God, whereas the Roman Catholic
funeral Mass, with its repeated prayers for eternal rest for the deceased, makes it
clear that Catholics believe in the possibility of further penance for sins after the
death of the body and before eternal union with the divine. In both systems,
however, which posit a body/soul dualism, the emphasis is on a kind of spiritual
existence in the afterlife, and there are many different interpretations of what that
might mean. Mormonism, on the other hand, which tends to blur the distinction
between spirit and matter, gives us another view of death and the afterlife, not as a
time of eternal rest but one of activity, much like earthly activity, which endures in
eternity. In fact, the Mormon view of eternity is not that of timelessness, but of an
endless extension of time. Mormonism holds that earthly relationships such as
marriage persist after death and also that the spiritual status of the individual can
be affected by those still on earth. Thus, Mormons engage in temple ceremonies
in which living persons are baptized in the names of those already dead, thereby
making them Mormons in the afterlife. Many Native American funeral rituals
emphasize the Indian belief that the deceased has set out on a journey to another
life, a passage that may take three or four days, and for which the body must be
prepared. It is the living who must make the preparations for the dead, and it is
also incumbent upon those who are left to preserve the memory of the person
among the living. Among the Ojibwa, or Chippewa, when the body was taken
from the home for burial, it was removed through the window rather than taken
out the door, to prevent the possibility that the door might slam behind the coffin,
thereby wiping out the memories in that household of the one who had died. The
Ojibwa believe, also, that the spirit of an ancestor lives on until the last person who
knew him or her chooses to forget that person. American Jews do not embalm
their dead, nor do they permit cremation or autopsies, unless it is legally
necessary. Thus, the body is buried very quickly, usually the day after death. This
practice proceeds from the Jewish belief that there will be a resurrection of the
bodies of the righteous at the coming of the Messiah. The belief in literal resurrection of the body is not common any longer, especially among Reform Jews, but
the practice of no embalming and early burial prevails nonetheless.

Third, a study of ritual behavior makes clear to us the many different ways
in which believers work out what forms of worship are most appropriate to their

theological systems—preaching, singing, dancing, wearing special robes, blessing with incense, ringing of bells. I have already emphasized that the dominant forms of worship in America have been relatively simple out of a conviction that the ceremonial elements of the rite must not distract from the primary purpose of worship—to "hear" the Word of God and to celebrate God's covenant with humankind. The question becomes, then, what is distracting and what is enhancing? The answer differs from religion to religion, but as believers come to grips with which forms of expression are appropriate for worship and which are not, the words, songs, and gestures associated with worship take on a moral quality—it is "right" to sing or say or do certain things in the church or the synagogue and "not right" to make use of others.

Music provides a good example of this fact. American Puritans sang in "plain song" and without musical accompaniment. Welcome as it was in their homes, instrumental music at meeting reminded the Puritans too much of the ceremonies of Roman Catholicism and Anglicanism, against which they had protested and had left behind. The Moravians, on the other hand, who came to America from Bohemia in the eighteenth century, built churches with organs and formed trombone choirs for use in worship services. The Moravians also contributed some of the first composers in the history of American music, John Frederich Peter and John Antes among them. It has been said that the Moravian trombone choirs provided the origin of the jazz funeral processions in New Orleans, but that may be an apocryphal story. Jewish congregations in the nineteenth century argued over whether or not an organ was appropriate for use in the synagogue, and in the 1960s there were many intense discussions about guitar music in churches. Dance has never played much of a part in the worship services of most American religions of European origins. Most contemporary attempts to introduce liturgical dance into worship services are likely to be met with nervous laughter rather than genuine appreciation. There have, however, been religious groups in America that have made use of sacred dance rituals, among them most Indian tribes and the American Shakers. The use of incense, the ringing of bells, and the wearing of vestments are usually confined, as has already been mentioned, to the more liturgically oriented denominations, whose rituals are highly regulated by the guidelines of the denomination for worship and are not a matter of arbitrary choice for either clergy or laity. Other denominations are more casual and informal in their regulation of ritual, but there may be unwritten laws to which members adhere.

As in every other aspect of religion in American life, worship customs, although having been influenced by Puritan Protestantism, are nonetheless endlessly diverse. But there are two points of a common nature that I'd like to emphasize: first, that what is considered appropriate in worship by any group is directly tied to its theology, even though the believers may have lost a sense of exactly what the connection is; and, second, that the forms of worship within a religious group are heavily laden with emotional meaning and with the weight of long-standing tradition. ("We have always done it this way and this is the way

God wants it to be.'') Making changes in ritual in most groups is a lengthy, difficult, and delicate matter. This leads to a final point about what we can learn from a study of different forms of worship in America—some factors that bring about changes in worship and how people react to those changes.

We have already seen some of the changes in ritual that Isaac Meyer Wise initiated in his attempt to put together a *Minhag America,* a guide for worship that would be suited to Jewish life in America. We recall, also, that the changes in ritual aroused so much antagonism in the synagogue Wise served in Albany that a split occurred in the congregation. Further, by the beginning of the twentieth century, many of the changes in worship adopted by even the most enthusiastic of Reform congregations had been modified in a return to a renewed emphasis on Hebrew and traditional customs. One hundred years after Wise's efforts in Reform Judaism, the Episcopal Church in America was debating two issues basic to the way the church conducted its worship—the ordination of women to the priesthood and changes in the *Book of Common Prayer* that would make the book more complex and twice as long as the previous version and offer alternatives to the Eucharistic service that stressed a mood of thanksgiving rather than of penance. Both changes were instituted in 1979 after debate at two national conventions, but not without much bitterness and unhappiness on the part of some members as well as the withdrawal of some congregations from the national organization. The ordination of women has prompted some male priests to leave the Episcopal Church, some of whom have been received into the Roman Catholic Church.

The point of these two examples is to show that changes are indeed made, but the old ways die hard. The rituals that might seem outmoded or empty repetitions of meaningless acts to the outsider have an intensely strong hold on those who practice them. Sometimes, however, the rituals do become empty—they lose their power to move and to instruct. One good example is the Sacrament of Penance, called ''Confession,'' in the Roman Catholic Church. Fewer than twenty years ago most American Catholics went to confession with great regularity, often every other week, a ritual that involved an examination of conscience, telling one's sins to a priest in a structure in the church called a confessional (a screen shielded the penitent from the confessor in order to ensure privacy), making a ''firm purpose of amendment'' to try to sin no more, and receiving absolution for sin through the priest. After Vatican II Catholics began to find less and less spiritual satisfaction in this ritual—it had become formulaic and without the power to move one to a true examination of the state of one's soul. They voted upon its efficacy with their feet—they stayed away. The modified ritual, now called the Sacrament of Reconciliation, may still be a private confession of sin to a priest, but it may also take the form of a face-to-face discussion of one's spiritual status with a priest or even a general penance service that includes many people; in all cases, absolution is given. The essential components of the sacrament did not change, but the form of the ritual was modified to meet a changing understanding of what the sacrament meant—a vehicle of reconciliation to God rather than of judgment and condemnation.

Up to this point the chapter has emphasized forms of worship in America that are chiefly of a communal nature, but Americans also engage in private prayer and devotions, some denominations encouraging such practices more than others. These include a daily reading of the Bible or the *Siddur,* the Jewish prayer book; attendance at daily Mass or the saying of the rosary; meditation, often with a Scriptural reading as a basis; the saying of meal prayers and morning and evening prayers; fasting, and doing good works out of a conviction that religious belief and worship both must have their natural consequence in action that benefits the world and one's fellow human beings. We also see examples in American culture of rituals with religious origins, such as fasting, meditating, and yoga, that have become secularized, that is, deprived of their obvious religious content, and used in order to foster good physical and mental health. The rituals we will now look at in detail—a Lutheran Sunday service, a Catholic baptism, a Jewish Bat Mitzvah, and an Ojibwa wake service—all are communal in nature, that is, they take place in the company of a number of worshipers, but they have import for the individual as well. The Sunday worship service, the weekly gathering or its equivalent that is the undergirding of religious worship in American culture, is an affirmation of the identity of the group and of its members' desire as "creatures" to "respond to the Eternal." It is also the opportunity for the individual worshiper to say publicly, "This is the religion to which I belong, and I wish to derive spiritual sustenance from participation in its rituals in the company of other believers." The baptism, the Bat Mitzvah, and the wake all mark the passage of an individual from one state to another, journeys that the particular religions consider to be of great significance and appropriately celebrated by means of prescribed rituals and in the company of other worshipers. There are two things to keep in mind when reading about these rituals. First, a description of a ritual in words cannot begin to convey the power that it exerts over the worshiper and even over the observer, who may be present only to try to understand how members of a particular group act out those beliefs that are central to their identity. Second, any religious ritual occurs not as an isolated event but within a particular context. The ritual events are revealing of the beliefs of the groups, but they also are likely to tell us something about factors of ethnic or racial heritage, the history of the group during its time in America, and the way members understand themselves and their religion in relationship to other religious movements in America and to American culture as a whole.

SUNDAY-MORNING WORSHIP
IN A LUTHERAN CHURCH

As I walked into a Lutheran Church with my neighbors on a Sunday morning, I couldn't help remembering the bad old days when the relationship between American Lutherans and Catholics was not as cordial as it is now. As a child raised in the Roman Catholic tradition, I nonetheless attended the many confirmations, weddings, and funerals of my mother's large Missouri Synod Lutheran family. In the very recent past, Catholics were admonished not to attend the services of other religions without good reason, the celebrations of relatives being one of them, and if they did attend not to participate in the service itself. I remember my mother saying, ''You don't have to sing''—we didn't know the hymns anyway—''but I want you to stand and sit at the right times. I don't want my children looking like lumps.'' I have no memory of family ''difficulties'' caused by my parents' different religions—instead an elaborate protocol prevailed among the members of both extended families—but as was typical of the times, and, perhaps of children, I was very attuned to the differences in the Catholic and Lutheran services. Now, many years later, I am struck by the similarities. The Lutheran church in Minneapolis to which I refer has a strong Norwegian background among its members, although they ''let in a few Germans,'' my neighbor has joked. It is a member of the American Lutheran Church, one of the three large Lutheran bodies, the others the Lutheran Church in America and the Lutheran Church–Missouri Synod, which together include 95 percent of the Lutherans in the United States.[3] Liturgically, the Lutherans represent middle ground, having more elaborate and more frequent rituals than denominations such as Congregationalism or Presbyterianism, but fewer than Catholics, Episcopalians, Greek Orthodox, or Conservative and Orthodox Jews. On this particular Sunday we see a good example of the middle ground of Lutheranism.

It is not a communion Sunday. Communion is held on the first Sunday of the month; members who wish to receive communion every Sunday may do so in a small chapel between the main services. The liturgy has as its focus the singing of hymns, the reading of Scripture, and the sermon. There are two ministers on the altar, the senior pastor and a retired pastor, who will give the sermon. Both are dressed in long white albs with green stoles around their necks (green is the liturgical color of hope) and thus more elaborately robed than their counterpart at the United Church of Christ a few blocks away and in fewer vestments than the Catholic priest who is saying Mass in another neighborhood church. Just before the service begins, the retired pastor announces that it is the senior pastor's birthday, and the congregation sings ''Happy Birthday'' to him.

One way to describe this Sunday-morning worship is simply to give the order of service, which opens with a hymn, ''Guide Me Ever, Great Redeemer,'' sung to a melody composed in the eighteenth century. Next comes the Hymn of Praise or Gloria, sung together by the minister and the congregation, which begins, ''Glory to God in the Highest, and peace to his people on earth.'' After the Gloria the minister and the congregation recite together the Prayer of the Day, which appears not in the book of worship, but in the weekly bulletin:

> Almighty and everlasting God, you are always more ready to hear than we are to pray, and to give more than we either desire or deserve. Pour upon us the abun-

---

[3] The American Lutheran Church and the Lutheran Church in America have agreed to merge by 1988 along with the Association of Evangelical Lutheran Churches, making the resulting denomination the fourth largest Protestant group in America after the Southern Baptists, the United Methodists, and the National Baptists. The Lutheran Church—Missouri Synod, with more than two and a half million members, has not taken part in the merger discussions.

dance of your mercy, forgiving us those things of which our conscience is afraid, and giving us those good things for which we are not worthy to ask, except through the merit of your Son, Jesus Christ our Lord. Amen.

This communal prayer is followed by readings from the Bible, the Old and New Testaments. On this particular morning, the retired pastor gives the sermon "Praise and Thanksgiving," which he bases on Psalm 34:1–8, "I will praise the Lord continually. . . ." The hymn that follows echoes the theme of the sermon and of the whole service, "Let all things now living / A song of thanksgiving / To God the creator triumphantly raise." Next is the recitation of the creed, sometimes the Nicene Creed (devised by the Council of Nicaea, which was called by the Emperor Constantine in A.D. 325 to foster church unity), but this morning we hear a shorter version, the Apostles' Creed, which sums up the beliefs of western Christianity in a trinitarian deity, in the redemption of human sin by Jesus Christ and his founding of a church, in Jesus' second coming, a final judgment and the resurrection of the body:

> *I believe in God the Father almighty,*
> *creator of heaven and earth.*
>
> *I believe in Jesus Christ, his only Son, our Lord.*
> *He was conceived by the power of the Holy Spirit*
> *and born of the virgin Mary.*
> *He suffered under Pontius Pilate,*
> *was crucified, died, and was buried.*
> *He descended into hell.*
> *On the third day he rose again.*
> *He ascended into heaven,*
> *and is seated at the right hand of the Father.*
> *He will come again to judge the living and the dead.*
>
> *I believe in the Holy Spirit,*
> *the holy catholic church* [''catholic'' here means ''universal'']
> *the communion of saints,*
> *the forgiveness of sins,*
> *the resurrection of the body,*
> *and the life everlasting, Amen.*[4]

Because there is no communion today, the Offertory, or Offering, which includes a collection of money from the congregation used for the maintenance of the church and its various missions, is followed by a series of short prayers "for the whole church, the nations, those in need, the parish, special concerns," and the Lord's Prayer. The minister blesses the congregation, raising his hand in the sign of the cross, and prays:

---

[4] Lutheran Book of Worship (Minneapolis, Minnesota: Augsburg Publishing House, 1978).

The Lord bless you and keep you.
The Lord make his face shine on you
and be gracious to you.
The Lord look upon you with favor
and give you peace.

After singing "O God, Our Help in Ages Past," the congregation leaves the church. The service has taken about an hour.

Describing a worship service such as this is one thing, but giving some idea of what it means to those assembled is another. These American Lutherans, many of Scandinavian descent, have come together on Sunday morning out of a double conviction: that it is right and necessary to worship the God they believe in and that it is incumbent upon them to do so together on what is for them the Sabbath, thereby obeying one of the Ten Commandments, "Remember thou keep holy the Sabbath." The designation on the bulletin that this is the "twelfth Sunday after Pentecost" (Pentecost occurs in the Christian calendar on the Sunday following the Ascension of Jesus into heaven forty days after Easter) tells us that the significance of this Sunday derives not from the fact that it is in August, but from its place in the church year, which proceeds in cyclical rather than linear fashion, sacred time rather than profane. The order of service reveals an interweaving of those prayers, hymns, and Scripture readings that change every week with those that remain the same, such as the Gloria, the Creed, and the Lord's Prayer. Perhaps the most "Lutheran" aspect of the service itself is the Prayer of the Week quoted previously, which places great emphasis on God's grace freely given and none on "works," or the need to make an effort to earn divine grace. In other respects, except for the absence of communion, the service would be highly familiar to both Catholics and Episcopalians. The very fact that the service is in English motivates us to remember that such was not always the case. When the church was founded as a Norwegian Lutheran Church in 1894, services and Sunday School were conducted in Norwegian. In this way the congregation is like many others of various denominations in America that were founded by a particular ethnic group, each one joking along the lines that "God understands only prayers in Norwegian . . . or Polish . . . or German." The service itself, however, does not convey that the Norwegian identity of the congregation is still very strong. Nor is there any way to discern from a description of the service the feeling of fellowship that prevails within the congregation. Members know and greet one another before entering church; visitors are asked to wear name tags so that people can introduce themselves. The departure from the service is slow because there are renewed greetings and conversations with the minister as well. The obvious affection with which members reacted to the retired minister's sermon and to news of the senior pastor's birthday reveal a strong sense of community among clergy and members of the congregation. The weekly bulletin makes clear that members are likely to encounter one another on days other than Sunday at choir practice, in a deacons' meeting, at a divorce recovery group, an Alcoholics Anonymous meeting, or a gathering of a group that visits at the state prison. Studied carefully, what appears to be an "ordinary" Sunday worship service in a mainstream Protestant church reveals itself to be a repository of theology and history. It contains within it the study of ancient church councils and a Reformation as well as highly contemporary decisions about how Lutherans in America should worship. The service and the congregation have their story to tell about Christianity in general, about Lutherans in particular, and even more specifically about Lutherans in America with their various synods and ethnic groups and the history of their worship.

BAPTISM IN ROMAN CATHOLICISM

When a child is born or adopted into a practicing Roman Catholic family, one of the important tasks during the first few months is to make arrangements for the baptism and to choose two sponsors, or godparents, who will take responsibility for the child's upbringing as a Catholic should the parents ever be unable to do so. Baptism, the sacrament of initiation into the Christian community, is one of seven sacraments in Roman Catholicism, the others being penance, eucharist, confirmation, matrimony, holy orders (ordination to the priesthood), and the anointing of the sick (formerly called *extreme unction,* administered to those near death). For Catholics these sacraments are outward or visible signs of inward spiritual transformation, of the infusion of divine grace and a change in spiritual status. Baptism is the first of the sacraments. Without it Catholics cannot receive the others, and proof of baptism in the form of baptismal certificate must be supplied when the time comes to receive other sacraments. For example, a Catholic cannot enter what the Church considers a valid marriage recognized by the Church without having been baptized. The Catholic Church finds support for its emphasis on baptism in the New Testament, in Jesus' being baptized by John the Baptist and in various passages that admonish the need for baptism in "water and the Holy Spirit," and in the teachings of church councils, among them the Council of Trent (1547), which declared that baptism is necessary for salvation. Among Catholics it is the custom to baptize infants by the pouring of water over the forehead rather than by immersion. The sacrament of confirmation, usually administered during adolescence, is in a sense a second baptism at which time the recipient reaffirms those vows and commitments that were made for him or her in infancy.

Most Catholic baptisms take place on a Sunday and are performed by a priest. Because of the importance, however, that Catholics place on baptism, an infant who is in danger of death can be baptized immediately by a layperson. Most often the parents and godparents bring the baby to church to be baptized either during Mass or in an early-afternoon service during which several babies are baptized. It is becoming more customary for baptisms to take place during Mass so that the whole congregation can witness the baptism of its new member, and those present are asked to renew their own baptismal vows. Sometimes the priest holds up the baby for all to see or carries the baby down the church aisles, saying, in effect, "This is our newest member; celebrate with the family." The baptismal ceremony itself is fairly brief, but it is a gold mine of words and gestures that reveal Catholic beliefs particularly about human nature, about the interrelationship between the material and the spiritual worlds, and about the reality of evil. The ceremony, as it is performed in most American Catholic churches, is divided into five parts: (1) a greeting and asking of questions; (2) Scriptural readings and prayers; (3) prayer of exorcism and the anointing; (4) the actual baptism, which includes the blessing of water, the renunciation of sin and profession of faith, the baptism itself, the anointing with chrism (holy oil), the clothing with a white garment, and the lighting of a candle, and (5) a conclusion in which those present say the Lord's Prayer and the priest blesses the mother, the father, and all those present. Some of these parts are either omitted or shortened if the ceremony is held during Mass.

The ceremony begins with the celebrant's greeting and his questions to the parents and godparents:

> **Celebrant** : *What name do you give your child?*
> **Parents** : *Elizabeth.*
> **Celebrant** : *What do you ask of God's Church for Elizabeth?*
> **Parents** : *Baptism.*
> **Celebrant** : *Elizabeth, the Christian community welcomes you with great joy. In its name I claim you for Christ our Savior by the sign of the Cross. I now trace the Cross on your forehead, and invite your parents to do the same.*[5]

After the Scriptural readings and prayers and the Prayer of Exorcism and the anointing, we enter the heart of the ceremony. It begins with the blessing of the baptismal water by the priest, a blessing by which the water becomes other than ordinary water. The following prayer of blessing is lengthy, but it is helpful for us to see the intense affirmation not only of the power that water holds as a symbol of spiritual life, but also of the history of that symbol in the teachings and traditions of Catholicism. It is also a kind of encapsulated lesson of how Catholics understand the relationship between the things of the earth and the spiritual realities for which they stand:

> *Father, you give us grace through sacramental signs, which*
>   *tell us of the wonders of your unseen power.*
> *In baptism we use your gift of water, which you have made a rich*
>   *symbol of the grace you give us in this sacrament.*
> *At the very dawn of creation your Spirit breathed on the waters,*
>   *making them the wellspring of all holiness.*

---

[5] "The New Rite of Baptism for Children." This is a pamphlet distributed in many parishes across the country. It contains no publication information. The quotations following are also taken from this source.

The waters of the great flood you made a sign of the waters of
baptism, that make an end of sin and a new beginning of
goodness.
Through the waters of the Red Sea you led Israel out of slavery,
to be an image of God's holy people, set free from sin
by baptism.
In the waters of the Jordon your son was baptized of John and
anointed with the spirit.
Your Son willed that water and blood should flow from his side as
he hung upon the cross.
After his resurrection he told his disciples: "Go out and teach all
nations, baptizing them in the name of the Father, and of the
Son, and of the Holy Spirit."
Father, look now with love upon your Church, and unseal for her
the fountain of baptism.
By the power of the Spirit give to the water of this font the
grace of your Son.
You created man in your own likeness: cleanse him from sin in a
new birth to innocence by the water and the Spirit.

The priest touches the water with his right hand and asks for God's blessing upon
it. During the Renunciation of Sin and Profession of Faith the celebrant reminds
the parents and godparents of their responsibility to bring up the child in the practice of Catholicism, to "see that the divine life which God gave her is kept safe
from the poison of sin, to grow always stronger in her heart." Next, the celebrant
asks of the parents and godparents, "Do you reject Satan . . . and all his
works . . . and all his empty promises?" after which the parents and godparents
make a profession of faith by reciting the Apostle's Creed almost word for word
the version recited by the Lutherans in their Sunday worship. Now it is time for
the baptism itself:

Celebrant : *Is it your will that Elizabeth should be baptized in the faith of the*
Church, which we have all professed with you?
Parents and
Godparents : *It is.*
Celebrant : *While pouring the water on the forehead of the child, the celebrant*
says, "Elizabeth, I baptize you in the name of the Father, and of the
Son, and of the Holy Spirit."

Finally, the baby is anointed with holy oil, and then a white garment is placed over
her while the celebrant says, "Elizabeth, you have become a new creation, and
have clothed yourself in Christ. See in this white garment the outward sign of your
Christian dignity. With your family and friends to help you by word and example,
bring that dignity unstained into the everlasting life of heaven." The father or

godfather then lights a candle to symbolize that the newly baptized baby is a child of the light rather than of the darkness.

Traditional Catholicism teaches that once the baby is baptized her spiritual status has changed—her baptism is a sign of this change. She is now a member of the worshiping community and a child of the light. There has been a change in the understanding of baptism in the American Catholic Church since Vatican II, from an emphasis on the more negative aspects of the sacrament to an interpretation of baptism as the sacrament of initiation as inclusion. As recently as the mid-1960s most Catholics who were asked about the meaning of baptism were likely to say that it "washes away the stain of original sin" or that it "releases the soul from the power of Satan." Contemporary Catholics have not lost the sense of connection between baptism and a belief in the Fall and in the reality of evil, but the ritual gestures and the prayers—the emphasis on newness, on innocence, on spiritual potential rather than debility—show a greater interest on the part of the Church and its members on what the sacrament "means" or signifies, the reality to which it points, rather than on what it "does," thereby reducing the danger, always present in any ritual, that the sacrament will take on a kind of magical quality and as a result become empty of the purpose for which it was intended—to point to a reality beyond itself and to affirm the faith and the hope of the community.

A JEWISH GIRL'S BAT MITZVAH

She had always been one of the little girls in the neighborhood, old enough now to be in junior high school and to babysit for our children. But she looked as if she had matured several years overnight as she entered the sanctuary of the temple with two rabbis and the cantor, ascended the *bimah,* and opened the doors to the ark that holds the Torah scrolls in their blue velvet covers. Thus began Julie's Bat Mitzvah, five months after her thirteenth birthday. Today was the day she "ascended to the Torah" for the first time and read and sang in Hebrew and English before her family, many of whom had come long distances for the celebration. Her friends and her parents' friends were gathered, too, both Jews and Gentiles, to see Julie become Bat Mitzvah, "a daughter of the commandment."

The history of the Bar Mitzvah, the coming of age for Jewish boys, and the Bat Mitzvah, the equivalent ritual for girls, is fairly recent, dating from nineteenth-century Jewish legal codes. According to the *Encyclopedia Judaica,* the ceremony for girls had its origin in France and Italy and quickly spread to other countries. The actual form of the ceremony may differ from synagogue to synagogue, from having the young girl say public prayers to conducting a less public celebration, or a group celebration, in the religious school or even at home.[6] Orthodox Jews in America celebrate the Bar Mitzvah, but not the Bat Mitzvah,

---

[6] "Bar Mitzvah, Bat Mitzvah," *Encyclopedia Judaica Jerusalem,* 1971, pp. 243–47.

although there might be some kind of ritual marking of girls' coming of age. Conservative and Reform congregations both conduct Bat Mitzvahs, and their popularity has increased with the contemporary feminist movement, which has questioned the very small role in religious ritual historically held by women, whether Christian or Jewish. Whether for boys or girls, this is the ceremony not only of physical coming of age in Judaism but of legal maturity as well, for after the ritual is completed the boy or girl is obligated to carry out the laws of Judaism.

Traditionally, obligations for men and women have differed, with women subject to negative laws (prohibitions against certain kinds of behavior) but not to positive laws (the duty to perform certain acts), which would necessarily take them outside the home. In recent times, particularly with the ordination of women rabbis in the Reform congregations, Jews, like members of most other religions in America, are grappling with the question of women's roles in religious ritual. Whatever the form that the Bar Mitzvah or Bat Mitzvah takes, it is impossible to think of a religious ritual in which a Christian child, Protestant or Catholic, has so much public and individual responsibility at a worship service. Preparation takes the form of many years of religious school, learning about the history and the traditions of Judaism, and of Hebrew school, in which the student learns to read and translate Hebrew. Because the coming-of-age ceremony seems to be so much the culmination, the end, of all these years of study, the candidates for Bar Mitzvah and Bat Mitzvah are warned that they must not see this celebration as the end of their studies but rather as an embarkation upon a more adult way of being a Jew.

In Julie's case, the Bat Mitzvah took place in a Reform temple as an individual ceremony that lasted about an hour and a half and was conducted in both Hebrew and English (in a Conservative synagogue, the ritual might have lasted three hours and there would have been much more Hebrew). Three themes dominated the service that were obvious to the observer: First was the affirmation of Jewish identity and tradition, along with the centrality of the reading of the Torah in Jewish ritual. Second was the strong emphasis on family bonds and of the passing of the Jewish heritage from generation to generation. Third was the frequent mention of the freedom to worship that Jews experience in America, this note underscored by the fact the Julie had chosen to ''share'' her Bat Mitzvah with a thirteen-year-old girl in Russia who was not legally permitted to have a Bat Mitzvah of her own. Because the ceremony was held on a Saturday morning it was incorporated into the Sabbath service. It was Julie's privilege and responsibility on this day to read the Torah portion and the prophetic reading. When the time came for her to begin, there was no mistaking the importance of the moment. Julie stood in front of the ark: ''Dear God, I am standing here in my temple before my family and friends about to become a Bat Mitzvah. . . .'' She prayed to be worthy; she prayed for the health and happiness of her family and she prayed that there might be an end to war, to world hunger and to assassination, this young girl coming of age during a time in history when news of assassinations and war are commonplace. After her prayer, Julie lifted the heavy scroll out of the ark and handed it to the rabbi. He held it aloft for the congregation to see and then interepreted its significance for the Jewish people:

> *This is our Torah; this is our banner.*
> *By it our ancestors lived; for it they often died.*
> *Herein is contained the history of our people;*
>
> *Herein is contained the quest of our people for the living God;*
> *Herein is contained the way that one should live;*
>
> *This is our Torah.*
> *Throughout the ages it was transmitted from generation to generation*
>   *that each generation might know it,*
>   *might cherish it,*
>   *might make it its own.*
>
> *And on this Sabbath as Julie becomes a Bat Mitzvah, once more do we*
> *transmit the Torah from generation to generation. We hand it down*
> *from the grandparents to the parents, from the parents to their daughter.* [7]

When the rabbi finished speaking, Julie's grandparents and parents came up to the platform that holds the ark. They had already joined Julie in the saying of prayers in Hebrew and English, and now in acting out the rabbi's words, they passed the Torah, the symbol of identity for the Jewish people, from the grandparents to the parents to Julie. Now a Bat Mitzvah, Julie moved to the lectern to do her reading.

The rabbi explained that Julie's reading came from the twenty-sixth chapter of Deuteronomy, the fifth book of the Tanakh, as Jews call it, or the Pentateuch, as Christians refer to it. This passage tells of Moses' admonition to the Jews as they are about to enter the promised land that they must give the "first fruits" of their land and their labor to God and that they must give part of their gain to the Levites, members of the priestly tribe who have no land of their own, and to the poor. It was Julie's task not only to read the passage but to sing parts of it in Hebrew as well, to translate it, and then to explain it. The theme of the passage is gratitude for survival and for good fortune, and it is upon the meaning of "gratitude" that Julie concentrated as she explained her reading. She related not only the "story" of the passage but also the historical context of this part of Deuteronomy, the entering of the Israelites into the land of Caanan. Then she related the message of the reading to her own life as a Jew in America. She recounted the history of religious persecution in her family, of her mother's grandparents, who left Russia for freedom of religious expression; of her father's grandparents, two of whom escaped Germany when Hitler came to power and two who did not survive a concentration camp. It was obvious that she had given much

---

[7] Rabbi Max Shapiro at the Bat Mitzvah of Julie Rothschild, Temple Israel, Minneapolis, Minnesota, September 4, 1982.

thought to what it means to be a Jew in America, to be free to celebrate a Bat Mitzvah. She contrasted her life with that of the young girl in Russia who is her counterpart, a thirteen-year-old whose parents lost their jobs after applying for papers to leave Russia for Israel. Julie prayed that she would not ever take for granted her happy and secure life in a loving family and the freedom that she has to practice Judaism. It was only when she thanked her cat, Snookers, for keeping her company and sleeping at the foot of her bed that the congregation was moved to remember that thirteen is not so old after all, and that the legacy of concern that American Jews carry from their histories of persecution can be a weighty yet inevitable burden for one so young.

The Bat Mitzvah ceremony ended with the rabbi's words of congratulations to Julie and his reminder that she must live a life that will make her family and friends grateful to know her. Her parents conveyed their own words of pride and love and helped her to put the Torah scroll back into its blue cover. Julie placed the scroll back into the ark and closed the doors. After memorial prayers for the dead, the Sabbath ritual also drew to a close. The relatives and friends gathered for a meal in celebration of the event, moved by the expression of a young girl's sense of her religious heritage, her gratitude for the opportunity to display her beliefs openly, and her efforts to take upon herself both the privileges and the responsibilities of the Jewish tradition as it has been shaped by the American experience.

OJIBWA WAKE SERVICE

The three rituals I have thus far described come from religious traditions with long, uninterrupted histories in the United States, subject, of course, to cultural influence, waxing and waning of membership, and changes in theological understanding. The Ojibwa wake service, a "watch" over the body of a deceased person, comes from a religious system that was nearly wiped out of American culture. As it is practiced in its present form by Ojibwa (designated as Chippewa by the United States government), who are Roman Catholics on the Red Lake reservation in northern Minnesota, the ritual reveals a combination of Indian and Catholic religious traditions regarding the dead. It is an Indian Catholic ritual, said the Ojibwa woman who described it for me, not Indian *and* Catholic; and it is fruitless to try to say whether it is more Catholic or more Indian, for the Ojibwa language does not provide for either/or constructions. The woman, too, considers herself an Indian Catholic, the product of Ojibwa culture and Catholicism. She has been trained in a degree program specializing in liturgics at a Catholic college and is at present in a Master of Divinity program at a Protestant seminary under the auspices of the Native American Theological Association. She is also looked upon as a holy woman by her people, a legacy from her great-grandmother, and considers herself a bridge person, one who can bring forth the rituals of the Ojibwa and Catholicism in such a way that they become mutually enhancing and illuminating to each other. The dual respect that she receives both from the Ojibwa and lay and clergy Catholics who are not Native Americans is testimony not only to her own integrity but also to the revitalization of Indian religious traditions that has characterized American culture since the 1960s.

The wake service has its basis in an Indian understanding of the meaning of death. In contrast with Christianity, Ojibwa belief regarding an afterlife does not distinguish between a place for the good and a place for the evil. Rather, they speak of a land for all spirits. When Frances Densmore did research among the Minnesota Ojibwa in the early part of the century, she found that there was not always unanimity of thought about "where" this land was. Tradition held that it was to the west, and thus burial was with the feet to the west. But an informant of Densmore stated that as a young man he was told that the land of departed spirits is "'somewhere—as though in *space.*' He said there was day and night in that place, but that during the day there was absolute silence. When night came the drums were beaten at some particular spot, and the spirits assembled from all directions and danced during the entire night, dispersing at daybreak."[8] Wherever the spirit land may be, the departed one does not enter it at the moment of death. Instead it embarks on a four-day journey along the Milky Way, a journey made perilous by the danger that the spirit might be tempted off the path, usually by the same sins for which the individual had a particular weakness in life, and be lost forever in oblivion.

The purpose of the wake, then, is not only to comfort the family but also to provide both company and assistance for the spirit on its journey. For this reason the body must never be left alone, and it is prepared with the journey in mind. Dressed in favorite clothes, the body is also given a little money for the journey, and perhaps other favorite items as well. Sometimes food enough for the journey is left at the grave after the funeral service is over. As is customary among many Catholics, a rosary is often entwined in the hands of the deceased, and in deference to Ojibwa tradition there is also an eagle feather placed in the hand that rests against the right shoulder. The feather is usually presented by a member of the family before the actual review of the body begins, and it often has a beaded spine (the feather is considered a prayer aid, just as is the rosary). It cannot be pinned or taped to the body because that would be desecration of a sacred object.

Depending upon the stature of the person in the community, the wake may last one or two days and nights, with the family present the entire time. What actually happens at the wake service? The leader, sometimes a priest and sometimes an Ojibwa holy person, begins with the sign of the cross and a prayer:

> Let us pray. My brothers and sisters it is good for us to gather here to honor our brother. He lived among us, sharing his life with each of us. Now he has returned to God, our Creator, from whom all of us have come. We are saddened, but we have hope. We pray for our brother and ourselves. Amen.[9]

---

[8] Frances Densmore, *Chippewa Customs,* Reprint Edition, Original Edition, 1929 (St. Paul, Minnesota: Historical Society Press, 1979), p. 75.

[9] Wilma Lawrence, "Bah Nee Mah: An American Indian Wake Service," a brochure that contains no publication information. Other quotations are also taken from this source. *Bah Nee Mah* means "awakening" in Ojibwa.

The singing of hymns begins at about nine o'clock in the evening. The songs are usually both Indian—these are accompanied by drums—and Christian, often the favorites of the deceased. Some of the Christian hymns are sung in the Ojibwa tongue. The hymns are interspersed with stories about the deceased told by relatives and friends and by prayers which reveal that two cultures have influenced this service. There are readings from the Old and New Testaments, the saying of the rosary, and the reciting of litanies such as the following, which is said antiphonally and reflects the Indian closeness to nature and to natural cycles:

> **Leader :** *Let us pray to our Creator, who gives us light:*
>
> **1 :** *I see the star that breaks the night; it is a sign of dawn.*
> **2 :** *The light comes; it joins me to all the life I see.*
> **1 :** *I am like a bird that sings in the dawn.*
> **2 :** *I am humble with love.*
> **1 :** *I walk in the circle of the greater love and the greater power.*
> **2 :** *Let me be like a ray of light.*
> **1 :** *Like a flower bright with light,*
> **2 :** *Like a waterfall laughing with light,*
> **1 :** *Like a great tree, mighty in its roots that split the rocks,*
> **2 :** *Mighty in its top that reaches the sky,*
> **1 :** *While its leaves catch the light and sing with the wind a song of the circle.*
>   ...
> **2 :** *Let me remember always the Great One, who gives light,*
> **1 :** *Who whispers to me in the breeze,*
> **2 :** *Whose words come to me out of the circle of life,*
> **1 :** *Whose command is like thunder: "Be kind; be kind;*
> **2 :** *Be brave; be brave*
>
> **All :** *Be humble as the earth; be as bright as sunlight!"*

Sometime during the night the body is blessed with sweet grass, cedar, or sage. Incense may be used, but that is less in keeping with Ojibwa tradition. At midnight a meal is served, often the favorite meal of the deceased, after which the singing and praying and story telling continue till dawn. The service ends with prayers of petition that the loved one may be remembered and remain a part of the lives of those who remain in the land of the living. It would be hard to find a prayer that better illustrates the "Indian Catholic" nature of the service, for it is a prayer that invokes the Great Spirit and concludes with the prayer for eternal rest that is part of the Roman Catholic funeral liturgy:

> We thank you, God, for our brother, who was so near to us and who has now been taken from us.
> Great Spirit, hear us.
> We thank you for the friendship that went out from our brother and for the peace our brother brought.
> Great Spirit, hear us.

We pray that nothing in our brother's life will be lost, but will be of help to all of us.
Great Spirit, hear us.

We pray that all our brother held sacred may be respected by those who remain after him.

Great Spirit, hear us.

We pray that everything in which our brother was great will continue to mean so much to us.

Great Spirit, hear us.

We pray that our brother may live with you and in the hearts and minds of all who knew him.

Great Spirit, hear us.

We pray that we who knew our brother may be even more united with each other now and that we who are united in peace and friendship here on earth may always be aware of your promise to be faithful to us always.

Great Spirit, hear us.

Eternal rest grant to our brother, Lord.

And let perpetual light shine upon him.

May he rest in peace. Amen.

May his soul and the souls of all the faithful departed through the mercy of God rest in peace.

The family remains with the body until it is time to leave for the funeral Mass. If the family and the deceased have chosen the traditional way, the body is taken through the window to prevent the closing of the door upon the memories of the person in that household. This practice is more common when the wake is held at home rather than in a community hall (the wake is never held at a funeral home, since that is thought to interrupt the passage of the spirit). After the Mass, family and friends accompany the body to the grave. The youngest person present throws the first dirt on the casket, and other relatives fill up the grave. Then the priest blesses the grave with holy water. No one leaves until the grave is covered. If Ojibwa tradition is followed, a small house will be built on the grave. Some Ojibwa indicate their wish to be taken from the coffin and buried wrapped in a blanket. Most present-day burials take place in a denominational cemetery, but it may also be within two hundred yards of the person's home with the body in a standing position and facing the rising sun. Again, this practice stems from the desire to preserve the person's memory within the community; if the body faces west, the relationship with the family is thought to end. The journey to the grave is the completion of the Ojibwa's travel back to the earth, and decay is the process of once again becoming one with the earth.

Given the histories of the native religions in America and of Roman Catholicism—one a story of ever-increasing growth and the other of virtual disintegration—it is astonishing, even miraculous, that a ritual such as the wake that combines the two traditions is in existence during the last quarter of the twentieth century. Sadly enough, the potential for that kind of blending was always there and might have been realized had events in the seventeenth century taken another turn. In *American Indians and Christian Missions* Henry Warner Bowden recounts the relationship between the Jesuits and the Hurons, like the Ojibwa an Algonquian-speaking people. The Jesuits, Bowden says, "recognized compatibilities between Huron spirituality and Christianity and used them." Both the Jesuits and the Hurons had faith in the existence of supernatural power located somewhere "above," a power that affected everyday lives. There was also a common belief in evil spirits and in the need to live in harmony with these supernatural realities. Both recognized the need for "ritual ceremonialism" as well as good conduct in relating to spiritual entities, and the nature of the vision quest among the Hurons (also characteristic of Ojibwa culture) was easily understood by the Jesuits, who likewise cultivated a private kind of spirituality in addition to public worship. Jesuits and Hurons alike believed that communication with the spiritual had an effect on the material, that is on the physical welfare of the individual and the community. There were, of course, areas of belief and practice that had no counterpart in each other. The Hurons could not comprehend the theology of the Fall or the need for redemption of human sin. The Jesuits could not countenance the practice of torturing captives, the Huron belief in many deities instead of one, and social customs such as easy and frequent divorce. Nor is there any denying that, finally, the Jesuit's object was conversion of the Hurons to Christianity. But the overall pattern was one of mutual respect rather than denigration of each other's religious practices, as in Father Jean de Brebéuf's use of red paint on crosses when he learned that the Hurons considered red to be a particularly significant color. Had the Iroquois not nearly obliterated the Hurons in 1648 and 1649, the survivors scattering both east and west, the Hurons and the Jesuits might have accomplished a widespread community of Hurons who manifested, as Bowden calls it, "a New World expression of the Old World faith."[10] The terms *new world* and *old world* are not much in common usage these days, but the Ojibwa wake service illustrates the basic point that Bowden makes—that two religious systems can come together and shed light on each other in ways that broaden each other's understanding of "the way things are" rather than causing each to retreat to a world view that is narrow, self-protected, and defensive.

[10] Henry Warner Bowden, *American Indians and Christian Missions: Studies in Cultural Conflicts* (Chicago: University of Chicago Press, 1981), pp. 75–95. Bowden describes the relationship of the Franciscans and the Pueblos in the Southwest as having the same potential for compatibility; it was never realized because the Franciscans chose to emphasize differences rather than similarities.

10

gathering together: some aspects of organization in american religion

Throughout the previous chapters, I have made occasional reference to the word *denomination*, using it synonymously with the terms *religion* or *religious group*. Although that use of the word is not technically correct as far as the sociology of religion is concerned, which sees the categorizing of religions as a much more complicated enterprise, most Americans understand a denomination to be a distinguishable religious organization with its own set of doctrines, rituals, and form of self-government. Often the word *sect* is used interchangeably with *denomination* (many dictionaries treat the two words as synonyms), even though early sociologists of religion, such as Max Weber and Ernst Troeltsch, distinguished between *church* and *sect*, using *sect* to refer to a religious movement that is newer and less established in its membership, and that sees itself in greater tension with the world than churches. Another organizational term familiar to Americans is *cult*, technically a religious group that grounds its teaching and practice in sources other than the Jewish and Christian scriptures and long-standing tradition. This meaning has virtually been lost, however, at least in the popular sense, and *cult* has come to mean a religious movement that is new, considered to be bizarre, and even dangerous. In present-day usage the word *cult* is so laden with negative connotations that its application to a religious movement is seldom interpreted as positive or even as merely descriptive.

The technical language of the sociology of religion can be extremely helpful in sorting out differences among religious organizations as to their origins, history, leadership, membership, and attitudes toward secular culture, but for the purposes of this chapter a more general description of the way Americans group themselves in various religions is appropriate. The basic unit or organization in American religion is the denomination, with the word used in the sense mentioned above. In fact, the United States was a land of denominations before it became a nation. In guaranteeing separation of church and state, with its dual promises of disestablishment and free expression, the First Amendment assured that the denominational system would continue and flourish. Denominationalism is undergirded by the principle of voluntarism, meaning that Americans are free to choose their own religions and that each religion is on its own as far as financing and governing itself and attracting new members. Voluntarism applies to all other organizations in American culture as well as to religion, but it is misleading to describe religion as just one of many other organizations for which an American is free to sign up. Legally, of course, this is the case. The state has no more to say about whether a citizen is a Methodist or a Christian Scientist than it does about whether that same person joins NOW or the Elks Club. But the social reality of voluntarism as applied to religion is a little different. The very fact that a person is born into a particular religion may have a greater influence on that individual than the principle of voluntarism as to choice of religion.

Definitional considerations aside, how have Americans chosen to group themselves in their choice of religion? The most generally accepted means of categorizing American denominations is into the "three great faiths," Protestant, Catholic, and Jew, although this scheme leaves out approximately five million Orthodox Christians (among them Greek, Russian, and Serbian) who are neither Protestant nor Roman Catholic, as well as Buddhists, Muslims, and others. This three-way breakdown is accurate up to a point, but it does not convey much about numerical realities. Protestants dominate American religion. They have done so historically, and that pattern continues. Protestants account for close to 60 percent of those who say that they are affiliated with a particular religion (not all persons who describe themselves as belonging to a religion practice it). Roman Catholics number about 22 percent of the population, and Jews make up 3 percent. Because there are so many separate denominations within Protestantism, it is necessary to look further at this group. Baptists of various kinds and Methodists are the most populous of the Protestant denominations. As Andrew Greeley has pointed out in *The Denominational Society,* Baptists and Methodists, together with Catholics, make up three-fifths of the American population. If we add Lutherans, Presbyterians, and Episcopalians, the total is up to three-fourths. Three percent of Americans designate themselves as "none," and another 3 percent are categorized as "other." The remaining 18 percent or so are members of the United Church of Christ, the Disciples of Christ, the "Christian" Church, the Mormons, the Seventh Day Adventists, the Church of the Brethren, and various Pentecostal churches.[1] Buried in these statistics and subsumed for the most part in the category "other" are groups such as the Quakers, the Unitarian Universalists,

---

[1] Andrew M. Greeley, *The Denominational Society* (Glenview, Illinois: Scott, Foresman and Company, 1972), pp. 89–90.

the Theosophists, members of the Native American Church, Muslims, Hindus, the Jehovah's Witnesses, Scientologists, and Unificationists. The ease with which the "big numbers" approach to religion in America permits us to forget groups other than those in the mainstream and with large memberships serves as a reminder that the statistical view of religion in America is illuminating but only one of many helpful perspectives.

How do we make all these numbers come alive? One unsophisticated but revealing research exercise is to survey "Churches" in the Yellow Pages of the phone book of a medium-sized city, with a population somewhere in the neighborhood of 100,000. I began with the Yellow Pages of Green Bay, Wisconsin, but as I noticed the predominance of Catholics and Lutherans, as is typical of many cities in the Upper Midwest, I speculated as to what I might find in the Yellow Pages of cities of similar size in different regions of the country. I expanded my survey to include the Yellow Pages of Springfield, Massachusetts; Pensacola, Florida; and Santa Barbara, California. Before beginning to count churches and synagogues, I indulged in a little pondering of regional stereotypes. Would the Congregationalists and the United Church of Christ, descendants of the Puritans, dominate religion in a New England city? Would there be many more evangelical, pentecostal, and holiness churches in a Southern city like Pensacola? Would Santa Barbara have a large number of metaphysical and so-called "California" religions? Finally, because I had grown up in Green Bay, my memory told me that anybody who wasn't Catholic was probably Lutheran, and I was interested in whether there was any accuracy to that perception or whether it was a distortion fabricated out of my own background.

There proved to be some accuracy to all my presuppositions about the different regions, and, in addition, the denominational percentages worked out pretty much the way most surveys and polls have indicated. Protestant groups are dominant by far in all four cities, even in a "Catholic" city like Green Bay, with regional differences accounting for which denomination has the most congregations: for example, Lutherans in Green Bay and Baptists in Pensacola. There are healthy representations of religious groups designated by polls as "other" in all four cities, also, and the number of synagogues ranges from seven in Santa Barbara to one in Green Bay (the Yellow Pages listing reads "Churches, Jewish . . . See Synagogues"). Baptists, who in their different denominations account for the largest Protestant group in America, have more churches than any other Protestants in Santa Barbara with fifteen and an overwhelming 116 in Pensacola, although many are bound to be very tiny congregations. In Springfield there are as many Baptist churches (eighteen) as there are Congregational and United Church of Christ. In Green Bay, however, Baptists are almost an unknown entity with seven congregations. Episcopalians, Methodists, and Presbyterians show up in the numbers that surveys would lead us to expect—four to ten congregations in all four cities.

Denominations that tend to be more evangelical in their piety, among them Assemblies of God and Church of the Nazarene, are represented, but not in startlingly high numbers in each city. The same is true of other holiness and pentecostal churches and of Mormons, Jehovah's Witnesses, and Seventh Day Adventists. Santa Barbara has the largest number of religions designated as "other" in polls, including two Buddhist groups, a New Age church, a Quaker meeting, three Christian Science churches, a Unity Church, an Integral Yoga Institute (listed, interestingly, under "churches"), and a Vedanta Society. Green Bay has the least number, but there is one Metaphysical church for which there is a phone number but no address. As far as regional stereotypes are concerned, there is some truth to the perception, then, that a California city is likely to have more "nonmainstream" religious groups, and that Congregationalists and the United Church of Christ have more congregations in a New England city than they do in other parts of the country. Green Bay does have more Catholic churches by far than all the other cities, twenty-three, and also more Lutheran churches, twenty-two. The surprise in Pensacola is not that Baptists are so numerous but that the actual number of churches in Pensacola, 287, exceeds that of the other three cities by more than 150, reinforcing a view of the South as a region in which religion is a more dominant, or at least more obvious, factor in the culture than it appears to be in other regions.

A Yellow Pages survey of churches and synagogues is obviously not exhaustive and is not grounded in the research tools of the professional social scientist. Any conclusions reached must be tentative and open to reservations about specific congregations in specific cities. For example, Catholic congregations tend to be larger than those in Protestant denominations, and there may be more Catholics in three congregations than there are Protestants in six. The Yellow Pages cannot tell us that three Catholic parishes in a city may have within them strong charismatic groups or that a Baptist pastor is under investigation for doctrinal errors. On the other hand, a look at the Yellow Pages of different cities confirms the reality of religious diversity in American life and the extent to which all the major denominations are represented in a particular city. And the very fact that churches and synagogues are listed in the Yellow Pages reminds us graphically that religion is not set apart from other organizations in America. We might contend that congregations are listed in the Yellow Pages in order to provide information as to their whereabouts rather than to sell services or goods, but they are nonetheless intermingled with references to Cement Products, Plastic Plants, Dentists, and Venetian Blinds. Whatever their theologies, the numbers of their memberships, or their orientations to the overall culture, all churches and synagogues are equal in the Yellow Pages, part of the American free-enterprise system that Americans "voluntarily" choose to patronize or not.

Voluntarism and regionalism are not the only factors in American culture that have affected religious groups. The rest of this chapter will be devoted to looking at four other areas of interest to the student of American religion: (1) the extent to which forms of self-government, or polity, as it is called, in denominations reflect the pressure in American culture for representation at many levels; (2) the influence of race and ethnic differences in the formation of denominations; (3) the struggle for religious groups to define the role of the clergy in a culture that separates church and state; and (4) the separation of roles of men and women in American religions.

POLITY IN AMERICAN RELIGIONS

Americans have devised a great variety of organizational units for subdividing their denominations and an equally diverse array of forms of government by which a denomination is sustained, decisions are made, and lines of authority are established. Looking at many forms of church polity is not just an exercise in comparative church politics, as interesting as that can be. Instead, it is a way to find answers to organizational questions: Where does the power to make decisions and changes lie in a particular denomination? With the clergy? With the laity? At the local level? At the national level or even at the international level? Most American denominations have some kind of national organization that includes subdivisions of a geographic nature—the region, the diocese, the conference, the stake—that break down further into local units—the parish, the congregation, the ward. The relative authority of each of these units depends on the overall organizational structure. In some denominations, authority filters down from the top and is mostly in the hands of the clergy. In others the laity has the most influence in decision making or else there is a sharing of authority between laity and clergy. There is a sense in the culture that the most ''American'' way to do things is to give the laity a great deal of power and to permit final authority in decisions to reside at the local rather than the national level, a carry-over from the congregational polity of the American Puritans. That is the case in the United Church of Christ, where voting on issues that affect the whole denomination takes place at the congregational level. Among the Presbyterians the local church is autonomous in spiritual matters, but issues of national significance are voted upon presbytery by presbytery (a geographic area composed of a minimum of twelve ministers and churches).

A comparison of the Roman Catholic and the Episcopal Churches in America gives us a good sense of differences in organizational structure and their consequences. From the outside it appears that Roman Catholics and Episcopalians have a great deal in common. And in many respects they do. They have very similar liturgies, even more so since English has replaced Latin in Catholic services. Both are considered ''sacramental'' churches that emphasize the celebration of the Eucharist. Both appear to be ''hierarchical'' in nature, that is, they have bishops in whom authority resides. It is at this point that the comparisons come to a halt, for these two denominations give very different kinds of power to their bishops—resulting, therefore, in correlative differences in decision-making patterns. In the Roman Catholic Church, the final arbiter of authority is the pope, and this denomination is a perfect example of an organizational structure in which authority filters down from the pope through the cardinals, archbishops, and bishops (all of whom the pope appoints) to the priests and finally to the laity. In Roman Catholic polity there is no power of decision making that officially belongs to the laity. This is not to say that the laity have no influence on church decisions, but rather that their "votes" are not built into the system. The laity must send their opinions and reactions back "up" through the chain of command. It should not come as a surprise that American Catholics, accustomed by the culture to the free exercise of their ideas, have had some difficulties with this system. One example is the hierarchy's bouts with "trusteeism" in the nineteenth century, marked by efforts of lay trustees in particular parishes to usurp the role of the priest in running the congregation.

Two contemporary examples give an idea of how the system works or doesn't work in the present, one involving a change in the liturgy and the other the practice of birth control. In 1981, the words of consecration of the wine at Mass were amended to omit "men" from the phrase ". . . blood which was shed for you and for all men," because the words were perceived to be gender exclusive. There is no doubt that this change was initiated from the grass roots as a result of the contemporary feminist movement, but it nonetheless involved the hierarchical process. The American Catholic bishops voted in conference on the change and then forwarded their request to the pope. After papal permission was received, the change was made in individual parishes. The birth control controversy has had another outcome, or, it may be more accurate to say, no outcome at all. Statistics show that the majority of American Catholics practice birth control, even though church doctrine forbids artificial contraception. In this case the system has broken down. The grass-roots action has not resulted in a change in doctrine, nor has the doctrine, at least since the 1960s, deterred many who consider themselves good Catholics from practicing birth control in good conscience. To sum up, the Catholic organizational system, part of a worldwide structure, is not typical of most American denominations. Jews and most Protestants give more power to the laity. But the Catholic system has at least one thing in common with others in America: Sometimes it works and sometimes it doesn't.

By contrast with Roman Catholicism, the Episcopal Church in America is run somewhat like a representative democracy. An Episcopal bishop is elected, not appointed, by a diocesan convention of clerical and lay delegates and then approved by the bishops and standing committees of other American Episcopal dioceses. Authority for decision making and change resides in two bodies that have been compared to the United States Senate and the House of Representatives: the House of Bishops and the House of Lay and Clerical Deputies. The national decision-making body of the Episcopal Church is the General Convention held every three years and attended by members of both the House of Bishops and the House of Deputies. It is at the General Convention that decisions such as those mentioned in a previous chapter, changes in the *Book of Common Prayer* and the ordination of women, are made. Obviously, in this denominational system bishops do not have the same power as do bishops in Roman Catholicism, even though their liturgical functions are very similar. What we see in Episcopal

Church polity is an Americanization of a hierarchical system, devised by some of the same people who put together the Constitution. Most eighteenth-century Anglicans in America did not want a state church. They did want to retain the ceremonial function of the bishop and his authority in doctrinal matters. If there is inherent in the Roman Catholic system the potential for rifts among laity, clergy, and hierarchy as well as for disagreements between the American Church and Rome, the Episcopal Church has built into it the problems of a representative democracy: the division and bitterness that can arise when the dissenting voices of the minority rise up against the vote of the majority. Nonetheless, the "majority rules" governance of American denominations has been the more typical pattern, not just in the Episcopal Church but also in many other Protestant and Jewish groups. The degree of centralization differs from denomination to denomination, with the Methodists able to tolerate more episcopal authority than members of the United Church of Christ, and Reform Jews historically more likely to look to national organizations than Orthodox Jews for leadership. On the whole, then, religious denominations in America have been more willing to take a chance on the pitfalls of relatively decentralized organization and of extending power to the laity than they have to devise systems in which most of the "official" power is retained by the clergy and the hierarchy, with Roman Catholicism being the large and notable exception.

Because the mainstream denominations include so many Americans in their ranks, it can be too easy to overlook some of the variations in organizational structure of less populous religious groups. America has been the birthplace of many new religions and thus has seen numerous examples of religious organization based on the role of the charismatic leader, often the founder of the movement. Two of the most obvious examples in the nineteenth century are Joseph Smith, founder of the Mormons, the Church of Jesus Christ of Latter-Day Saints, and Mary Baker Eddy, who "discovered," as she said, Christian Science. Both of these religious movements are American in their origins, and yet their organizational structures remain to this day much more centralized than congregational. Some new religions do not survive the deaths of their founders, but in these two cases the churches not only endured, but the power over doctrine and practice remained vested in a central authority. The Mother Church in Boston with its Board of Directors continues to hold sway over Christian Science churches throughout the world. The Salt Lake City Mormons have an elaborate priesthood of many gradations open to "worthy males," which in one sense opens up many opportunities of participation to the rank and file, but great power nonetheless remains with the office of the First Presidency and the Council of the Twelve. The president is regarded as prophet and seer for the Mormons, and because revelation remains as yet unfinished, also the revealer of new doctrines that are divinely inspired (one of the most recent was the approval for black men to enter the priestly ranks). Examples of charismatic leaders still living who have great power over the religions they have founded are the Reverend Sun Myung Moon of the Unification Church (Moon is a Korean citizen), and Elizabeth Clare

Prophet, "guru ma" of the Church Universal and Triumphant. How power and authority will be distributed in these movements upon the deaths of the leaders remains to be seen.

RACE AND NATIONAL ORIGIN

If one way to learn about differences among denominations in America is to compare their organizational styles, then another is to look at the influence of race and ethnic background in the makeup of their members. The development of separate black churches in Protestant denominations, particularly among the Baptists and Methodists to which churches most American blacks originally belonged, provides a good example of how race has operated as an organizing factor in American religion. And as "immigrant" religions, Judaism, Catholicism, Lutheranism, and Eastern Orthodoxy all were shaped in their acculturation to life in America by the various nationalities that composed their membership. It goes almost without saying that the realities of race and ethnicity have a dual potential: both for variety and vitality and as the cause of divisiveness. It is not easy to find the positive elements in the reality of separate black denominations and congregations in America, other than the fact that they provided some autonomy for blacks in matters of religion away from the supervision of whites. Further, they spared blacks some of the humiliations encountered when they worshiped in the same congregation as whites, among them entering the church through a side door and sitting in seats segregated from the white worshipers, or even having services at different hours or in a separate building on the same grounds. Beyond that, the Protestant theologian H. Richard Niebuhr's assessment that racism was the underlying motivation for separation is the most accurate. Niebuhr could find no differences in theology, worship, or organization so marked between blacks and whites that they could account for the need for separate denominations and churches. "But on the whole," he said, "the sufficient reason for the frankness with which the color line has been drawn in the church is the fact that race discrimination is so respectable an attitude in America that it could be accepted by the church without subterfuge of any kind."[2]

When Niebuhr wrote these words in 1929, he named four denominations that were "purely Negro": the National Baptist Convention, the African Methodist Episcopal, the African Methodist Episcopal Zion, and the Colored Methodist Episcopal (now called the Christian Methodist) churches. However, there had been separate black churches, if not denominations, in both the North and the South since the end of the eighteenth century. As the nineteenth century wore on and with it the fears that blacks gathered together in churches might revolt against slavery, there was less willingness on the part of whites to tolerate the idea

---

[2] H. Richard Niebuhr, *The Social Sources of Denominationalism* (Hamden, Connecticut: The Shoe String Press, 1929), p. 236.

of separate black churches without white supervision. It was only after the Civil War and emancipation that separate black denominations (Baptist) were founded in the South, the Methodist groups having been founded in the North early in the century. Historians tend to agree that for the most part, black churches did not take an active part in combating racism in America until the 1960s. Instead, the pattern was to help blacks accommodate themselves to a society that discriminated against them. In addition, many black clergy had a vested interest in keeping things the way they were since most likely the authority of black ministers would have been diminished in an integrated system. In this respect the black and white churches were not much different from each other, with notable exceptions in both cases. The 1960s brought the protests against institutionalized racism in America led by Martin Luther King, Jr., who was joined by other black and white religious leaders. The 1960s saw also the growth of black religions, such as the Black Muslims, whose purpose was not just to help blacks put up with their place in society but to celebrate in a militant way both blackness and separateness.

Not all American Blacks have participated in the patterns just described. Many belonged to no church at all; others were members of integrated congregations. Although the majority of blacks who espoused a religion belonged either to Baptist or Methodist churches, there were others who were Presbyterians, Congregationalists, or Episcopalians. There are also black Catholics, many of whose ancestors came from Maryland or Louisiana; and there are black Lutherans. Many others joined pentecostal groups or organizations such as Father Divine's Peace Mission Movement, whose members (most of them now over fifty) still gather for banquets in the headquarters city of Philadelphia. In spite of all these different manifestations of black religious experience in America, the overall reality until very recently has nonetheless been one of separation based on color more than any other factor.

Americans from Asia and the Middle East, too, have experienced separation from American culture in matters of religion, but their stories are different from that of black Americans. Blacks have worshiped separately primarily for reasons of race, not theology, since they have had Christianity in common with whites. Americans from Asia and the Middle East, on the other hand, have practiced religions almost completely unfamiliar to most Americans, with some exceptions among the highly educated in both the nineteenth and the twentieth centuries. Thus, until recently, Americans have remained ignorant of the religions of the Hindus and the Sikhs from India, Buddhists of various schools from Japan and China, and Muslims from such countries as Syria, Egypt, and Iran. Among the more recent immigrants to America, members of all these groups have tended to live together in enclaves, as have generations of newcomers before them, and to be more visible in western states—California and Hawaii, for example—than others. As a result, their various religions, along with their cultures, have remained set apart and have seemed mysterious.

The situation began to change somewhat in the 1950s and 1960s as Protestant, Catholic, and Jewish Americans began to look beyond their own traditions for insights that religions of the East could offer about those age-old questions concerning the nature of reality, the divine, and the human. Americans found appeal in the emphasis of Eastern religions on mental discipline, ascetic practices, and cultivation of the interior life, often in contrast with the more action-oriented religions of the West. The attraction of West for East in matters of religion is evident in the growth of interest in Zen Buddhism, in the use that black Americans have made of Islam (already noted in Chapter 6), in the development of offshoots of Hinduism such as Hare Krishna, the Healthy-Happy-Holy Organization of Sikh origin, and in the secularized versions of Eastern religious practices such as Transcendental Meditation. In spite of all these examples, however, the religions of the East and the Middle East and the people who practice them are by no means completely assimilated into American culture, and for many Americans they retain the flavor of the exotic.

Jewish Americans have experienced separations from one another not as a result of race but through differences in practice and worship and varying patterns of immigration. It is the separation caused by immigration that concerns us here. Sephardic Jews from Spain and Portugal were the first to arrive in America (the famous Touro Synagogue in Newport, Rhode Island, was built in 1763, but the congregation had been in Newport since the 1660s). By the time other Jews began to arrive, chiefly from Germany, in small numbers in the eighteenth century and large numbers in the nineteenth, the Sephardim were not only well established; to the newcomers they represented a kind of aristocracy. In *Judaism in America* Joseph Blau speculates that this is why the German and Dutch Jews were so willing to join synagogues that practiced a ritual different from their own. In addition to the prestige offered by the Sephardim, there was the practical matter that the small number of Jews in most places could not support two synagogues: "So, the Ashkenazim joined the Sephardic synagogue, sometimes married into Sephardic families, were elected to office in the synagogue, and learned to tolerate and in some cases to love the strange sound of the Sephardic *minhag.*"[3] The next wave of immigration brought with it a different outcome as far as the merging of Jewish communities of different ethnic backgrounds was concerned. By the time the Jews from Eastern Europe arrived in America at the end of the nineteenth century, many of German heritage had achieved middle-class status and had left Orthodox Judaism for Reform temples, where worship services, as we have already seen, were more in keeping with Protestant ritual. As was typical of many immigrant groups, these newcomers clung to one another and to their old-world ways of worshiping and living; many of their customs were derived not just from the country they had left, but from the *shtetl,* the specific community, that had been their home. The result was separate synagogues and mutual suspicions on the part of both groups. The Germans were embarrassed by the immigrant ways of the newer arrivals, both in the synagogue and the marketplace; and the Eastern European

[3]Joseph Blau, *Judaism in America: From Curiosity to Third Faith* (Chicago: University of Chicago Press, 1976), p. 26.

Jews accused the Germans of excessive pride in their Germanic heritage and the dilution of Jewish tradition in their new-found American ways. In a sense, it was the kind of intense quarrel that erupts among family members, occasioned by small issues rather than large, but its consequences lingered long into the twentieth century.

Among Lutherans and Catholics we find a repetition of the separation by ethnic background pattern. For many years of their history the Lutherans in America maintained separate denominations on the basis of national origin, whereas the Catholics, with only a few exceptions, housed many different nationalities under the same denominational roof. Lutherans came to America from Germany, Norway, Sweden, Denmark, Finland, Iceland, and scattered parts of the Austro-Hungarian empire. The complexities of Lutheran denominational differences are almost overwhelming. Some of the differences had to do with worship style, often an evangelical versus a less enthusiastic mode. Others stemmed from theology and the difficulties Lutherans have traditionally had in America in coming to an agreement as to what their stance should be toward other Christians. The most dominant basis for organization, however, was that of nationality. The result was many, many separate Lutheran denominations: among them the Danish Lutheran Church in America, the Norwegian Lutheran Church of America, the Slovak Evangelical Lutheran Synod, the Augustana Synod (Swedish), the Finnish American National Evangelical Lutheran Church, the Wisconsin Synod, and the Lutheran Church–Missouri Synod (both German). The gradual movement of Lutherans toward church unity, particularly in the twentieth century, has had to take into account these differences in national heritage as much as they have theological disagreements. Although the Lutheran denominations are no longer officially based on national origin, most Lutherans in the Midwest, where Lutheranism has its largest membership, can still point out the heritage and history of particular congregations in small towns, cities, and rural areas. And it would be a rare Lutheran who could not distinguish Lutheran colleges in this manner—for example, St. Olaf's is Norwegian; Gustavus Adolphus is Swedish; Wartburg is German. Thus, although the ethnic identifications have waned in importance in American Lutheranism, they have not completely disappeared and still figure into the ways that Lutherans look upon themselves.

American Catholicism never broke apart into many separate denominations based on ethnic distinctions, but the potential was certainly there. One need only look at the names of parish churches, particularly in urban areas, to discover that identification with the old-world homeland for many decades formed the basis of parish structure: St. Patrick's, the Irish church; St. Boniface, the German church; St. Willebrord's, the Dutch church; St. Stanislaus, the Polish church. Many of the churches were built in close proximity to one another, another indication that the parish was meant to serve not a geographic area but an ethnic constituency. The ethnic bonds were strong enough that an Irish American family might walk right past St. Stanislaus two blocks from their home to attend St. Patrick's a mile away.

Generally, at least in the late nineteenth and early twentieth centuries, a bishop assigned a priest of the same background as pastor to a parish. If he didn't there was likely to be trouble, occasionally resulting in pressure among parishioners for a separate, ethnic denomination. Almost always the attempts at separation were defused, an exception being the formation of the Polish National Catholic Church in America at Scranton, Pennsylvania, in 1904. This breakaway had its origins in the chafing of Polish parishioners at the domination of an Irish bishop. Because the Irish did indeed dominate the American hierarchy from the mid-nineteenth century until very recent times, rebellion of later immigrants, particularly Italians and Poles, was not at all uncommon. The Irish, for their part, were just as reluctant to be served by a priest who was not Irish. There is a joke in Wisconsin that the Italian Dominican Samuel Mazzuchelli (1806–1864), a missionary to the Indians of the Midwest as well as a parish priest, was tolerated by the Irish only because they thought his name was Father Matthew Kelly. Only rarely, however, did the push for ethnic control of a parish become anywhere near as extreme as it did in Scranton.

The desire of immigrant Catholics to become Americanized, coupled with the move to suburban areas where ethnic distinctions were blurred, worked to diminish the importance of ethnic identity in American Catholicism. Yet, when Gerhard Lenski published *The Religious Factor,* his sociological study of religion in Detroit, in 1961, he was severly criticized for lumping Catholics together and failing to take into account their ethnic differences and the effects those differences would have on education, political stance, and economics.[4] In *The American Catholic,* published in 1977, Andrew Greeley still distinguished among Irish, German, Italian, and Polish Catholics.[5] Finally, any study of American Catholics done in the 1980s would certainly have to take into account the fact that one of every three Catholics in America is of Hispanic descent. It may be that the age of ethnic distinction is not yet over in American Catholicism, but that the focus of attention will shift away from the immigrants of the nineteenth and early twentieth centuries to concentrate on those peoples who have been called "the new ethnics."

A last example of ethnic distinctions stems from the presence of Eastern churches in America, the most populous being the Greek and Russian Orthodox, followed by others of national origin, such as the Serbian, Bulgarian, Rumanian, Albanian, Ukranian, and Syrian Orthodox churches. In addition, there are other separate eastern, but not Orthodox, churches, such as the Armenian Apostolic Church of North America. There are some interesting parallels with Lutheranism in the maintaining of national churches. Because the Lutherans have had a longer history in America, they have had time to go through a period during which the national churches were separate from one another and after which began the process of unification that has been characteristic of Lutheranism in the twentieth

---

[4] Gerhard Lenski, *The Religious Factor: A Sociologist's Inquiry* (Garden City, New York: Anchor Books, 1961).

[5] Andrew M. Greeley, *The American Catholic: A Social Portrait* (New York: Basic Books, Inc., Publishers, 1977).

century. The eastern churches are products of early-twentieth-century immigration, and so far they have exhibited a greater tendency to split from one another than to unify, the splits often occasioned by disputes over the process of Americanization. Thus, it remains an open question as to whether some of the beginning steps to unity taken late in the twentieth century will become the trend of the next several decades.

CLERGY AND LAITY

The respective roles of clergy and laity in American religious groups yield another area of study that is helpful in looking at divisions within denominations as well as differences among them. Expectations for clergy vary across denominations, of course. Members of Free Church traditions who deemphasize an ordained ministry are bound to want different things from their ministers than do Roman Catholics, who stress a sacramental priesthood. But if there is one thing that seems to characterize most American denominations during this second half of the twentieth century, it is a preoccupation with what the role of ''minister'' (priest, rabbi, or minister) actually means in a culture that is highly secular and that separates church and state. It is not only the clergy who are wondering about their roles. Lay people, too, are concerned about where they fit into the scheme of organized religion and are no longer so willing to give over all forms of ministry to the clergy; nor are they quite so docilely led as was once the case. For many denominations the shepherd and sheep metaphor for minister and congregation is no longer an appealing one. Clergy are frustrated about several things, among them the gradual diminishing of their influence on American culture during the last 150 years.

No longer one of the only educated persons in the congregation or even the community, the minister is often perceived as just one among many professionals, a situation that leads to a questioning of the validity of the divine ''call'' to ministry, once such a vital part of the clergy identity. Further, there may be an assumption about ordained clergy that they don't know much about the ''real world'' of politics, finance, and science, and thus what they have to say cannot be taken very seriously. Ironically, clergy often feel, also, that they are called upon to function as experts in areas for which they are really not trained: marriage or drug or financial counseling, for example. Another difficulty arises when laity and clergy have differing ideas as to what functions are most important for ministers to perform. Related to this point is the way in which lay people perceive what the minister actually does with his or her time. Many lay people think that the clergy spend the majority of their time on ''priestly'' matters, such as preparing sermons, conducting worship, and making sick calls, and these are the tasks of which parishioners are most approving. The minister, however, often feels overwhelmed by the many hours that must be spent on the administrative work of running a congregation, with little time left to engage in contemplation, theological reading, or even prayer. In the case of large urban or suburban congregations, various duties may be assumed by both lay and ordained staff members, but in this case senior pastors or rabbis need to function with some sophistication at the level of manager. There is another problem that further burdens clergy. In spite of the waning role of the ministry in secular culture, the ordained person is often placed on a pedestal by members of a congregation and perceived as somehow above ordinary human beings. This kind of adulation with its high expectations can take its toll in the pressure to be all things to all people without showing one's own weaknesses. There are also pressures unique to different denominations. Whereas the celibate Catholic priest may suffer a sense of isolation and loneliness, his married counterparts in Protestantism and Judaism may be overwhelmed by the frustration of not being able to give sufficient time to both family and congregation.

The situation just described makes the present state of the ministerial profession in America seem rather gloomy. But the concern over clergy roles has generated a great deal of the kind of vitality that comes from self-assessment on the part of clergy, laity, and seminary faculty, producing in turn some very revealing projects to determine just what it is that Americans want in and from their clergy. One of the most recent and exhaustive surveys was undertaken in the 1970s by the Association of Theological Schools, an organization of 200 seminaries in the United States and Canada. Five thousand clergy and laity were selected at random from many denominations to complete a questionnaire that ranked major themes (with many subcategories) as to their importance for the beginning minister. The resulting statistics and their interpretations were published in 1980 in *Ministry in America.*[6] The volume also included essays by eighteen denominational leaders who interpreted the results for their own particular groups. The material generated by the study and its potential for interpretation are almost endless, but some of the major themes that emerged are very helpful in understanding not only what Americans expect from their clergy and what clergy expect of themselves, but how these perceptions differ between laity and clergy and across denominations. In some instances the areas of agreement are more startling than the points of disagreement.

What qualities, then, do clergy and laity alike agree are most valuable in a minister in all the denominations? As it turns out, it is not the ability to lead a congregation or to engage in theological reflection and interpretation or to conduct worship, although these functions were ranked third, fourth, and sixth out of eleven and considered "quite important." What people agreed on to the greatest extent, regardless of denomination, clerical or lay status, age, or gender, was the need for the minister to have an "open, affirming style," which included such qualities as "flexibility of spirit," acceptance of the clergy role, the ability to handle diversity and to risk change, doing tasks responsibly whether one liked them or

[6] *Ministry in America,* ed. David S. Schuller, Merton P. Strommen, and Milo Brekke (San Francisco: Harper & Row, Publishers, 1980).

not, and responding warmly to people.[7] All of these points have more to do with style than function, with what the minister is rather than with what the minister does. This is an interesting result in a nation that sees itself as action-oriented and pragmatic in spirit and is testimony to the intensely high value that Americans at this period in history place on the quality of relationships. The second-ranked category was "caring for persons under stress," revealing the great extent to which Americans expect their clergy, whether trained for it or not, to be counselors. It may also indicate a widespread perception that life in contemporary American society is indeed filled with stress and whatever its source, a priest, rabbi, or minister is the person to whom one turns for help.

The categories just mentioned elicited much agreement across denominations as to their importance. The characteristic ranked fifth, "Ministry from Personal Commitment to Faith," was the source of greatest controversy among separate denominations. To put it broadly, this category dealt with the minister's obvious commitment to an exemplary moral life and a "born again" style of piety, as well as fairly aggressive evangelizing. Denominations that heartily endorsed obvious manifestations of the minister's piety and faith commitment were Lutherans, Southern Baptists, Evangelicals of two types, and Free Church members. Those less enthusiastic in their approval were the Episcopalians, the Roman Catholics, and members of the United Church of Christ. The category ranked very low for Unitarians and Jews (Reform) who, interestingly, were grouped together in one "denominational family" for purposes of analysis because their concepts of ministry are so similar. Researchers also found that the older the respondents and the more often they attended services, the more likely they were to find an evangelical piety in their clergy desirable. Although there had to be widespread agreement that "personal commitment of faith" is an important quality for ministry in order for it to be ranked fifth, the disagreement seemed centered on how one was to show that piety. As one interpreter explained, a display of piety that one denomination considers essential in its clergy would be embarrassing for members of another denomination. There was also disagreement as to whether "ministry to the community and world" was an important quality in a minister, reflecting a parallel dispute in the culture at large as to whether ordained clergy should get involved in areas outside the congregation, such as social action and politics, probably an obvious quandary in a culture that separates church and state. A final area of controversy centered upon the importance of a "priestly sacramental ministry"—that is, a ministry highly involved with the performing of rituals and administering of the sacraments. It isn't hard to guess that this category received high ratings from Catholics and lower ratings from most Protestants, especially the evangelical denominations. A last revelation of the questionnaire concerned qualities that were agreed upon by all denominations as detrimental to a member of the clergy: "privatistic, legalist style," resulting in autocratic decision making, a theological emphasis on God's punish-

---

[7] Ibid., p. 30.

ment, and avoidance of social change; and "disqualifying personal and behavioral characteristics," which included everything from immaturity to drinking too much.

The ATS study also revealed areas of disagreement, or at least different emphases, between clergy and laity. It appears that the person entering the ordained ministry is correct in assuming that the laity have tremendously high expectations of the clergy, even though they may differ among denominations as far as personality and style of life are concerned. On the other hand, there is confusion as to what role they want the clergy to play in areas outside those concerns that are obviously related to religion. Although there are people in America who want their clergy to walk picket lines, to run for Congress, to feed the poor, and to take strong stands on social issues, there are many more who prefer to see their minister or priest or rabbi in the sanctuary or at the side of a dying parishioner. Clergy, too, are torn on this issue, but the ATS study shows that they are much more likely to see their role as extending outside the congregation than are the laity. Ministers also value their functions as theologians, which we might look upon as the intellectual side of the job, more than do the laity. The laity tend to see the minister as having learned enough theology at seminary, certainly enough to carry on the running of a congregation, whereas the clergy as a group value and feel that they need further theological study in order to provide insights on both personal faith and social issues for their congregants. It is the widespread experience of clergy in America that their listeners prefer a sermon that deals with "real-life issues," something "useful," rather than one that displays a highly structured theological argument or a complicated bit of Biblical exegesis. Further, clergy of many denominations sense that those to whom they minister are disconcerted by clergy admissions of doubt, worry, or personal problems and would prefer that they keep their difficulties to themselves.

The evaluators of the ATS study, those who interpreted the data for specific denominations and those who devised the study in the first place, saw the data gathered as useful on several levels: a clarification of the expectations of specific denominations for their clergy; the opportunity for denominations to see their own understandings of ministry in comparison with others in America; and a chance for the individual contemplating the ordained ministry to see whether his or her interpretations of that role coincide with the denomination's. The study also revealed that ministry takes place in many different contexts in American society, not just in the congregation but also in prisons, hospitals, chemical dependency centers, educational institutions, and "on the street." On the negative side the results of the study make it clear that persons entering the ordained ministry in America should expect confusion and frustration and even "burnout" in their work, not unlike the pitfalls of any profession, but perhaps more frightening to persons, both lay and ordained, who had expected the ministry to be protected and set apart from life's ordinary problems.

It is interesting to note that those who devised the study did not upon its completion lash out against the confusion that adheres to ministry in America, saying, "If only we could define the minister's role more effectively once and for all, there would be no more problems." Instead, David Schuller, one of the editors, developed a theological concept of the minister as human being, one who cannot minister to others without also having been in need of ministry. Schuller concludes that the ordained clergy in America will have to expect ambiguity and tension as normal parts of their lives and not fool themselves into thinking that if only they could stop going to meetings, or being interrupted by the phone or having to work on the church budget, they could get on with the work of "real ministry." But, says Schuller, "these excuses vanish with the realization that those very misunderstandings, intrusions, and tedious expectations present the moment and context for ministry." Schuller concludes that "Only the one who has experienced the pain, the frustration, the struggle of living fully in a moment such as ours—and has both glimpsed meaning and has personally heard the word of hope—dare speak to us."[8] It may be that at this point in time American clergy are better able to accept Schuller's interpretation of the minister than are the laity, but the seeds are planted for an understanding of the minister in America both as human and as set apart, a double identity that has inherent in it the potential for a kind of liberation of the minister but also for frustration as well.

MEN AND WOMEN

Traditionally in American religions the roles of women have been more tightly prescribed and restricted than those of men. Although women were generally perceived as more pious, more spiritually oriented, and more faithful in their church attendance, in most denominations they could not be ordained nor could they serve on parish boards and councils. Women were considered to be by their very nature unsuited for ordination. Cotton Mather (1663–1728) called women the "hidden ones." He noted their piety and at the same time their absence from the pulpit and the council room, and he concluded that because Eve had been the "first transgressor" in the Garden of Eden, women had rightfully inherited a legacy that made them subject to the authority of men in both religious and civil affairs and caused them to suffer pain in childbirth. Further, Biblical injunctions in the New Testament, particularly in the writings of Paul, that women keep their heads covered, remain silent in church, and be subject to their husbands were all interpreted as the foundation of the divine plan for women that they be second to men in the hierarchical structures of both church and society. As early as 1636 Ann Hutchinson was exiled from Boston on the basis of this understanding of social structure. Hutchinson was accused of heresy and of upsetting the social balance. But her transgressions were considered worse because as a woman she had "preached" and taught, thereby usurping a privilege that did not belong to her.

---

[8] Ibid., p. 8.

By the nineteenth century there were many women who considered institutional religion to be among the chief instruments of their oppression. The writings of women who founded or joined religious movements that gave equal status to women (among them the Quakers, the Shakers, the Spiritualists, the Christian Scientists, and the Theosophists) were full of references to the bondage in which traditional Christianity had kept women. In 1895 Elizabeth Cady Stanton and a "revising committee" began work on *The Woman's Bible*, which included interpretive comments on passages in the Pentateuch and other Biblical books that made reference to women or else excluded them in ways that these women considered inappropriate. Stanton also asked prominent women of the times to respond to her by letter concerning two questions: "Have the teachings of the Bible advanced or retarded the emancipation of women?" "Have they dignified or degraded the Mothers of the Race?"[9] One answer was from Frances E. Willard, founder and president of the Woman's Christian Temperance Union, who defended the Bible. Willard subscribed to the theory that women must exert the influence of their superior moral natures upon the evils of the world, and her answer to Stanton reflects this position: "To me the Bible is the dear and sacred home book that makes a hallowed motherhood possible because it raises woman up, and with her lifts toward heaven the world. This is the faith taught to me by those whom I have most revered and cherished; it has produced the finest characters which I have ever known; by it I propose to live; and holding to the truth which it brings to us, I expect to pass from this world to one even more full of beauty and hope."[10] A letter from a woman who signed herself "E. M." is typical of those who agreed with Stanton: "The truth of the matter is . . . that whatever progress woman has made in any department or effort she has accomplished independently of, and in opposition to, the so-called inspired and infallible 'word of God,' and . . . this book has been of more injury to her than has any other which has ever been written in the history of the world."[11] As it turned out, *The Woman's Bible* was too controversial a volume to gain widespread approval, even among many ardent suffragists. In 1896 a resolution was adopted at the annual convention of the National-American Woman Suffrage Association stating that the organization was nonsectarian and had no connection with the "so-called" *Woman's Bible*. There was fear among the members that approval of *The Woman's Bible* would alienate too many church members who were at that point in favor of women's suffrage, and in spite of President Susan B. Anthony's plea that the group had to make room in its platform for many different opinions without condemning any of them, the resolution passed.

However many American women repudiated religion entirely or else elected to join new or nontraditional movements, millions more chose to remain within

---

[9] Elizabeth Cady Stanton and the Revising Committee, *The Woman's Bible* (Seattle: Coalition Task Force on Women and Religion, 1974), p. 185.

[10] Ibid., p. 201.

[11] Ibid., p. 203.

the mainstream of Protestantism, Judaism, and Catholicism and do what they could. The histories of different denominations in the nineteenth century are filled with examples of the ways in which women exercised influence in matters of religion even though they could not be ordained. For Protestant women one outlet was the mission society, which many historians see as the basis for the formation of women's organizations in both the church and the community. Up to the beginning of the nineteenth century, mission societies were male organizations. By 1800 there is historical record of women's "cent" societies, based on the assumption that most women could afford a penny a week for the missions. At this point women began to gather in groups to pray for the missions and to educate themselves concerning missionary activities, some of them fearful that the Bible prohibited women from assembling to pray without a minister present to lead them. The next step for women was mission societies, followed by all-female boards for these societies, free of supervision by men. The growth of widespread and highly sophisticated women's mission organizations in America paralleled the careers of women missionaries. Women were sent into the mission fields, both foreign and domestic, first as "wives," considered essential to the operation but subordinate and subject to their husbands. By the mid-1800s single women were being sent out as independent missionaries, and the women's missionary societies and boards had argued for their elevation to "missionary" in their own right. Through their work with the missions, Protestant women of many denominations gained experience in organization, administration, and financial managing. While doing so, they improved the lot of women within the mission fields as well as within the church structures at home, deriving in addition personal benefit from the friendship and support for one another that grew out of mutual effort.[12]

Many of the changes in status for Jewish women came out of Reform Judaism, which permitted women to be more active and more visible in the synagogue, whereas previously their chief religious duties had been performed at home. In "Jewish Woman's Encounter with American Culture," Ann Braude suggests that Jewish women "provided all the physical elements that allowed men to conform with Jewish ritual practice," such as making food in accordance with dietary laws, preparing ritual objects for special occasions, being seated separately in the synagogue so as not to distract the men, and avoiding their husbands during menstruation and bathing in a ritual bath afterwards because a man was not permitted to have intercourse with a menstruating woman. "Tradition," says Braude, "taught that piety in this life led to heaven in the next. But a woman could get to heaven only through her husband's godliness, so she could never place anything before her constant striving to aid him in the fulfillment of his religious obligations."[13] Not all women, of course, belonged to the Reform movement; nor

---

[12] This account is taken from R. Pierce Beaver, *All Loves Excelling: American Protestant Women in World Mission* (Grand Rapids, Michigan: William B. Eerdman's Publishing Company, 1968).

[13] Ann Braude, "The Jewish Woman's Encounter with American Culture," in *Women and Religion in America, Volume I: The Nineteenth Century* ed. Rosemary Radford Ruether and Rosemary Skinner Keller (San Francisco: Harper & Row, Publishers, 1981), p. 151.

did all Jewish women remain practicing Jews in America, but for many women the changes initiated by Reform Judaism lessened the dichotomy between the religious roles of Jewish women and men, resulting in fewer ritual duties to be performed by women at home and more freedom to participate in synagogue life. In addition, like Protestant women, Jewish women achieved prominence and influence within Judaism through women's organizations, among the best known The National Council of Jewish Women, which had its origins in the Congress of Jewish Women, part of the World Congress of Religions held in Chicago in 1893.

One way for Roman Catholic women to achieve not only a measure of autonomy, but also an education and a profession, has been to join a religious order of nuns. The many different orders of nuns—Dominicans, School Sisters of Notre Dame, Franciscans, Sisters of St. Joseph, and Ursulines, to name a few—came to America to found missions, schools, and hospitals and generally followed close behind a missionary priest who had sent back to Europe for help. The European nuns saw themselves as missionaries to a foreign country probably in much the same way as did American Protestant women going to serve the missions in China and India. As parochial-school teachers, nuns participated in the Americanization of Catholic children of many different ethnic groups, at the same time often preserving the ethnic backgrounds of their own orders well into the twentieth century. Nuns were also instrumental, probably more so than priests, in gaining greater acceptance for Catholics in an American society that was often suspicious of and hostile toward not only lay Catholics but particularly nuns and priests. Rumors abounded about strange goings-on in convents and orphanages filled with the offspring of nuns and priests. Occasionally convents were attacked. However, the excellent schools and hospitals run by different orders and the nursing of the wounded during the Civil War helped to convince the American public that nuns were productive and respectable citizens.[14] Convent life and the distinctive habits of the nuns came to be looked upon favorably as signs of a pious life rather than as marks of a bizarre and un-American way of being religious. Nuns had other battles to fight as well. Subject to the authority of the bishop of the diocese in which they worked, mother superiors of convents experienced ecclesiastical attempts to limit authority over their own communities. In addition, nuns could not be ordained and thus could not say Mass, hear confessions, or perform marriages; they could baptize only in an emergency. A priest was needed to perform these sacramental offices; and so in the hierarchical structure of the Catholic Church nuns were always considered a notch below the priests.

In spite of gains in status made by women of many different faiths and a broadening of their roles during the nineteenth century, at the beginning of the twentieth century most denominations still did not ordain women or permit them to preach. The struggle for ordination continues to the present, and there are a significant number of American religions that do not ordain women, among them the Southern Baptists, the Roman Catholics, and Missouri Synod Lutherans, the

---

[14] Mary Ewens, O.P., "The Leadership of Nuns in Immigrant Catholicism," in *Women and Religion in America*, pp. 101–06.

Eastern Orthodox, and Orthodox Jews. In those denominations that do ordain women, female ministers often have a difficult time obtaining a "call" to a congregation or keeping it once they're there. This is true of denominations that have only recently begun to ordain women—the American Lutheran Church, the Lutheran Church in America, Reform Judaism, and the Episcopal Church—and it is also the case among members of the United Church of Christ, Methodists, and Presbyterians, who have a longer history of women ministers.

Ordination is not the only subject that presently occupies feminist critics, both female and male, of religion in America. Another is the use of male language in reference to the divine, which pervades the prayers of Judaism and Christianity. Many persons see a direct connection between the fact that women have generally been subject to the doctrinal authority of men in American religions and the fact that God imagery in Western religion is male. Language that refers to God only as "father" and never as "mother" and only as "he" and never as "she" reinforces the image of a God who is male and is not conducive to an association of the female with the divine. Thus, religious feminism at this point in history seeks inclusion in church structure for those women who feel called to an ordained ministry; it also looks for changes from exclusively male imagery in the language of prayers, hymns, and liturgies on the theory that change of consciousness is essential to bringing about change in outward reality.

A third effort has gone into the recovering of the history of women's roles and of particular women in American denominations. For many years denominational and church history was given over to the recording of theological disputes, growth statistics, and biographies of the clergy, all areas in which women's names and deeds were not likely to be recorded. Searches in women's letters and diaries and in the minutes of women's meetings have yielded a different kind of history that points to the contributions of women to religious life in America that had been previously overlooked. In sum, denominations in America have responded to women's seeking of extended roles with differing degrees of alacrity and enthusiasm, to say nothing of hostility and opposition. In the nineteenth century many denominations were able to avoid the need to deal with the question of women's roles on a broad scale. In the latter half of the twentieth century it would be difficult to find a religious group that has not had to consider at least on some level how it is that women are perceived and to what extent they participate in the life of the denomination.

CONCLUSION

Religions in America have all been shaped by their participation in the denominational system, one that gives religious groups the freedom to respond as they will to the influences of American culture that come from many quarters. Denominations fight separate and individual battles as to where they want to stand not only on matters of theology and appropriate expressions of piety, but also on more socially oriented issues: lay participation, racial discrimination, poverty, women's ordination, sexual morality. The configuration of responses to these and other issues determines whether denominations are considered liberal, moderate, or conservative. However, given the diversity of opinion that exists in most denominations today, it is not possible to label at least the mainstream denominations very accurately; their memberships encompass a continuum of opinions on both theological and social issues. It has become a sociological truism to say that liberal Baptists may have more in common with liberal Catholics, for example, than they do with conservative Baptists. It goes almost without saying, then, and this chapter has provided numerous examples, that denominations in America are not necessarily groups of people who agree with one another. The freedom afforded by the denominational system brings with it all the risks of disagreement. Most Americans appear willing to chance the dangers of freedom. If denominationalism and voluntarism are viewed as the alternative to a state church, these principles are perceived not only in a highly positive way but also as the only possible way for religions to organize in a pluralistic society. But it doesn't hurt us to listen to a dissenting voice on the subject of denominationalism, that of H. Richard Niebuhr (1894–1962), who wrote in 1929 that "Denominationalism . . . represents the moral failure of Christianity." Niebuhr was advocating Protestant unity, certainly not a state church and not even unions of Catholics and Protestants or Christians or Jews. Niebuhr saw the sources of Protestant denominationalism as social rather than theological and therefore reflecting the injustices inherent in American culture: "It [denominationalism] represents the accommodation of Christianity to the caste system of human society." Niebuhr condemned this caste system that he saw reflected in the membership of separate denominations and in the ways that various groups were related to one another: "The division of the churches closely follows the division of man into the castes of national, racial, and economic groups. It draws the color line in the church of God; it fosters the misunderstandings, the self-exultations, the hatreds of jingoistic nationalism by continuing in the body of Christ the spurious differences of provincial loyalties. . . ."[15] These are strong words, but they remind us that the history of America's coming to terms with religious pluralism has not always been cause for celebration. The very fact of diversity, even though it is guaranteed by law, does not necessarily mean equality of privilege and power within the culture. Niebuhr's is considered one of the "prophetic" voices in American religion, one whose task it is to remind us that any cultural system has within it the potential for both freedom and oppression.

---

[15] H. Richard Niebuhr, *The Social Sources of Denominationalism*, p. 6.

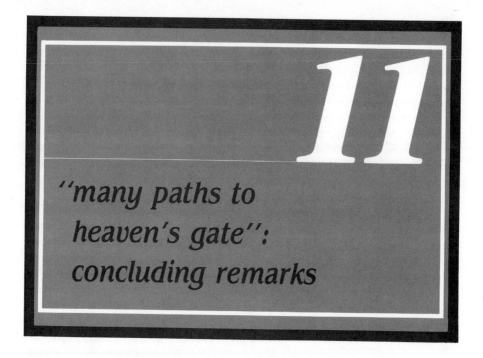

11

"many paths to heaven's gate": concluding remarks

As I sat in the synagogue waiting for our neighbor's Bat Mitzvah ceremony to begin, I thumbed through the prayer book I found in front of me. In the introduction was a passage written to affirm the variety of beliefs and practices in Reform Judaism in America, all directed toward the worship of one God. "There are many paths to heaven's gate," the introduction said. It struck me that these words were particularly appropriate to describe the conviction underlying freedom of religious practice in American culture, and the following excerpt from which they were taken had a significance for all of us:

> We are a diversified people. . . . There is disagreement among us on many issues. . . . We do not assume that all controversy is harmful; still less do we wish to stifle the expression of views sincerely held. Therefore in this prayerbook we have followed the principle that there are many paths to heaven's gate, that this prayer and that one, this service and that one, may both have the power to lead us to the living God. Faithful to this view, we have tried to provide room for many ways of worship.[1]

These few words sum up the spirit that underlies the structure of religious pluralism in America: the deeply held conviction that the dangers which lie in differences, in conflict, in controversy over matters of religion are much less to be feared than those inherent in the attempt "to stifle the expression of views sin-

---

[1] *Gates of Prayer* (New York: Central Conference of American Rabbis, 1977), p. xi–xii.

cerely held." Americans have chosen diversity as a means to unity in the matter of religion out of the strong belief that many voices are better than one, that it is more appropriate to have many paths to the gate of heaven rather than just one that would be too narrow to accommodate all who want to travel there. The American religious system, then, is based on a paradoxical proposition: Unity lies not in oneness of religious belief and practice, but in the agreement that such oneness is neither possible nor desirable. The preceding chapters have dealt with the results of that devotion to pluralism of religious expression: many different religions freed by the Constitution to be as creative and enterprising as they have wanted to be or as faithful to ancient traditions in developing answers to questions of ultimate concern, rituals that would express those answers in worship, and organizations that suited their perspectives of right order.

After so long an emphasis on religious diversity in America, it is time to ask a question: "Has the devotion to pluralism, no matter how firm, really been enough to hold the whole system together over two centuries?" We know from American religious history that the First Amendment has never put an end to religious disputes and hostilities or the social domination of some groups over others. Why, then, we are led to ask, is there such faith in American culture that religious pluralism is still the most desirable state of affairs? How is it possible that a culture as religiously heterogenous as that of the United States has never, since 1791, experienced a serious or effective attempt by any one faction to establish a state religion? How can it be that America has never suffered the agonies of religious warfare? One easy answer can be couched in negative terms: It is that fear of any one denomination or group of similar denominations taking over the government that is the motivating force behind religious pluralism. Another easy answer is to look at the old phrase "divide and conquer" and speculate that, given the divisions within the denominational system, it would be impossible to find enough like-minded people to support any one religion for a state church. A third answer might issue from the fact that Protestantism, no matter how divided, has always been the dominant religion in America, so that there has really been, in a sense, an established religion all along. None of these answers, of course, can be completely discounted; they all have bits of truth in them. But if we are searching for a more positive answer as to why the system of religious diversity is so successful in America, we must look to a more complex solution. It lies in one of the true ironies of American culture: the fact that although the First Amendment could guarantee separation of government from *organized* religions, it simply could not separate religious *values* from the fabric of American culture. It could not, by means of one amendment or ten amendments, erase the early history of America or efface from the culture the sense that God had chosen America from all other nations, much as God had once chosen Israel, to be the Promised Land of modern times, the source of endless plenitude and opportunity, the home of the homeless from many lands, and the site, finally, of the perfect social order.

This strong sense of being a nation set apart by God has pervaded American culture from its early history and forms the basis of a religious value system. One of the most compelling beliefs of the system is faith that the very fact of living in America and of participating in the American way of life has the potential to turn diversity into unity, to render diversity creative and vital rather than divisive and destructive. It has been these high expectations in the transforming powers of American culture that have brought "the tired, the poor, and the huddled masses longing to breathe free," beginning with the Puritans in the seventeenth century and continuing through the arrival of refugees at the end of the twentieth century from Southeast Asia, Haiti, Cuba, and Mexico. In spite of the fears of many that the economy cannot support these later immigrants, that America has lost its promise as the land of endless resources, the faith still prevails on the part of millions of others that the uniquely transformative powers of the American way of life can accommodate and assimilate the many pluralities of the new immigrants—religious, economic, racial, and social—just as it has done in the past.

Again, we ask, haven't there been some discernible vehicles in the culture that have sustained this belief in the transforming of diversity into unity? It is only recently that scholars have begun to point to and describe some of the outlines of these vehicles of value transmission in the culture. One of them has been identified as civil religion or public religion. In 1967 the sociologist Robert Bellah advanced a theory that alongside the institutional and visible religions of America had grown up a religion of the nation, of American-ness, whose prophets, saints, rituals, holy days, and sacred scriptures could be perceived and analyzed in much the same way as those of Lutheranism, Judaism, Methodism, or Catholicism.[2] To look at a religious system in this way, as lying outside the boundaries of organized religions, requires departure from the way in which most Americans understand religion.[3] But once supplied with the idea and the basic framework, it is not difficult for someone new to the idea to sit down and name George Washington, Thomas Jefferson, Andrew Jackson, Abraham Lincoln, Franklin D. Roosevelt, and John F. Kennedy as the prophets and saints; Memorial Day, Flag Day, the Fourth of July, Labor Day, Veterans Day, and Thanksgiving as the holy days; the Declaration of Independence and the Constitution as the sacred scriptures; and ceremonies ranging from a simple flag raising to the inauguration of a president as the rituals. In spite of debate about details of the civil religion since Bellah articulated its structure, the alacrity with which Americans have recognized its existence and the speed with which most listeners nod in agreement as to their own experiences of the civil religion are testimony to the fact of its reality in American

---

[2] Robert Bellah, "Civil Religion in America," in *Religion in America,* eds. William G. McLoughlin and Robert N. Bellah (Boston: Beacon Press, 1968). This essay has been reprinted in numerous sources.

[3] Most Americans still understand religion as a matter of organized groups. For example, in a recent study of *Time* magazine, three communications professors found that in *Time* articles religion is portrayed as an "overwhelmingly institutional affair." Because of the widespread circulation of *Time,* it is probably safe to come to some conclusions about Americans' perception of religion based on this survey. Roderick P. Hart, Kathleen J. Turner, and Ralph E. Knupp, "A Rhetorical Profile of Religious News: *Time,* 1947–1976," *Journal of Communication,* 31 (Summer 1981), p. 60.

culture. In fact, there seem to be some parallels with what Mary Baker Eddy called her "discovery" of Christian Science in Bellah's formation of the concept of the civil religion. Eddy intentionally chose the word *discover* to indicate her belief that God had revealed to her that the Bible had always been a document of healings. According to Eddy's understanding, she didn't invent or found Christian Science; she came upon it already in existence. In much the same way, although without claim of divine inspiration, Bellah came to recognize and was able to put forth convincingly a description of what had been there all along.

The historian Catherine Albanese likewise confirms the unifying powers of the civil religion in America, but she also looks to another source just as compelling in accounting for the unity within American religious diversity that she calls "public Protestantism." The Protestant way of being religious in America has exerted its influence on all other religions of the culture, and we have seen in previous chapters how the beliefs, rituals, and forms of self-government of many denominations have been shaped by the Protestant penchant for action and moral rectitude over intellectual probing; simplicity over complexity; and widespread participation over hierarchical forms of polity. Albanese is particularly convincing in her description of the ways in which public Protestantism has brought a measure of uniformity to the rituals of many different religions: Reform Jews' moving their worship services to Sunday instead of Saturday; Catholics' simplifying the Mass so that it was closer to Protestant forms of worship; Mormons and Adventists' preaching the optimism of liberal Protestantism; Japanese Buddhists' speaking of churches, Sunday services, and bishops; and black Americans' either moving to integrated congregations or imitating the format of white Protestant worship.[4] As forceful as public Protestantism has been in bringing a semblance of uniformity to American religions, sometimes its power has degenerated into a kind of coercion, not legal but social, expressed particularly in criticisms of "foreign" or new religions and urgings that they conform to cultural expectations.

The civil religion has had its underside also. That same sense of chosen-ness, of God-given purpose and privilege, has had a stultifying effect on the process of national self-criticism and prophetic vision. It has tended to cultivate an excess of self-righteousness and pride in national identity, leading to grave problems in both foreign and domestic policies. In a nation in which there is a strong sense that "God is on our side," it is not easy to assemble very quickly a majority of people to speak out against government actions. The war in Vietnam and the Watergate scandal are ample evidence of that fact. When things appear to be going badly, the confidence in God-given national imperatives has too often fostered the tendency to look outward for the causes of trouble, to try to purge and purify the culture of what are perceived as dangerous elements—whether they be alcohol, communists, or the governments of foreign nations. Like other institutions of the culture, the

---

[4] Catherine Albanese, Chapter Ten, "Historical Dominance and the One Religion of the United States," *America: Religion and Religions* (Belmont, California: Wadsworth, 1980), pp. 247–81.

churches, too, are susceptible to the pull of the civil religion and may be drawn into affirming an unthinking uniformity of purpose rather than responding to their expected roles as critics of the culture. To use an historical example, it is one of the scandals of American religious history that so many American religions failed to cry out against the practice of slavery and in fact often defended it. And in the twentieth century the call to action in the civil rights movement was not heard, at least at first, by many churches. It may be that in cases such as these, when American culture condoned first slavery and in the twentieth century segregation, religious groups responded slowly to issues of social justice because, perhaps even unwittingly, they sensed that they were up against not just "the world" or "government" but another religious system immensely more powerful because it was not split into many different denominations but instead had a hold on the whole culture. At such times the function of the civil religion as an agent of national unity is distorted, for it has deprived the culture of the diversity it needs to remain critically self-aware of its own limitations and sins.

Thus, we come around again to the role that religious diversity plays in American culture as it is lived out in the denominational system and acts as a safeguard against a religious or political unity that is unthinking, unyielding, and deprived of the life-giving energies of many voices. We have seen that the system is not flawless. The First Amendment has been able to guarantee only freedom of religious practice, not absence of religious bigotry. We are reminded, also, of H. Richard Niebuhr's criticism of the denominational system—that it imitates the economic, racial, and social caste system of other aspects of society. But on the whole the system works, confirming the agreement of Americans that we are indeed a diverse people and that we therefore need many paths to heaven's gate.

EPILOGUE

I remember reading many years ago a description by Joseph Blau of the instant forming of community when a small child runs smiling down the aisle of a bus and brings all the other riders together in common delight and concern. The little incident has served for me as a reminder that much "book learning" can come alive through a very ordinary and simple experience.

Just previous to beginning the conclusion of this book I spent a few days at an ecumenical retreat center in the woods of Minnesota. My companions at dinner the first evening were the Lutheran theology professor and his wife who had begun the community; a Roman Catholic nun who is an art history professor; the Quaker director of ministries at an urban Friends' Meeting; several Lutheran youth pastors from across the country; a woman who belonged to a Congregational Church; and another young woman serving a year with the Church of the Brethren Volunteer Services. We engaged in an informal kind of shop talk, exchanging stories of childhood encounters with and stereotypes of "other" religions, telling a few Catholic/Protestant jokes, reminiscing about a Jewish-led service held in the chapel a few weeks earlier, admiring a painting of Elijah the Prophet on the wall outside the chapel that was the product of a Greek icon painting retreat held the previous year. All of us had stories to tell of unhappy encounters with religious prejudice; all of us likewise had experienced some participation in the rituals of religious traditions different from our own. It was not a momentous occasion: There were no sermons made; no petitions signed; no manifestoes put forth; no conversions experienced. And yet the evening remains for me a reminder both of the diversity of religion in America—only minimally represented by the few of us—and of the strong sense of community, of tolerance, and the sharing of insights that, at its best, underlies that diversity.

Bibliography

In keeping with this book's overall theme of diversity, the following bibliography is meant to indicate not just basic references in each section but also different approaches to subject matter. For example, the three histories in the first section are all very different from one another. Ahlstrom employs the standard method of historical writing; Albanese treats many varieties of American religions separately, what she calls the "manyness" of religion in America and then goes on to describe the "oneness" of religion in America; and Gaustad makes use of quotations from many primary sources. In addition, the references are not necessarily the last word in a particular discipline or area of study. The information in Lenski's *The Religious Factor,* for example, is out of date, but there is much value in analyzing the methods he used to study religion in Detroit. There is a final section included in the bibliography of literary works, on the theory that such writings capture the spirit of a particular religious system or an era in ways that are not possible in scholarly works.

HISTORY AND BIOGRAPHY

AHLSTROM, SYDNEY E. *A Religious History of the American People.* New Haven, Connecticut: Yale University Press, 1972.

ALBANESE, CATHERINE L. *America: Religions and Religion.* Belmont, California: Wadsworth, 1981.

BOWDEN, HENRY WARNER. *Dictionary of American Religious Biography.* Westport, Connecticut: Greenwood Press, 1977.

GAUSTAD, EDWIN SCOTT. *A Religious History of America.* San Francisco: Harper & Row, Publishers, 1974.

————. *A Documentary History of Religion in America to the Civil War,* Vol. I. Grand Rapids, Michigan: Eerdman's, 1982.

PROTESTANT HISTORY AND THEOLOGY

BRAUER, JERALD C. *Protestantism in America: A Narrative History,* rev. ed. Philadelphia: Westminster Press, 1965.

HANDY, ROBERT T. *A Christian America: Protestant Hopes and Historical Realities.* New York: Oxford University Press, 1971.

MARSDEN, GEORGE M. *Fundamentalism and American Culture: The Shaping of Twentieth Century Evangelicalism: 1870–1925.* New York: Oxford University Press, 1980.

MARTY, MARTIN. *Righteous Empire: The Protestant Experience in America.* New York: The Dial Press, 1970.

MATHEWS, DONALD G. *Religion in the Old South.* Chicago: University of Chicago Press, 1977.

MILLER, DONALD EARL. *The Case for Liberal Christianity.* San Francisco: Harper & Row, 1981.

NIEBUHR, H. RICHARD. *Christ and Culture.* New York: Harper & Row, Publishers, 1951.

SOCIOLOGY

GLOCK, CHARLES Y., and RODNEY STARK. *Religion and Society in Tension.* Chicago: Rand McNally & Company, 1965.

HERBERG, WILL. *Protestant, Catholic, Jew: An Essay in American Religious Sociology.* Garden City, New York: Doubleday & Co., 1955.

LENSKI, GERHARD. *The Religious Factor.* Garden City, New York: Doubleday & Company, Inc., Anchor Books, 1963.

MARTY, MARTIN. *A Nation of Behavers.* Chicago: University of Chicago Press, 1976.

ROMAN CATHOLIC HISTORY AND THEOLOGY

ELLIS, JOHN TRACY. *American Catholicism,* rev. ed. Chicago: University of Chicago Press, 1969.

———, ed. *Documents of American Catholic History.* Milwaukee: Bruce Publishing Company, 1961.

GREELEY, ANDREW M. *The American Catholic: A Social Portrait.* New York: Basic Books, 1977.

HENNESEY, JAMES, S.J. *American Catholics: A History of the Roman Catholic Community in the United States.* New York: Oxford University Press, 1981.

MCBRIEN, RICHARD P. *Catholicism,* Study Edition. Minneapolis: Winston Press, 1981.

JUDAISM

BLAU, JOSEPH L. *Judaism in America: From Curiosity to Third Faith.* Chicago: University of Chicago Press, 1976.

GLAZER, NATHAN. *American Judaism.* Chicago: University of Chicago Press, 1957.

NEUSNER, JACOB, ed. *Understanding American Judaism: Toward the Description of a Modern Religion,* Vol. II, Sectors of American Judaism: Reform, Orthodoxy, Conservatism, and Reconstructionism, 1975.

———. *The Way of Torah: An Introduction to Judaism.* Belmont, California: Dickenson Publishing, 1974.

DISSENTING AND NEW RELIGIONS IN AMERICA

ELLWOOD, ROBERT S., Jr. *Alternative Altars.* Chicago: University of Chicago Press, 1979.

GOTTSCHALK, STEPHEN. *The Emergence of Christian Science in American Religious Life.* Berkeley: University of California Press, 1973.

HANSEN, KLAUS J. *Mormonism and the American Experience.* Chicago: University of Chicago Press, 1981.

JUDAH, J. STILLSON. *The History and Philosophy of the Metaphysical Movements in America.* Philadelphia: Westminster Press, 1967.

NEEDLEMAN, JACOB. *The New Religions,* rev. ed. New York: Simon and Schuster, Pocket Books, 1972.

———, and George Baker, eds. *Understanding the New Religions.* New York: The Seabury Press, 1978.

ZARETSKY, IRVING I., and MARK LEONE, eds. *Religious Movements in Contemporary America.* Princeton, New Jersey: Princeton University Press, 1974.

CIVIL RELIGION

ALBANESE, CATHERINE. *Sons of the Fathers: The Civil Religion of the American Revolution.* Philadelphia: Temple University Press, 1976.

BELLAH, ROBERT. *The Broken Covenant: American Civil Religion in Time of Trial.* New York: Seabury, 1975.

WILSON, JOHN F. *Public Religion in American Culture.* Philadelphia: Temple University Press, 1979.

NATIVE AMERICAN AND BLACK RELIGIONS

BOWDEN, HENRY WARNER. *American Indians and Christian Missions: Studies in Cultural Conflict.* Chicago: University of Chicago Press, 1981.

DELORIA, VINE, Jr. *God Is Red.* New York: Grosset and Dunlap, 1973.

NEIHARDT, JOHN G. *Black Elk Speaks.* Lincoln: University of Nebraska Press, 1961.

SIMPSON, GEORGE EATON. *Black Religions in the New World.* New York: Columbia University Press, 1978.

WASHINGTON, JOSEPH R., Jr. *Black Sects and Cults.* Garden City, New York: Doubleday, Anchor Books, 1973.

WOMEN IN AMERICAN RELIGION

CHRIST, CAROL P., and JUDITH PLASKOW. *Womanspirit Rising: A Feminist Reader in Religion.* San Francisco: Harper & Row, Publishers, 1979.

PORTERFIELD, AMANDA. *Feminine Spirituality in America: From Sarah Edwards to Martha Graham.* Philadelphia: Temple University Press, 1980.

RUETHER, ROSEMARY RADFORD. *New Woman/New Earth: Sexist Ideologies and Human Liberation.* New York: Seabury Press, 1975.

LITERATURE

BRADSTREET, ANNE. *The Works of Anne Bradstreet,* ed. Jeannine Hensley. Cambridge, Massachusetts: The Belknap Press of Harvard University Press, 1967.

DICKINSON, EMILY. *The Complete Poems of Emily Dickinson,* ed. Thomas H. Johnson. Boston: Little, Brown and Company, first published in 1890.

CATHER, WILLA. *Death Comes for the Archbishop.* New York: Vintage Books, 1971, first published in 1927.

FAULKNER, WILLIAM. *Light in August.* New York: Modern Library, 1959, first published in 1932.

FREDERIC, HAROLD. *The Damnation of Theron Ware,* ed. Everett Carter. Cambridge, Massachusetts: The Belknap Press of Harvard University Press, 1960, first published in 1896.

HAWTHORNE, NATHANIEL. *The Scarlet Letter,* ed. Harry Levin. Boston: Houghton Mifflin Company, 1960, first published in 1850.

MOMADAY, N. SCOTT. *House Made of Dawn.* New York: Harper & Row, Publishers, 1968.

O'CONNOR, FLANNERY. *The Complete Stories.* New York: Farrar, Strauss & Giroux, 1980 (sixteenth printing).

ROTH, HENRY. *Call It Sleep.* New York: Cooper Square Publishers, Inc., 1965, first published in 1934.

WHITMAN, WALT. *Leaves of Grass,* eds. Harold W. Blodgett and Sculley Bradley. New York: W. W. Norton & Company, Inc., 1965, first published in 1855.

Glossary

This glossary provides some basic information about a wide variety of religious groups in America along with some terms that the beginning student is likely to encounter frequently. Since the glossary cannot possibly be inclusive of all the religious groups in America, it is meant to be representative in its references to large and prominent denominations with a long history in American culture as well as to smaller groups and religions that are relatively new.

Adventists trace their history to the nineteenth-century Baptist preacher William Miller, who foretold the imminent end of the world. The largest of the Adventist groups is the Seventh Day Adventists, who look expectantly to the Second Coming of Christ, practice dietary restrictions, and worship on Saturday.

The Amana Church Society is descended from an eighteenth-century German pietist group that came to America in 1842 and lived communally, first in Buffalo, New York, and then in Iowa, site of the Amana Colonies. The community was disbanded in 1932, but the Church continues to function.

The Assemblies of God, the largest Pentecostal Church in the United States, was founded in 1914. It puts great emphasis on gifts of the Holy Spirit, such as speaking in tongues and divine healing, and has a congregational form of self-government in which local churches have authority over their own affairs.

Baha'i came to America from Persia in the nineteenth century. Its foundations are in Islam; it has little creed or ritual and insists on the unity of all religions and seeks world peace. Baha'i headquarters in the United States is in Wilmette, Illinois.

Baptists form the largest Protestant group in the United States and trace their history in America to seventeenth-century New England. Baptists practice baptism of believers (that is, they do not baptize infants) and insist upon the autonomy of the local congregation. Baptists in America are divided into many separate groups, among them the Southern Baptists (the largest), the American Baptists, the General Baptists, the Free Will Baptists, and the Primitive Baptists.

Buddhism, one of the world's great religions, came to America in the nineteenth century and was for many years practiced chiefly by Japanese and Chinese immigrants. Interest in forms of Buddhism such as Zen and Nichiren Shoshu began to grow in America in the 1950s and 1960s. The Jodo Shinshu sect of Buddhism is represented by the Buddhist Churches in America, which has incorporated Protestant influences into its organization and worship.

The Church of the Brethren has its roots in eighteenth-century Germany. Brethren are pacifists, abstain from alcohol, and practice the "simple life," one of frugality and avoidance of luxury. The Church of the Brethren operates a volunteer service for young men and women, including conscientious objectors.

The Church of Christ, Scientist, more popularly known as Christian Science, was founded by Mary Baker Eddy on the basis of her healing experience in 1866. Christian Science denies the reality of matter and thus also of evil, pain, and sickness. Healing proceeds from true understanding of the perfection of God's creation. There is no ordained clergy in Christian Science, but there are readers, practitioners, and teachers.

The Church of God is a Pentecostal denomination founded in the early twentieth century that puts emphasis on justification by faith rather than works and on the gifts of the Holy Spirit. It is one of many similar groups in America, among the others the Church of God (Cleveland, Tennessee), the Church of God (Anderson, Indiana), the Church of God by Faith, and the Church of God in Christ.

The Church of Jesus Christ of Latter-day Saints (the Mormons) was established by Joseph Smith in 1830 based on a series of visions that led to the discovery of golden tablets from which he translated the *Book of Mormon.* The major Mormon group has its headquarters in Salt Lake City, Utah. There are several offshoots of Mormonism, the largest the Reorganized Church of Jesus Christ of Latter-day Saints with its headquarters in Independence, Missouri.

The Church of the Nazarene was founded in Texas in 1908 and has its theological foundations in Methodism. It is a holiness group and does not practice speaking in tongues.

The Church Universal and Triumphant was founded in 1958 by Mark and Elizabeth Clare Prophet, mother and son. Mark has since died and Elizabeth is known as Guru Ma. This group's teachings are eclectic and similar to those of Theosophy in its understanding that Ascended Masters communicate universal truths to human beings.

The Church of Scientology was founded by L. Ron Hubbard in 1955. It was at first primarily a system of self-improvement and self-knowledge called Dianetics. Scientology takes its teachings from a variety of sources. Scientology has experienced an ongoing battle with the Internal Revenue Service over its tax-exempt status.

Congregationalism has two meanings in American culture. In a general sense it refers to a system of church government by which separate congregations are autonomous. More specifically, Congregationalism has historical reference to the Puritan religion of New England and today points to those groups who did not join in the merger to form the United Church of Christ in 1957. The Congregational Christian Churches are the largest of these groups and are sometimes referred to as ''continuing Congregationalists.''

Deism grew out of the Enlightenment, or Age of Reason, of the eighteenth century. It was not an organized religion and departed from traditional Christianity in its insistence that human reason, unaided by revelation, could make sense of the universe, which operated according to natural law. In this view God created the universe but does not interfere in its workings or in human affairs.

The Disciples of Christ (also called the Christian Church) originated in the nineteenth century on the American frontier. Disciples espouse no creed other than the Scriptures, and the basic unit of the denomination is the local church.

The Episcopal Church is a mainstream denomination with theological and liturgical roots in the Church of England and a history in the United States since the seventeenth century. It is a part of the Anglican Communion but governs itself independently as a representative democracy.

Ethical Culture societies were formed by Felix Adler in 1876. Ethical Culture is humanistic rather than theistic in emphasis, has no creed or ritual system, and encourages freedom of thought and social action.

Evangelicalism has several different meanings in American culture, among them an emphasis on the Bible or the "Gospel" as the foundation of faith rather than creeds or theological systems. The term also refers to religion based on an individual conversion experience that results in a life of piety. Sometimes the term is used to refer to conservative Christians in contrast to liberals.

Friends are more commonly known as Quakers and have been in America since the seventeenth century. Historically devoted to freedom of conscience, Quakers were persecuted in some colonies for their dissenting views. Today the Society of Friends continues its tradition of social activism and pacifism and sponsors the American Friends Service Committee, one of the most effective relief agencies in the world.

Fundamentalism refers to a conservative Protestant theology that seeks to hold on to what it considers the essential truths of Christianity as found in the Bible. The term implies reliance on a literal interpretation of the Bible and came into currency in the 1920s as the opposite of Modernism (which see).

The Holiness Movement began in pre–Civil War America and particularly influenced Methodism. The movement stressed that salvation is the work of the Holy Spirit and not of sacraments or churches and put great emphasis on living a pious life.

The International Church of the Foursquare Gospel was founded in the 1920s by Aimee Semple McPherson, whose teachings included an emphasis on love, healing, and self-fulfillment. "Foursquare" refers to four roles of Jesus Christ: savior, baptizer, healer, and king.

The International Society for Krishna Consciousness, better known as Hare Krishna, was founded in America in 1967. Members are devoted to Krishna as Supreme God. They practice an ascetic lifestyle and spend their days in a disciplined regimen of work and prayer.

Jehovah's Witnesses, known early in their history as Russellites, were organized by Charles Taze Russell in 1884. Witnesses are adventists who look to the imminent Second Coming of Jesus Christ, and they actively spread their beliefs. They look upon business, government, and the "false" teachings of other churches as agents of Satan.

Judaism in America has three divisions: the Orthodox, the most observant of Jewish customs and rituals; the Conservative, which has looked for middle ground between Jewish beliefs and practices and the pressures of a secular American culture; and Reform, which is most liberal in orientation and has simplified rituals and practices in the course of its assimilation into American culture.

Lutherans are theological descendants of the sixteenth-century German reformer Martin Luther, who argued that salvation comes through grace received by faith instead of through works. Lutherans were present early in American history, but the denomination did not grow greatly until the nineteenth century. Lutherans have traditionally been divided into separate churches based on ethnic differences—for example, German, Danish, Norwegian, and Swedish—as well as theological, but movement toward unity has been a constant factor in twentieth-century American Lutheranism.

The Mennonites originated in sixteenth-century Switzerland under the leadership of Menno Simons, an Anabaptist who denied the validity of infant baptism. Mennonites live a simple life and are usually pacifists. The Old Order Amish belong to this group.

The Methodists make up the largest Protestant denomination in the United States after the Baptists and have their roots in the teachings of the eighteenth-century English dissenter John Wesley. Methodism has produced many offshoots during its history in America, among them the largest, the United Methodist Church. Other Methodist bodies include the Free Methodist Church, which emerged from the Holiness movement of the nineteenth century, and the African Methodist Episcopal Church and the African Methodist Episcopal Church Zion, both black denominations.

Millennialism is a belief that Christ will establish his kingdom on Earth for 1,000 years of peace and prosperity either before (premillennialists) or after (postmillennialists) the Second Coming and a battle between the forces of good and evil. There are a number of millennial groups in America, all with their own interpretations of this belief, among them the Seventh Day Adventists and the Jehovah's Witnesses.

Modernism is a term that came into common use in the 1920s to refer to a liberal kind of Protestantism that cut across denominations and looked to science as well as to religion for inspiration. Modernism emphasized an optimistic view of human nature, the possibility of moral progress, a more figurative than literal interpretation of the Bible, and a greater stress on the humanity of Jesus than his divinity. The term was frequently used as an opposite to Fundamentalism.

The Moravians, of Bohemian descent, arrived in America in the eighteenth century and settled in eastern Pennsylvania, North Carolina, and, later, northeastern Wisconsin. The Moravians produced some of America's first composers and also did missionary work among the Indians. Today they are a small Protestant denomination.

The Native American Church was incorporated in Oklahoma in 1918. It draws Indians from a number of different tribes and uses peyote, an hallucenogenic plant, in its rituals, a use that has been declared legal by the United States government.

Neo-Orthodoxy refers to a theological movement that emerged in the 1930s as a rejection of liberal Protestantism's optimism about human nature and the possibility for social and moral progress. The movement renewed the Reformation emphasis on an omnipotent God and a sinful and helpless humanity.

The Orthodox churches represent eastern European Christians who do not accept papal authority. Similar in some respects to Roman Catholicism, they are sacramental and highly liturgical. Orthodoxy began to grow in America at the beginning of the twentieth century, and its churches are separated according to nationality; among them are the Greek, the Russian, and the Serbian Orthodox Churches.

Pentecostalism is a form of Christianity that stresses the charismatic gifts conferred by the Holy Spirit upon the Apostles at Pentecost, such as speaking in tongues and divine healing. In America the term is applied to a variety of denominations, many of them offshoots of the Baptists and the Methodists, and it can also refer to movements within other denominations.

Pietism began as a seventeenth-century German movement to bring new life to Lutheranism and gave rise to such groups as the Moravians. Now the term is used more generally to refer to an emphasis on living a life free of corruption and one devoted to piety. Pietistic groups tend to be more concerned with religious experience than with theological reflection and generally expect that their members refrain from smoking, drinking, and gambling.

The Presbyterians are a mainstream Protestant denomination with Scottish roots. "Presbyterian" refers to their form of self-government, that is, by teaching elders who are ordained ministers and ruling elders, lay members elected from the congregation, both of whom are called "presbyters." In 1983 the northern and southern branches of Presbyterianism, separated since before the Civil War, merged into The Presbyterian Church (United States).

Revivalism is a form of religious expression that centers on an emotional acting out of the drama of sin and salvation. Revivalism may refer to a way of being religious that is the dominant focus of a particular denomination, or it may refer to a wave of renewed religious feeling that sweeps across a denomination or a geographic area. Essentially a Protestant phenomenon, revivalism has also found expression in American Catholicism.

The Roman Catholic Church constitutes the largest single denomination in America, and its members number about 22 percent of the population. The central act of Catholic worship is the Mass, and the church is governed by a hierarchical system headed by the Bishop of Rome, the Pope. Present in America as early as the sixteenth century, Catholicism did not grow in large numbers until the nineteenth century, when millions of immigrants came from northern and western Europe and later southern and eastern Europe. Ethnic distinctions among such groups as the Irish, the Germans, the Italians, the Poles, and the Hispanics are important in understanding American Catholicism.

The Salvation Army was founded by a British Methodist, William Booth, and came to America in 1880. This group functions both as a church and as a social agency and is better known in American culture as the latter.

The Shakers were founded by Mother Ann Lee, an Englishwoman, in the late eighteenth century and brought by her to America. The Shaker communities, based on celibate living and belief in a Mother/Father God and governed by male/female leadership, were at their strongest in mid-nineteenth-century America. Today there are fewer than ten Shakers, all women, in two communities in Maine and New Hampshire.

Spiritualism, a belief in the power of certain persons called *mediums* to communicate with the spirit world, began in America in 1848 and acquired a widespread popularity that lasted until the Civil War. Even though interest in Spiritualism waned somewhat after that, there have been revivals of interest, particularly after the two world wars, and Spiritualist groups remain a part of American culture. The most prominent group is the National Spiritualist Association of Churches.

The Social Gospel movement began to emerge at the end of the nineteenth century as an expression of liberal Protestantism that based its hope for the improvement of industrial society on an optimism about the possibilities of human perfection and a conviction that humanity with God's help could gain control over social forces, particularly poverty and the suffering experienced by workers in a capitalist society and that working for a better society was an important Christian obligation.

Transcendentalism was a nineteenth-century movement that originated in New England with Ralph Waldo Emerson and other members of the Transcendental Club, most of them Unitarians. Transcendentalists emphasized intuition over reason as a means of deriving truth and preached a highly optimistic view of human nature. Never an organized religious movement, Transcendentalism had a great influence on American literature and on the "positive thinking" religions.

The Unification Church was founded in Korea in 1954 by the Reverend Sun Myung Moon. This group has aroused a great deal of antagonism, but it has a sophisticated theology with similarities to various kinds of adventism and looks to the restoration of human innocence that existed before the Fall.

The Unitarian Universalist Association was formed in 1961 by a merger of the Unitarians, whose chief doctrine was originally a denial of the trinity, and the Universalists, who affirm that salvation is for all. Unitarian Universalists are liberal in their emphases. They look upon Jesus Christ as an ethical leader rather than as a divine/human being, and they stress reason and personal experience rather than revelation as the guides to truth.

The United Church of Christ, a mainstream Protestant denomination, grew out of a merger in 1957 of the Congregational Christian and the Evangelical and Reformed churches. In this denomination the local church is autonomous in managing its own affairs, and its relationship to regional and national bodies is voluntary.

The Unity School of Christianity, founded by Charles and Myrtle Fillmore in 1887, is a New Thought religion, that is, it stresses an optimistic theology, "positive thinking," and mental healing. Unity has many similarities to Christian Science, although its governing system is not as tightly structured, and it is a close relative of Divine Science and Religious Science.

The religion of **Wicca** is described by its followers as a renewal of an ancient nature religion that had as its central focus worship of the Mother Goddess or Earth Mother. Referred to also as contemporary witchcraft and a form of neo-paganism, this movement is not to be confused with Satanism.

Index

Abolition, 23, 71
Abortion, 6
Adler, Felix, 44–45
Adventists, 23, 99, 141, 163
African Communities League, 75
African Methodist Episcopal Church, 145
African Orthodox Church, 75
Afterlife, 42, 120, 134
Agee, James, 90n
Ahlstrom, Sydney, 15, 21, 75
Albanese, Catherine, 163
Amana Colonists, 23
"Amazing Grace," 31
American colonies, 15–16, 18–20, 34
American Factor, The (Greeley), 149
American Gothic (Wood), 91–92
American Humanist Association, 118
American Indians and Christian Missions (Bowden), 137
"Americanist" controversy, 43–44
American Lutheran Church, 124
American Plains Indians, 67
American Revolution, 20, 21
Amish, 67
Anglicanism, 20, 21, 69
Antes, John, 121
Anthony, Susan B., 155
Anti-Semitism, 27, 44, 86
Apostles' Creed, 125
Appraisal, The (Wood), 92
Aquinas, Saint Thomas, 44, 110, 115
Architecture, 78–86
Armenian Apostolic Church, 149
Art, 78–93
Assemblies of God, 140
Association of Evangelical Lutheran Churches, 124n
Association of Theological Schools, 151–54
Atheism, 108
Augustana Synod, 148
Austin, Ann, 69
Awakenings, 30, 33–36

Bacon, Margaret H., 69, 70
Bahái, 66
Baird, Robert, 24
Baldwin, James, 75–77
Baptism, 123, 127–30

Baptists, 3, 8, 20, 22, 23, 139, 140
 black denominations, 67, 145, 146
 clergy, role of, 152
 worship, 119
Barth, Karl, 59
Bar Mitzvah, 123, 130–33
Batterham, Forster, 62
Belief, 94–115
Bellah, Robert, 162–63
Bemes, Peter, 82
Benton, Thomas Hart, 91, 93
Biblical interpretation, 56, 66, 98
Birth-control controversy, 143
Black Muslims, 25, 67, 74–77, 146
Blacks, 27, 33, 57–61, 67, 70, 71, 145–46
Blau, Joseph, 147, 164
Blavatsky, Helena, 42
Book of Common Prayer, 122, 143
Bowden, Henry Warner, 137
Braude, Ann, 156
Brebéuf, Jean de, 137
Breuer, Marcel, 82–84
Brook Farmers, 23
Bryant, Robert, 9
Buchanan, James, 65
Buddhism, 67, 99, 141, 146, 163
Budenz, Louis, 112

Carnegie, Andrew, 40
Catholicism, 3, 9, 16, 19, 22–24, 27, 140, 163
 "Americanist" controversy, 43–44
 anti-, 43
 architecture, 83–84
 baptism, 127–30
 beliefs, 96, 99
 clergy, role of, 152
 Day, Dorothy, and, 61–64
 funeral rituals, 120
 literature, 79, 80, 86–90
 national origin and, 148–49
 Ojibwa wake service, 133–37
 organizational structure, 142–43
 percentage of population, 139, 141
 science and, 43
 Sheen, Fulton J., and, 100, 101, 110–15
 Vatican II, 25, 44, 87, 110, 122, 130
 women and, 157
 worship, 119, 120, 122, 127–30

Catholic Worker, 63
Catholic Worker Movement, 62–64
Central Conference of American Rabbis, 105
Christian Church, 3, 139
Christianity and Progress (Fosdick), 56
Christian Science, 3, 9, 23, 27, 141, 163
  organizational structure, 144
  theology of, 42, 66, 72–74, 97, 98
  women and, 72–74
Church and state, separation of, 4, 20, 139
Church of Christ, Scientist (*see* Christian Science)
Church of Jesus Christ of Latter-Day Saints (*see* Mormonism)
Church of the Brethren, 139
Church of the Nazarene, 140
Church Universal and Triumphant, 9, 67–68, 99, 145
Civil religion, 162–64
Civil-rights movement, 58–60, 164
Clergy, role of, 142–44, 150–54
Colonial Church of Edina, 81–82
Colored Methodist Episcopal (Christian Methodist) Church, 145
Communion, 119, 124
Confession, 113–14, 122
Confirmation, 127
Conflicts in Religious Thought (Harkness), 106–9
Congregationalism, 3, 8, 20, 22, 24, 81, 140
Conscientious objection, 26
Conservative Judaism, 105, 131
Constitution of the United States, 16, 25–26
Council of Nicaea, 125
Council of Trent, 127
Creationism, 6, 39, 67
Cults, 3, 27, 66, 138
Curry, John Steuart, 91

Dance, 79, 121
Danish Lutheran Church, 148
Darwin, Charles, 39
Davis v. Beeson (1890), 26
Day, Dorothy, 47, 61–64
Deism, 22, 67, 97
Dennis, James, 92–93
Denominationalism, 138–59
  clergy and laity, 150–54
  organizational structure, 142–45
  race and national origin, 145–50
  women, roles of, 154–58
Denominational Society, The (Greeley), 139
Densmore, Frances, 134
Dickinson, Emily, 78, 80
Dinner for Threshers (Wood), 92–93
Disciples of Christ, 3, 139
"Displaced Person, The" (O'Connor), 88
Dissent, religious, 65–77
Divine Science, 99
Dolan, Jay, 36n

Drew, Timothy, 75
Dworschock, Baldwin, 83, 84

Ecumenical movement, 27, 87
Eddy, Asa Gilbert, 72
Eddy, Mary Baker, 42, 72–74, 97, 144, 163
Edwards, Jonathan, 3, 30–32, 47, 48–53, 55, 57, 100
Eisenhower, Dwight D., 95, 118
Ellwood, Robert, 68
Elmer Gantry (Lewis), 29
Emerson, Ralph Waldo, 74, 78, 99, 100
English settlers, 18–19
Enlightenment, 21, 22, 34, 49
Ephrata Cloister, 22
Epicureans, 74
Episcopal Church, 3, 8, 24, 122, 139, 140
  ordination of women, 158
  organizational structure, 142, 143–44
Ethical Culture Society, 45
Eucharist, 119, 142
Evangelicalism, 22–24, 107, 140, 152
Evans, Walker, 90n
Evolutionary theory, 6, 39, 67

Failure of Modernism, The (Horsch), 56
Faith for Tough Times, A (Fosdick), 57
Fard, W. D., 75, 76
Fasting, 123
Father Divine's Peace Mission Movement, 25, 146
Finney, Charles Grandison, 32
Finnish American National Evangelical Lutheran Church, 148
Fire Next Time, The (Baldwin), 75
First Amendment to the Constitution, 26, 139, 161, 164
First Great Awakening, 20–21, 31, 33–35, 48, 52
Fisher, Mary, 69
Ford, Henry, II, 112
Fosdick, Harry Emerson, 47, 53–57, 107
Foundling, The (Spellman), 87
Fourth Great Awakening, 33, 35
Fox, George, 69
Franklin, Benjamin, 22, 31
Free Church, 152
Freedom of religion, 4, 16, 21–22
Freethinkers, 98
Friends (*see* Quakers)
Frost, Robert, 79
Fullenwider, S. P., 60
Fundamentalism, 25, 42, 53, 55–57
Funeral rituals, 119–20

Gaines, W. H., 59–60
Gandhi, Mohandas K., 59, 60
Garvey, Marcus, 75
Gaustad, Edwin, 66–67

Ghost Dance religion, 67
Gill, Sam, 17
Gladden, Washington, 58, 59
Glock, Charles, 3
God and Intelligence (Sheen), 111
"Good Country People" (O'Connor), 88
"Good Man is Hard To Find, A" (O'Connor), 88-89
Gortner, Marjoe, 29
Gospel of Wealth, The (Carnegie), 40
Gottschalk, Stephen, 74
Graham, Billy, 29
Great Awakening (*see* First Great Awakening; Fourth Great Awakening; Second Great Awakening; Third Great Awakening)
Greek Orthodox Church, 9, 149
Greeley, Andrew, 43, 139, 149
Gropius, 83

Half-Way Covenant, 52
Halsey, William M., 113, 115
Hare Krishna, 3, 27, 66, 147
Harkness, Georgia, 94, 100, 101, 105-10
Harmonists, 23
Hawthorne, Nathaniel, 78, 80
Healthy-Happy-Holy Organization, 147
Hebrew Union College, 105
Heller, James G., 104
Herberg, Will, 5, 95
Hinduism, 42, 140, 146
History of Human Redemption, The (Edwards), 52
Holiness churches, 140, 141
Holocaust, 25
Horsch, John, 56
"How My Mind Has Changed in This Decade" (Harkness), 108
Hudson, Winthrop, 20
Humanists, 67
Human nature, theology of, 98-99
Huron Indians, 137
Hutchinson, Ann, 154

I Am movement, 25
Ingersoll, Robert C., 40
Integral Yoga Institute, 141
International Society for Krishna Consciousness (*see* Hare Krishna)
Ireland, John, 44
Islam, 75, 147

James, William, 2, 3
Jefferson, Thomas, 4, 22
Jehovah's Witnesses, 6, 16, 65, 99, 140, 141
Jesuits, 137
Jesus Christ, divinity of, 94, 98, 109
Jesus People, 32
"Jewish Woman's Encounter with American Culture" (Braude), 156
Jones, Rufus, 70

Judaism, 3, 9, 16, 19, 22-25, 27
anti-Semitism, 27, 44, 86
architecture, 84-86
Bat Mitzvah, 123, 130-33
beliefs, 96, 99
Conservative, 105, 131
funeral rites, 120
immigration and, 147-48
literature, 79
ministry, role of, 152
organizational structure, 144
Orthodox, 103, 105, 130
percentage of population, 139
Reform, 45, 84-85, 102-3, 105, 131, 147, 156-58, 163
science and, 44-45
Wise, Isaac Meyer, and, 100-105
women and, 104-5, 130-33, 156-57
worship, 119, 122, 123, 130-33
Judaism: Its Doctrines and Duties (Wise), 104
Judaism in America (Blau), 147

Kacmarcik, Frank, 83
Kampf, Avram, 85
Kennedy, John F., 27
Killens, John, 60
King, Coretta Scott, 58
King, Martin Luther, Jr., 47, 57-61, 75, 146
Kissinger, Henry, 27
Knox, Israel, 104
Korean War, 26
Kreisler, Fritz, 112
Kuhlman, Kathryn, 29

Laity, clergy and, 142-44, 150-54
Lenski, Gerhard, 149
Leo XIII, Pope, 43
Let Us Now Praise Famous Men (Agee and Evans), 90*n*
Lewis, Sinclair, 29
Liberals, 53, 55-57
Life Is Worth Living (Sheen), 112
Literature, 78-80, 86-90
Living of These Days, The (Fosdick), 53
Long Loneliness, The (Day), 61, 62, 64
Luce, Clare Booth, 112
Lutheran Church in America, 124
Lutheran Church-Missouri Synod, 66, 67, 124, 148
Lutheran Church-Wisconsin Synod, 148
Lutheranism, 3, 9, 22, 24, 139, 140
clergy, role of, 152
national origin and, 148
ordination of women, 158
worship, 123-27

Madison, James, 4
Malcolm X, 75-77
Male imagery, 158

Marty, Martin, 65
Maryfarm, 63
Mather, Cotton, 154
Maurin, Peter, 62–64
Mazzuchelli, Samuel, 149
McLoughlin, William, 33, 34, 36–37
Meditation, 123
Meeting houses, 81–82
Meher Baba, 3, 66
Meliorism, 108
Melville, Herman, 78
Mendelsohn, Eric, 84–85, 118
Mennonites, 67
Metaphysical church, 141
Methodism, 3, 8–9, 20, 22–24, 139, 140
    black denominations, 67, 145, 146
    Harkness, Georgia, and, 105–10
    ordination of women, 106, 158
Millennialism, 67
Mind and Mood of Black America, The (Fullen-
    wider), 60
Ministry of America (eds. Schuller, Strommen,
    and Brekke), 151–54
Mission societies, 23, 156
Modernism, 53, 55–57
Moon, Sun Myung, 3, 144
Moorish Science Temple of America, 75
Moral Majority, 27
Moral Universe, The (Sheen), 110
Moravians, 121
Mormonism, 3, 23, 24, 27, 65, 98, 139, 141,
    163
    funeral rituals, 120
    organizational structure, 144
    polygamy issue, 16, 26, 66
    theology of, 42, 66, 99
Mott, Lucretia, 71
Mount Zion Temple, St. Paul, Minnesota, 84,
    118
Muhammad, Elijah, 75–77
Muhammad, Wallace D., 76, 77
Muhlenberg, Henry, 31
Music, 78, 79, 121
Muslims, 140

National Baptist Convention, 145
National Council of Jewish Women, 157
Nation of Islam (*see* Black Muslims)
Native American Church, 140
Native American religions, 16, 17–18, 27, 67
    funeral rituals, 120
    Ojibwa wake service, 133–37
    Quakerism and, 70, 71
Native American Religions (Gill), 17
Neo-Thomism, 44, 115
New Age church, 141
New Light Baptists, 67
Nicene Creed, 125

Niebuhr, H. Richard, 58, 59, 100, 145, 159,
    164
Noonan, D. P., 111, 112
Norwegian Lutheran Church of America, 148
Nuns, 157

O'Connor, Flannery, 79, 80, 86–90
Ojibwa wake service, 120, 133–37
O'Keeffe, Georgia, 80
On Being a Real Person (Fosdick), 57
Oneida Perfectionists, 23
On the Freedom of the Will (Edwards), 51, 52
Optimism, 22, 108
Ordination of women, 27, 106, 109, 122, 143,
    157–58
Organizational structure, 142–45
Origin of the Species, The (Darwin), 39
Orthodox churches, 9, 149
Orthodox Judaism, 103, 105, 130
Our Christian Hope (Harkness), 109

Pacifism, 54, 57, 70, 71
Paine, Thomas, 22
Painting, 78–81, 90–93
Parker, Theodore, 103
Parks, Rosa, 58, 59
Peace of Soul (Sheen), 111, 113
Peale, Norman Vincent, 101
Pentecostal churches, 139, 140, 141
Percey, Walker, 79
Personalism, 63
Personal Narrative (Edwards), 50
Pessimism, 108
Peter, John Frederich, 121
Pittsburgh Platform, 45
Poe, Edgar Allan, 38–39, 45
Polygamy, 16, 26, 66
Pope, 142–43
Positive thinking, 74
Potok, Chaim, 79
Prayers, 94
Presbyterianism, 3, 8, 20, 22, 24, 139, 140
    ordination of women, 158
    organizational structure, 142
    worship, 119
Privatization of religion, 6, 117–18
Prohibition movement, 25
Prohme, Rayna Simons, 61
Prophet, Elizabeth Clare, 144–45
Protestant, Catholic, Jew (Herberg), 5
Protestantism, 3, 21–25
    clergy, role of, 152
    denominations, 139–41
    funeral rituals, 120
    liberal/fundamentalist debate, 53, 55–57
    organizational structure, 142, 143–44
    public, 163
    revivalism, 29–37

women and, 156
worship, 116–17, 119, 121, 122
Psychoanalysis, 113–14
PTL (Praise the Lord) Club, 29
Public prayer, 117
Puritanism, 15, 16, 18–19
architecture, 79, 81–82
Edwards, Jonathan, and, 48–53
Quakerism and, 69–70
theology of, 49–50

Quakerism, 9, 15, 139, 141
doctrines of, 69–71
history of, 68–69
women and, 70–71
worship, 119

Race, 145–50
Racism, 58–61
Rappites, 23
Rauschenbusch, Walter, 41, 58, 59
Reformation, 18, 30, 117
Reformed Union of American Congregations, 105
Reform Judaism, 45, 84–85, 102–3, 105, 131, 147, 156–58, 163
Regionalism, 91, 141
Religion, definitions of, 3
Religions in America (Rosten), 5
Religious Factor, The (Lenski), 149
Religious History of the American People, A (Ahlstrom), 15
Religious Science, 99
Religious Society of Friends (*see* Quakers)
Reminiscences (Wise), 102, 103, 105
Revivalism, 20–21, 29–37, 42
Ritual, 116–37
Riverside Church, New York, 54, 57
Roberts, Oral, 29
Roman Catholicism (*see* Catholicism)
Rosten, Leo, 5, 118
Roth, Henry, 79
Ruether, Rosemary Radford, 106
Russian Orthodox Church, 149

Saarinen, Eero, 83
Sacraments, 119, 123, 124, 127–30, 142
Salem Witchcraft trials, 19
Schismatics, 66–67
Schlesinger, Arthur M., 39, 45
School prayers, 6, 117
Schuller, David, 154
Science, 34, 38–46, 53, 57, 72–74
Science and Health with Key to the Scriptures (Eddy), 72, 73
Scientology, 27, 66, 140
Scopes trial, 39
Second Great Awakening, 22, 32–34

Second Vatican Council, 25, 44, 87, 110, 122, 130
Segregation, 58–60, 164
Seminex, 66
Sephardic Jews, 147
Seventh Day Adventism, 23, 99, 139, 141
Shakerism, 22–24, 66, 121
"Shall the Fundamentalists Win?" (Fosdick), 54, 55
Sheen, Fulton J., 100, 101, 110–15
"Sinners in the Hands of an Angry God" (Edwards), 30–31, 48
Skeptics, 67
Slavery, 164
Slovak Evangelical Lutheran Synod, 148
Smith, Joseph, 42, 144
Snake handling, 96
Social Gospel movement, 23, 25, 41, 115
Society for Ethical Culture, 118
"Sonnet—To Science" (Poe), 38–39, 45
Southern Christian Leadership Conference, 59
Spalding, John, 44
Spanish settlers, 17, 18
Spellman, Francis Cardinal, 87, 111
Spiritualism, 3, 23, 42, 97, 98
St. John's Abbey and University Church, Collegeville, Minnesota, 82–84
Stanton, Elizabeth Cady, 155
Stark, Rodney, 3
Stevens, Wallace, 80
Stoddard, Solomon, 52
Sunday, Billy, 32, 35
Sunday services, 116, 123–27
Supreme Court of the United States, 4, 16, 26, 59

Temperance, 23
Ten Commandments, 94
Theosophy, 3, 23, 42–43, 97, 140
Third Great Awakening, 33, 34–35
Thoreau, Henry David, 59
Tillich, Paul, 3, 58, 59, 90
Tocqueville, Alexis de, 5
Transcendentalism, 67, 74
Transcendental Meditation, 147
Treasure in Clay (Sheen), 114
Tribe, Laurence, 26
Troeltsch, Ernst, 138
Trusteeism, 143
"Two revelations" theory, 41

Underhill, Evelyn, 118
Unificationism, 27, 66, 98, 140, 144
Unitarianism, 9, 22, 24, 152
Unitarian Universalists, 96, 139
United Church of Christ, 96, 139, 140, 142, 152, 158
United States v. *Seeger* (1965), 26

Unity School of Christianity, 99, 141
Universal Negro Improvement Association, 75

Varieties of Religious Experience, The (James),
    2, 3
Vatican II, 25, 44, 87, 110, 122, 130
Vedanta Society, 141
Vietnam War, 27, 163
Violent Bear It Away, The (O'Connor), 88
Virgin Birth, 56, 109
Voluntarism, 139, 141, 159

Wake, 123, 133–37
Warren, Robert Penn, 79
Washington, George, 22
Watergate Scandal, 163
Watson v. Jones (1872), 4
Weber, Max, 138
"What Are Christian Liberals Driving At?"
    (Fosdick), 56
What Christians Believe (Harkness), 94
Whitefield, George, 31, 34, 52
Whitman, Walt, 78
Willard, Frances E., 155

Williams, Roger, 4
Winslow, Ola Elizabeth, 48–49
Wise, Isaac Meyer, 7, 100–105, 122
Wise Blood (O'Connor), 88
Witchcraft, 3
Woman's Bible, The, 155
Women, 23, 61–64, 100, 101, 105–10, 154–58
    Catholicism and, 157
    Christian Science and, 72–74
    Judaism and, 104–5, 130–33, 156–57
    Methodism and, 106, 158
    ordination of, 27, 106, 109, 122, 143, 157–
        58
    Protestantism and, 156
    Quakerism and, 70–71
    revivals and, 32–33
Women in Church and Society (Harkness), 109
Wood, Grant, 81, 90–93
Woolman, John, 71
Worship, 116–37

Yoga, 123

Zen Buddhism, 3, 9, 25, 66, 147
Zimmerman, Phillip D., 82